*The Reputation of the
American Businessman*

The Reputation of the American Businessman

BY SIGMUND DIAMOND

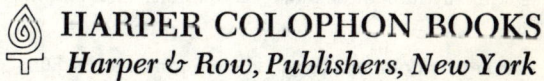
HARPER COLOPHON BOOKS
Harper & Row, Publishers, New York

This book was originally published by Harvard University Press, Cambridge, Massachusetts, in the United States of America, and is here reprinted by arrangement.

First HARPER COLOPHON edition published 1966 by Harper & Row, Publishers, Incorporated, New York.

LIBRARY OF CONGRESS CATALOG CARD NUMBER: 54:8623

To My Wife

ACKNOWLEDGMENTS

It is with a sense of deepest gratitude that I record my indebtedness to Professor Frederick Merk, of the History Department of Harvard University; in countless ways he gave me advice and encouragement, and I deem it a privilege to have been his student. Professors Arthur H. Cole and Leland H. Jenks of the Research Center in Entrepreneurial History at Harvard University have been my friends as well as my teachers, and for their kindness and their counsel I express my deep appreciation. To Mr. Yehoshua Arieli, of The Hebrew University, I am indebted for many pleasant and — to me — profitable hours of discussion. Miss Ruth Crandall eased my tasks with her patient and friendly aid. I wish to acknowledge, too, the financial assistance given me by the Research Center in Entrepreneurial History and by the Committee on Research in Economic History; it was that assistance which made possible the writing of this book.

I am indebted to Dr. Hugh G. J. Aitken, editor of *Explorations in Entrepreneurial History*, for permission to reprint in Chapter Two material which originally appeared in somewhat different form in that journal; to Random House for permission to reprint from W. H. Auden's "Heavy Date," which appeared in the *Collected Poetry of W. H. Auden;* to the editor of the *National Republic* for permission to quote from the article by Ira Bennett; to the Ford Motor Company for permission to reprint a stanza from a poem by Edgar Guest, which first appeared in the *Ford Times;* to John Dos Passos for permission to quote from his *U.S.A.*, published by Houghton Mifflin Company; and to George Sylvester Viereck for permission to reprint the Morgan poem from his *My Flesh and Blood.*

S. D.

CONTENTS

*The Reputation of the
American Businessman*

Introduction

"*Hero, Prophet, Poet,* — many different names, in different times and places, do we give to Great Men; according to varieties we note in them, according to the sphere in which they have displayed themselves! . . . The Hero can be Poet, Prophet, King, Priest, or what you will, according to the kind of world he finds himself born into." [1] So Thomas Carlyle informed his London audience in 1840. Significantly, there was in Carlyle's analysis no room for the Hero as Entrepreneur; the Hero as Divinity, Prophet, Poet, Priest, Man of Letters, and King exhausted the categories. But perceptive readers, if they took note of Carlyle's comment that the "Hero can be . . . what you will, according to the kind of world he finds himself born into," would have concluded that the categories were not exhaustive, that each society, to the degree that it differed from others and transformed itself through the course of history, would create heroic types sufficient unto itself.

So it happened that the triumphal entry into London in 1853 of Commodore Cornelius Vanderbilt, America's most renowned business-man, gave opportunity to the London *Daily News* to probe more deeply into the relation of hero to society and to advance specific reasons for the higher prestige afforded men of his kind in the United States than in England. "America . . . is the great arena in which the individual energies of man, uncramped by oppressive social institutions, or absurd social traditions, have full play, and arrive at gigantic development," the *Daily News* observed:

It is the tendency of American institutions to foster the general welfare, and to permit the unchecked powers of the highly gifted to occupy a place in the general framework of society which they can obtain nowhere else. The great feature to be noted in America is that all its citizens have full permission to run the race in which Mr. Vanderbilt has gained such immense prizes. In other countries, on the contrary, they are trammelled by a thousand restrictions . . .

Your men of rank here — your makers of millions for themselves, and tens of millions for the country — too often spend their time, their intellect, their labor, in order that they may be able to take rank among a class of men who occupy their present position in virtue of what was done for them by some broad-shouldered adventurer, who, fortunately for them, lived eight hundred years ago in Normandy . . . Here is the great difference between the two countries. In England a man is too apt to be ashamed of having made his own fortune, unless he has done so in one of the few roads which the aristocracy condescend to travel — the bar, the church, or the army . . .

It is time that the *millionaire* should cease to be ashamed of having made his own fortune. It is time that *parvenu* should be looked on as a word of honor. It is time that the middle classes should take the place which is their own, in the world which they have made. The middle classes have made the modern world. The Montmorencis, the Howards, the Percys, made the past world — and they had their reward. Let them give place to better men.[2]

The factor which so impressed the London *Daily News* — the absence of feudal-aristocratic traditions in the United States as compared with England — is undoubtedly of great importance in accounting for the difference in the prestige the parvenus of each country could hope to attain. But what of the United States itself? Has the great American man of business always had the assurance that the community would elevate him to a position of distinction? Has his status in American society undergone no alterations? Has that status been associated always with the functions called for by his business position, or has it — undergoing its own historical mutation — become identified with the nonbusiness functions of businessmen? To what factors, in the various periods of our country's history, has entrepreneurial success been attributed? Has there been no change in the conception of the practices and activities which the community has associated with the entrepreneur? To isolate the various conceptions of the entrepreneur's significance to society and the ingredients of successful entrepreneurship held at the same time by different groups within the community, and to examine the changing conceptions of the entrepreneur's significance during more than a century of our country's history are, then, the two major subjects of this investigation.

In the belief that the retrospective discussion characteristic of journalistic obituaries reveals, not necessarily the truth about the subject, but basic assumptions and evaluations concerning the social ideals of their writers, the method of this study has been to analyze the comment elicited by the death of six of the most famous American businessmen: Stephen Girard, John Jacob Astor, Cornelius Vanderbilt, J. Pierpont Morgan, John D. Rockefeller, and Henry Ford. Since, then, the bulk of the evidence which has been examined has come from the press, it is necessary to comment on the nature of that evidence and how it has been treated.

No one should read this study under the misapprehension that, having read it, he will know what "public opinion" was on the questions here examined or what "the American mind" thought about these questions. The content of mass communications, properly interpreted, may teach us many things, but that it can ever fully reveal the state of public opinion is greatly to be doubted. To believe that newspaper editorials reflect "public opinion" is to assume that those editorials express precisely the state of mind of the audience to which they are directed. It hardly seems necessary at this late date to belabor the point that such an assumption is unwarranted. The decision of a newspaper editor to print a report or discussion of an event depends not only on the nature of that event but on his judgment of it, a judgment which by no means is necessarily shared by all members of the community. To state that such sources have limitations upon their usefulness, however, is not to state that they are of no use at all. If the decision to print a newspaper article or editorial rests upon a judgment made by an editor, then a study of such material, at the very least, throws light upon the systems of values which underlie those judgments. If it is remembered that newspaper editors and publishers can bestow or withdraw prestige from persons, legitimate or repudiate social movements, and under certain circumstances persuade others to similar beliefs, then understanding of the values which support those decisions and of the techniques by which those values are propagated is of considerable significance.[3]

These values and techniques, moreover, influence human action as well as human thought. "Preliminary to any self-determined act of behavior," we are told, "there is always a stage of examination and deliberation which we may call the definition of the situation. And actually not only concrete acts are dependent on the definition of the situation, but gradually a whole life-policy and the personality of the individual himself follow from a series of such definitions." [4] In any highly complex society, the media of mass communications indicate acceptable forms of behavior, suggest that deviance from those forms is to be deplored, lend authority to certain persons within the community, and give weight to some opinions rather than others. They are, therefore, a potent instrumentality for defining the situations that members of society are called upon to meet. Moreover, as Mr. Clyde Kluckhohn has stated, definitions are important for behavior as well as understanding: "Mainly, language is an instrument for action. The meaning of a word or phrase is not its dictionary equivalent but the difference its utterance brings about in a situation . . . The primary social value of speech lies in getting individuals to work more effectively together and in easing social tensions." [5] Such a study as this becomes, then, at least in part, an inquiry into the nature of the consensus which keeps a society together, the function of the press in sustaining that consensus and in altering it to take account of changing circumstances, the means by which social discipline is maintained, and the relationship of competing definitions and disciplines.

Whatever has been said here about the limitations on the use of newspapers in general applies with special emphasis to the material which has been the major source of this investigation — obituaries. Petroleum V. Nasby's ironic definition of an obituary as a "post-mortem endorsement" serves to underscore the necessity for probing beneath the journalist's definition — an obituary is an attempt "to 'place' the dead person in history with emphasis upon his importance and contributions." [6]

No sophisticated notions of sampling were employed to determine which newspapers and magazines were to be examined for this study. All were deemed relevant; and every effort was made to include representatives from the widest possible list of categories — geographical region, size of place of publication, nature of the audience to which the medium was directed, chain or independent, and the like. In the case of each of the entrepreneurs studied, the decision that sufficient material had been examined was made long after the point at which additional sources ceased to disclose opinions different from those already ascertained. In each case, too, the decision to quote excerpts from the press was based on their representativeness of the class of material of which they were held to be samples. This is, then, a qualitative rather than a quantitative approach to the data. The basic procedure of quantitative content analysis — the counting of all statements which are held to be examples of one or another of a series of categories — was rejected because of the difficulty of drawing up a list of categories which would fully exhaust all aspects of the discussion created by the death of each of these entrepreneurs, because categories established on the basis of interests contemporary to each of these men are of limited significance when applied to the others, and because categories constructed in such a way as to apply to all are so general as to be almost meaningless. The qualitative approach has at least the virtues of preserving something of the flavor of the original discussion, of being a flexible instrument for the analysis of that discussion, and of allowing emphasis to be placed, not on static analysis, but on historical change. Besides, the scientific appearance of quantitative analysis may be more illusory than real; whether the analysis be quantitative or qualitative, the major problem is that of determining the categories to be investigated, and quantitative analysis provides us with no more nor better guides for the selection of those categories than does qualitative analysis.[7]

I

Stephen Girard

On May 20, 1948, when President Harry S. Truman spoke in Philadelphia at the centenary celebration of the founding of Girard College and the one hundred ninety-eighth anniversary of the birth of Stephen Girard, he remarked that he "was always a very great admirer of Stephen Girard . . . The vicissitudes of Stephen Girard are an example to every American boy." In thus expressing his approval of the activities of Girard and in pointing to his career from cabin boy to merchant-banker as a model for youth, President Truman was but echoing, as representative of the latest generation of Americans, the appraisal of Girard's own contemporaries. But in adding that Girard "has the typical American story," [1] President Truman was introducing into the discussion an element which was wholly absent from contemporary judgments concerning Girard's status and function in society. For Americans of the first third of the nineteenth century, the explanation of individual destiny was to be sought, not in any magical properties imputed to a particular time and place, but in the personal qualities of body, mind, and spirit. The verdict of Stephen Girard's contemporaries was set forth not when President Truman spoke on the one hundredth anniversary of the founding of his college, but when Nicholas Biddle spoke at the laying of its cornerstone, on the Fourth of July, 1833. For Biddle and the men of his generation, the explanation of Girard's success lay not in opportunities offered by his country and the period in which he lived, but in personal character — in his plain appearance, simple manners, frugal habits, intense and untiring industry, judicious enterprise, above all, in the fact that his "very relaxation was only variety of labor." [2] "We may cease to wonder," said another celebrant at the same event, "at the magical transformations of his Midas touch. His secret lay in the patient application of a remarkably clear and sagacious intellect to the single work of accumulation, aided by inexpensive personal habits and the observance of general frugality." [3]

If contemporary evaluations of the life of Stephen Girard contained little or nothing of the notions of the unique advantages afforded by the time and place in which he lived and the peculiarly American quality of his career, what, then, were the standards by which his performance was judged, what reasons were proposed to account for his success, and what conclusions were drawn from the analysis of his activities?

When on December 26, 1831, Stephen Girard died during an influenza epidemic in Philadelphia, the reaction of the newspapers of that city to the event was immediate and widespread. Despite his reticence and the solitude of his life, Girard had been, even during his own lifetime, the object of considerable curiosity and discussion. The Harvard College student who commiserated with Girard over his lack of an heir "to succeed to" Girard's "possessions" and offered himself as "a candidate" to "fill up" the void was simply expressing one aspect of popular thought concerning the banker.[4] And the offer of Auguste Baton, ex-officer in the French army, past Grand Master of the Masons, bankrupted billiard-parlor operator, dancing master, and promoter of subscription balls, to write a biography of Girard because it would "serve for the instruction of future generations by demonstrating to youth the means . . . used to rise to the height of fortune" [5] suggests that there was sufficient interest in Girard during his life to warrant the notion that a market existed for a book about him. For the most part, however, such curiosity and interest in Girard seem to have been confined to the private correspondence he received and the gossip of barrooms and countinghouses. But with his death the floodgates were opened, and a veritable torrent of discussion, indicative of the American people's attitudes toward the great man of business, poured forth into the public press.

Philadelphians first learned of the death of the most eminent citizen of their community when on the morning of December 27, 1831, the *National Gazette* reported the event. Girard's death, the *National Gazette* stated, had created a sensation "in consequence of the vast wealth and extensive enterprizes of the deceased." He had contributed substantially to the development of the city of Philadelphia, had won extraordinary success as a merchant, and as a banker had "flourished beyond all example in this country." In emphasizing that Girard was "the richest *merchant* in the world" with a net capital of $10,000,000; in attributing his remarkable achievements to possession of acuteness, industry, and good faith; in insisting that the explanation of his steady progress from "humble poverty to princely opulence" need take account of no factors external to Girard himself; and in indicating concern over the disposition of his estate, the *National Gazette* sounded the basic themes which, with few exceptions, were to be echoed by newspapers the country over.

The Philadelphia *United States Gazette* — a Whig paper — obliged its readers with a full-scale review of Girard's life, a review in which the events of his life were made to serve the cause of Nicholas Biddle and Henry Clay. "Up to the year 1811," the *United States Gazette* reported, "Mr. Girard was exclusively engaged in commerce, which he pursued with unwearied and successful industry. But when the Congress of that year committed an act of almost political suicide, by destroying the charter of the Old Bank of the United States, or, what amounted to the same thing, refused to renew it, Mr. Girard purchased the building which belonged to the institution, and commenced the business of a banker." His success in that enterprise, the *United States Gazette* suggested, might be gauged by the fact that he had "left the largest fortune, perhaps, in the new world." Public attention was devoted now to discover "in what manner he has disposed of it."

The Philadelphia *Inquirer* was even less restrained in its praise of Girard: "The death of no citizen could have been an event of more general anxiety — the demise of none could have constituted a greater calamity for Philadelphia." And as to the reasons for Girard's financial success, the *Inquirer* was at least as emphatic as other newspapers in asserting that they were to be sought in the area of character and not of environment. "His immense wealth was accumulated solely through his own industry, exertions, and enterprise. His character through life was distinguished for sobriety, honesty, and consistency throughout, and his whole career presents a beautiful example of the success of industry and economy, when added to good sense, perseverance and the moral virtues." The *Inquirer*'s concern with the relationship between Girard's character and career was matched only by its interest in the disposition of his estate. If that paper is to be believed, Philadelphians talked of nothing else, and so numerous, vague, and contradictory were the rumors that the *Inquirer* decided to "forbear to repeat any of them" until the authentic document was made public.

Before the appetite of Philadelphians could be satisfied, however, it had still to be whetted — whetted by a funeral of a magnitude and solemnity never before seen in the city and by the insertion into newspapers of notices deliberately calculated to intensify the already existing curiosity.

Two days before the funeral, the *National Gazette,* possibly at the behest of William J. Duane, Girard's attorney, carried the following advertisement:

The late Stephen Girard, Esq., having by his will left very handsome bequests to the City of Philadelphia, as well as during his lifetime very extensively contributed to its beauty and improvement, it is respectfully suggested to all citizens who are not conscientiously scrupulous to close their windows at *least* from the hours of ten to twelve o'clock as a testimony of gratitude and respect to the memory of their liberal benefactor.

The *United States Gazette* transformed an appeal that the public give visible evidence of mourning into a general invitation to participate in the funeral services. The obsequies would have all the characteristics of a civic ceremony, it indicated, with participation in the cortege by the appropriate political authorities of the city, wardens of the port, officers and members of the Grand Masonic Lodge and subordinate lodges, members of the Society for the Relief of Distressed Masters of Ships and their Widows, officers of the Pennsylvania Hospital, controllers and directors of the public schools, and members of various charitable organizations. The journal assured its readers that even the lowliest would be welcome: "It is not practicable to give special invitations to individuals, nor is it supposed that invitations will be expected. All those who knew Mr. Girard personally or by reputation, and who revere his example and memory, are respectfully invited to attend his funeral."

The Common Council of the city added its voice to the general chorus of praise for Girard. On the motion of William Duane its members adopted a resolution which found that the "merits and means" by which he acquired his immense estate "were probity of the strictest kind, diligence unsurpassed, perseverance in all pursuits, and a frugality as remote from parsimony as from extravagance." As tokens of their respect, the Council voted to have the City Hall hung with mourning and to participate as a body in the funeral service.

Small wonder, then, that Philadelphians, their curiosity piqued by insinuations of favors to be received and their civic spirit exhorted by newspaper editorials, poured into the streets on the day of the funeral. Following the coffin, which was draped with black cloth and decorated with silver trappings, marched at least one thousand mourners, according to one estimate, nearly twenty thousand, according to another. All business appeared to have been suspended "in the general desire to pay homage" to Girard. A vast array of "heads and head-dresses, solemnly disposed," poked forth from the windows of the houses, and "countless multitudes" of spectators lined the streets. It was an "immense assemblage," the largest ever to have gathered for a funeral in Philadelphia; but before the morning was over there were to be still more exciting stories for busy tongues to relate over coffee cups and brimming glasses. Those who had attended the burial at the Catholic Church of the Holy Trinity witnessed the refusal of Archbishop Francis Patrick Kenrick to proceed with the burial rite because "the free masons . . . decked out with gems . . . were making a great display in honor of their brother"; though he did permit burial in consecrated ground because Girard had been born a Catholic and had never formally "renounced communion with the Church." [6] Religious controversy concerning Girard was soon to take new forms, but for the moment it seemed less important than authentic information concerning the question which, according to the newspapers at least, was uppermost in the minds of most Philadelphians: Who was to get Stephen Girard's estate? When the answer to that question was known — and within a few days it was to become a matter of public knowledge — discussion of Girard's place in the social order and of correct modes of business procedure and the reasons for business success received a new impetus from the public prints.

The text of Girard's will first became widely known when it was printed in the January 2, 1832, issue of the *United States Gazette*. At the same time the *United States Gazette* announced the impending publication of the first full-length biography of Girard, by Stephen Simpson, publicist and son of the late treasurer of the Girard Bank. Later issues of that newspaper carried extended accounts of the same story, embellishing them with anecdotes illustrative of various facets of Girard's character; and within a few days other Philadelphia newspapers entered the discussion.

The *National Gazette* felt the document to be of sufficient importance to print its most important sections and, when the full text became known, to devote to it its entire front page. *Hazard's Register* used seven full pages to print the complete text of the will, and for fully five months kept its readers informed of the activities of the Mayor and Common Council in the administration of the estate.

The focal point of discussion was the immense bequests left by Girard for what was termed "public purposes," especially his endowment of a college for poor white orphan boys. A fortune of such magnitude had never before been accumulated in the United States and the bequests for charitable purposes were unparalleled. Of a total estate estimated at nearly $7,500,000, only $140,000 was bequeathed to relatives and $65,000 was left as annuities to friends and retainers. Various Philadelphia charities received the sum of $116,000; $500,000 went to the city of Philadelphia to improve the Delaware River waterfront; the state of Pennsylvania was granted $300,000 for internal improvements; and 280,000 acres of rich plantation land with its slaves were left for the benefit of the cities of Philadelphia and New Orleans. The residue of the estate — cash and real estate to the value of slightly more than $6,000,000 — was left for the improvement of Philadelphia and for the establishment of a college. [7]

The reaction of Philadelphia newspapers to the news of Girard's bequests and the philosophy upon which their approval rested were expressed by the *Saturday Evening Post:*

. . . this munificent donor considered himself merely as an agent, or steward, who was to account for the manner in which he disposed of his vast wealth; and . . . his anxious wish was to make such a disposition of it as would produce the greatest possible good . . . he has discharged his duty, and fulfilled his destiny like a philanthropist and benefactor, and left behind him those who for generations will revere his name and cherish his memory . . . Mr. Girard looked upon the wealth and prosperity of individuals as blessings that are given in trust, to be used and disposed for the common good of society.

The verdict was unanimous; no Philadelphia paper dissented. They differed from one another, not in substance, but only in the degree to which each could find more glowing adjectives in which to express its approval. The Whiggish *Daily Advertiser,* for example, after citing Girard's will as "one of the most important documents ever promulgated," went on to consider him as one of the great constructive geniuses of world history. "Never was more effectual means taken by any one man to perpetuate his name and the benefits of an active life, not even the pyramids of Egypt," it continued. As founders of great schools, even Cardinal Wolsey and Thomas Jefferson were less significant than Girard: "Mr. Jefferson's scholars will be useful to adorn the world of letters; Mr. Girard's the Republic itself." [8]

Otherwise warring with the Whig *Daily Advertiser* over the issues involved in the impending presidential election of 1832, the Democratic *Banner of the Constitution,* edited by Condy Raguet, a leading spokesman of Jacksonian Democracy,[9] could yet agree with its political enemy in its evaluation of the significance of the life of Girard. If anything, the Democratic newspaper was even more lavish than the Whig in praising the preëminent banker of the Western Hemisphere and in sanctioning his activities.

The standards applied by Raguet in measuring the significance of Girard were by no means antagonistic to business enterprise; indeed, Girard rose in the esteem of the Jacksonian editor precisely because he was considered the embodiment of business virtues and because his manner of living allowed for none of the frivolity and extravagance of the men of rank and privilege who were the real objects of Raguet's scorn. The "economical style" of Girard's life, Raguet editorialized,

has induced some persons to entertain very erroneous views of the influence of his mode of living upon the welfare of the community. You would hear people say, "It is a pity that Mr. Girard does not make a better use of his money — he ought to live more affluently, and by that means, give employment to tradesmen and other poor people." It is very certain, that Mr. Girard contributed very little to the support of livery servants, footmen, coachmen, pastry-cooks, French restaurateurs, ice-cream-makers, dancing masters, musicians, play actors, hair-dressers, fancy shopkeepers, jewellers, and many other callings; but his income was not, on that account, less unexpended. His fancy was to set in motion the industry of ship-builders, riggers and sailmakers, seamen, stevedores, and dray-men, and of late years, that of carpenters, bricklayers, brickmakers, masons, plaisterers, painters, glaziers, marble masons, and all the other mechanics employed by him in building houses. What portion of his capital he did not expend, he lent to others to be expended as they might see fit.

So far, indeed, was Raguet from criticizing Girard on the grounds that large accumulations of wealth in the hands of a single person necessarily deprived others, that he deliberately repudiated that notion. The road to wealth, Raguet argued, lay not through limitation or division of property accumulations: "Cannot any one perceive," he wrote, "that the superintendence of so frugal and industrious a steward, has been the means of accumulating an immense fund in the City of Philadelphia, which could never have existed, but owing to the cheapness with which so large a capital was managed? The same sum divided into a hundred portions, could never have produced the same accumulation; and for this single reason, that, in its management, a hundred individuals or families would have had to be supported, whereas, in this case, only one individual was to be supported, and he too, very frugally." Clearly, for Raguet, there was no conflict between the apex of the economic pyramid and its base when the entire pyramid rested on what he conceived to be productive enterprise. As to Girard in particular, "so far from his mode of expenditure operating disadvantageously to the working classes, it has been, of all others, the one which was calculated to produce the greatest good to the community."

With respect to the other vital points in the analysis of Girard the Democratic paper was at one with the Whig press. There was agreement that Girard's public life was an extension of his private qualities, that his financial success was to be attributed solely to the virtues he possessed — his pleasure in work, his scorn of indulgence, his plainness of dress and simplicity of manner — and that the crucial test of the value to society of a rich man's life lay not so much in the means by which his fortune was acquired as in the uses to which it would be put after his death. As to that test, Girard passed it with flying colors. "He resembled . . . the Steward of some great Proprietor," Raguet wrote, "and we trust that a monument may decorate some conspicuous spot" as a memorial to one "who set so bright an example for the imitation of the poor and industrious." Raguet quoted the statement attributed to Girard just one month before his death as epitomizing his character: "When death comes for me, he will find me busy." [10]

For those members of the community who were sufficiently interested, and who could afford the price, there were other sources in which additional information, albeit information which supported the general verdict, could be obtained. Thomas and Robert Desilver, Philadelphia printers, were among the first to capitalize on the possible cash value of interest in Girard's life by publishing a pamphlet containing a brief biography and the full text of the will.[11] The analysis by Girard's biographers served primarily to make perfectly explicit what had been less fully developed in the previous discussion. Like the newspaper editors, the Desilvers agreed that private character determined individual destiny, but the character of the man, they believed, was implicit in the character of the child. "A spirit of enterprise, a love of adventure, and a thirst of new scenes and untried institutions" — precisely the qualities to which his success was due — "very early distinguished him." It was not "parental oppression" that forced Girard from his Bordeaux home; "it is most likely, taking into consideration the peculiar structure of the mind of *Stephen Girard,* that he was impelled by the natural enterprise of his vigorous spirit, to quit the parental roof." The qualities of untiring industry and unremitting effort, of frugality and abstemiousness which thrust him forward from cabin boy to "the most opulent banker in the country" were qualities of the boy as well as of the man. This, indeed, was the secret of success and of life itself. The precise methods by which Girard attained his wealth were not yet known, his biographers explained, and, besides, "were not material to our proper estimation of his character. 'By their fruits ye shall know them!'" — and Girard had reaped a gigantic harvest.

Step by step the stages of Girard's career were traced: cabin boy; mate of a small schooner; "aquatic pedlar" on the Delaware; shopkeeper, selling "segars and groceries"; tavern owner; merchant and overseas trader; savior of Philadelphia during the yellow fever epidemic of 1793; organizer of the Bank of the United States; heavy investor in public lands and the public debt; owner of the Girard Bank. But the culmination of this career was surely his bequests. His "great PUBLIC BENEFACTIONS . . . proclaim him as one of the FIRST PHILANTHROPISTS OF THE AGE; and . . . an enlightened benevolence will rejoice, that his great wealth has been devised, with unparalleled patriotism and public spirit, for the BENEFIT OF THE COMMUNITY; and not the gratification of private passions, or individual avarice." The conclusion tersely summarized the two major elements in the thinking of Girard's contemporaries: "The architect of his own fortunes — he has reared a durable monument of his fame in the benefactions he has bequeathed to posterity."

Still other enterprising publishers apparently saw economic opportunity in catering to the curiosity concerning what manner of man Girard had been. On February 8, 1832, Porter's Literary Rooms, publishers of the *Journal of Health,* the *Journal of Geology and Natural Science,* the *Journal of Instruction,* and *Causes, Cure, and Prevention of Sick Headache,* brought forth the first issue of a new magazine — the *Girard Journal of Wealth and Record and Depository of Benevolence,* priced at $2.00 for twenty-four issues. Despite the claim in its prospectus to be "not a temporary and transient journal," there is no record that the *Girard Journal* survived its first issue. Businessmen who felt the need for approval of their activities found it in the columns of the *Girard Journal;* indeed, they could hardly have laid down their copy of the *Journal* without a renewed and invigorated sense of their significance to society. "Whatever relates to the acquisition of Wealth, national or individual, must always be considered of the utmost importance to mankind; as it implies the practice of all the virtues that make men happy, and countries prosperous. The history of Wealth is, in other words, the history of virtue; and he who can attain a knowledge of the means by which to gain it, will at once consider himself both wiser and happier; and he will necessarily command more influence in society, and extort more respect from his fellow men." The identity of private striving and public welfare, of wealth and virtue, wealth and wisdom, wealth and happiness, wealth and prestige — surely businessmen who received these assurances could pursue their calling with confidence. But it was for businessmen-to-be, as well as for businessmen, that the *Girard Journal* had words of comfort. "The Philosopher's Stone was no fable, but a reality"; Girard and many others had found it and it had guided their steps to success as it would all who but chose to follow. "It consists in industry, economy, and virtue; but first in *industry,* which is the fountain, while the other virtues are but the channels, that convey it off to its proper destination." Blood and privilege meant nothing and the concept of "Luck" was not understood. Character ruled, and anyone might have that; it was not a function of birth or rank or the opportunities offered by social systems. All men alike were encouraged to strive to become Girards. If they tried and succeeded, they were assured of the respect and esteem of the community; if they tried and failed, they had no one to blame but themselves. And in either case, whether they succeeded or failed, so long as men modeled their conduct on that of Girard, they would contribute to the development of business enterprise by virtue of their voluntary acceptance of its goals and methods.

But the first book-length biography of Girard that appeared shortly after his death — still another evidence of the extraordinary interest that had been aroused — while not disagreeing with the philosophical foundations upon which the basic evaluation of Girard rested, nevertheless entertained some doubts as to whether the banker in fact incarnated virtues to the degree that others had implied.[12] Stephen Simpson, its author, had had a varied career. Son of the former cashier of the Girard Bank, publicist, newspaper editor, self-styled advocate of the cause of labor, he had gradually moved politically from support of Andrew Jackson to support of Clay's American System and the Bank of the United States.[13] It may be that his strictures concerning Girard stemmed from disappointment at not having been promoted from clerk to cashier of the Girard Bank;[14] but whatever the reason, he did express certain attitudes concerning Girard which were somewhat at variance with the majority report and which indicate, therefore, however small in scope and feebly articulated, the existence of a minority view.

To begin with, Simpson made no effort to conceal the fact that his biography would not fully take its readers inside Girard. Concerning any biography, "it is better to suppress a little, than to disclose too much," [15] he wrote. And as for a biography of Girard, "Even a *Boswell* would have found it a difficult task, to *paint to the life,* a character so mysterious, mercenary, and *anti-literary* as that of Stephen Girard." [16] The banker, it seems, was no Dr. Johnson. Still, while there were omissions from the book — "because the cause of virtue was considered superior to the gratification of an idle curiosity" — whatever facts the book did contain were nothing but the truth, truth obtained on the basis of personal knowledge of the subject and diligent inquiry among the friends of Girard.[17]

But in what specific respects did Girard fail to measure up to Simpson's implicit model? Girard, it seems, lacked compassion and sympathy for his fellow men, never permitted friendship to affect his business dealings, was chilly and rigid in his personal affairs, did not appreciate the importance of fidelity except in business transactions, indulged in fits of anger and tyrannized his associates, venerated "ancient families" despite his "republican character" and the fact that he himself was a "novus Homo," overvalued the importance of money, treated his employees as "machines or instruments," failed to patronize literature and the arts, and condoned and even supported the existence of slavery.[18]

The judgment seems negative, yet there were on the other side of the ledger credits not only more than enough to compensate for Girard's defects but also to indicate that, in the final evaluation of a business career, other considerations were more important than these.

In the first place, the blame for many of his less desirable qualities could not be placed on him. The "hard buffeting of a rude world, and his arduous struggles to escape from the gripe of its selfishness, to independence and competency . . . early misfortune and peculiar hardships" — these had conspired to harden his heart against its own "natural *basic . . .* purest benevolence." He had not been "treated very kindly by the world"; indeed, he had felt its "iron foot . . . upon his heart." Under the circumstances it was perhaps less to be wondered that he turned from "the world to its treasures" than that his natural "sympathy and good nature would occasionally shine out." [19]

In any case there was more to be said for Girard than against him, and with respect to the fundamental issues Simpson was in complete agreement with other commentators. Girard had not inherited his wealth; he had earned it, and earned it by the possession of qualities and the practice of virtues beyond reproach. A "poor, outcast, ignorant, and wandering boy," he had by force of "sobriety, prudence, economy, and industry" — properties which "extort applause and challenge imitation" — climbed from "the lowest point of existence . . . to the highest." His intellectual faculties, his incredible knowledge of market conditions, his creative character, his "passion for production" and belief in the duty to work — it was to these that he owed his success. That Girard was "the architect of his own fortunes" and that the qualities which permitted him to attain his fortune were really the important ones to be considered in evaluating a man's life, Simpson, no less than others, agreed.[20]

But there was agreement on other points as well. In the final analysis, it mattered little that one might look dubiously at some aspects of Girard's character and career. That which overshadowed all else was the ultimate purpose to which his money was put — "public utility, laudable enterprises, and noble benefactions." Consideration of the destination of his money overcame all questions as to the legitimacy of its source or the propriety of the means by which it had been earned. Money, wrote Simpson, "in itself, is nothing. Its *application* decides its character; and it is in this, that the fortune of Mr. Girard, in its destination to the *happiness and improvement* of mankind, excites the noblest ideas, together with the most exalted reflections of *moral sublimity*." That Girard had accumulated his wealth not for the "gratification of his own passions, or a frivolous vanity" but for "the improvement of a great commonwealth"; that he had acted "merely as the *steward* of his great fortune," discharging his "trust . . . with liberality and taste," was the final consideration which impelled a favorable verdict on his career. For Simpson, "*posthumous philanthropy*" had to "be balanced against a life of avaricious accumulation, in order to arrive at a just estimate of the man"; and the scales weighed in favor of Girard, for "his will redeemed him from a load of errors." As with Simpson, so with others: "The moment the true character of his bequests were known, a loud shout of applause and admiration, filled the public press, and flowed from every tongue; succeeded by a profound sentiment of gratitude and esteem for the man, the citizen, and the philanthropist." [21]

Such, then, was the framework of the discussion erected by the journalists of Stephen Girard's own city and, with minor exceptions, it served to contain the utterances of other editors from the seaboard metropolitan centers of the East to the frontier hamlets of West and South.

New York newspapers, for example, varied little from those of Philadelphia in their amazement at the size of Girard's wealth, in their attribution of it to his qualities of mind and temperament, and in their applause at the magnanimity of his bequests to the public. In part, of course, this similarity arose from their dependence upon Philadelphia newspapers for information concerning Girard — highly developed newspaper "morgues" were still in the future[22] — but there is no evidence that they disagreed with what they printed, and when they did comment on their own account it was largely to add their approbation to what had already been said.

New Yorkers first learned of the death of Girard on December 28, 1831, and from then until well into January they were kept informed by the press of various estimates of the size of Girard's estate, its distribution, and the details of his career. The portrait of the man with which they were presented was drawn with the old familiar brush strokes; character stood clearly delineated in the foreground, setting disappeared into the mist. The subject of the painting could at once be recognized. He was the unmalleable man, the man of "utter exemption from any foible or weakness," as the *Morning Courier* for December 28 put it, the man of a "strong, discriminating, and capacious mind"; the "artificer of his own great wealth and distinguished reputation," the *Atlas* added.

Only with respect to that provision of his will by which Girard sought to forbid ministers of any denomination from ever setting foot in the college he endowed was there a discordant note. One correspondent of the New York *Evangelist* noted bitterly that "Voltaire could not have showed his malignity to the gospel, more plainly than Mons. G. has done . . . It is an insult to christianity." But social reformers Frances Wright and Robert Dale Owen agreed with Girard: "The place of the clergy is with their congregations, and not in Public Schools."

The newspapers of Albany provide an especially clear example of the degree to which Girard's activities could find a broad basis of approval among otherwise conflicting groups. The *Evening Journal*, supporting National Republican candidate William Wirt for the presidency, and the *Daily Advertiser*, supporting Whig candidate Henry Clay, competed in the praise which they bestowed upon Girard. But their praise was pallid beside that of the *Argus*, official paper of Martin Van Buren's staunchly

Democratic Albany Regency — Girard was virtuous, Girard would be deeply mourned, Girard had been patriotic and public-spirited, Girard might even, with no risk to his own reputation, be compared with Thomas Jefferson.

As in New York and Albany, so it was in Boston. After the first terse reports of Girard's death and the descriptions of his funeral had been printed, Boston's newspapers vied in publishing the stereotyped account of his career and character and in speculating upon the amount and distribution of his estate. The conjecture of New Englanders, too, it seemed, had "often exhausted itself in attempts to divine how . . . Mr. Girard (*the rich Mr. Girard*) . . . almost as famous as Mr. Rothschild" would dispose of his property. "Curiosity" was "on tiptoe to learn how" such a vast sum, earned by "acuteness, industry, and good faith," had been disposed of. And no wonder. The imaginations of otherwise sober Bostonians boggled at the idea of an estate worth fifteen million dollars. Even a child could do the arithmetic: "Calculating the interest at 6 per cent and the year at 360 days, it will furnish the following curious results: Income per annum, $900,000; Income per month, $75,000; Income per day, $2,500; Income per hour, $104.16⅛; Income per minute, $1.73⅕."

Whig, Democrat, and Anti-Mason, Baptist, Congregationalist, Presbyterian, and Unitarian, Boston's press agreed with the *New-England Magazine* that the foundation of Girard's fortune was "to be found in his great industry and frugality." For the most part, it gave blanket approval, as well, to the judgment that Girard's will "established his claim to a high rank among the benefactors of his kind" and proved his "nobility of soul." The Boston *Post,* more inquisitive than most, made an effort to account for the civic character of Girard's generosity. That there was something in the atmosphere of Philadelphia the *Post* was certain: "The public spirit of Penn was the bright exemplar of Franklin; the liberality of Franklin an example for the munificence of Girard. All these great benefactors were remarkable for the tolerance of their religious creeds." Could this in turn be traced to the influence of the Quakers, the *Post* inquired? But most Boston papers were content to accept the portrayal of Girard without examining it too closely.

A few papers, like the *Telegraph* and the *Christian Herald,* objected indignantly that the will of Girard the "benefactor (?)" would deprive the students of his college of the solace of "that religion which affords the only light and happiness to miserable men," and excoriated the banker as a Deist. The indecisive *Weekly Messenger* could not make up its mind whether it should admire Girard's extraordinary career or deplore his extraordinary will. But none of these papers, it should be noted, raised questions concerning Girard's business activities or departed from accepted views as to proper behavior for a businessman. And even with respect to the issue which concerned them, Girard was not without defenders. "O!" said the *Trumpet and Universalist Magazine,* "the sectarians groan and writhe in agony . . . Their tongues are let loose, and every vile epithet their heated brains can devise, is bestowed on Mr. Girard . . . Does not the reader perceive, that unless a man will truckle to these dominant sectarians — live in fear of them, and bequeathe them his property when he dies — they will say all manner of evil of him? They live for their sect . . . alone . . . If you oppose that, you oppose God . . . We are sick of such arrogance."

Only two of Boston's newspapers went beyond the accepted pale of discussion and raised questions concerning the source and not the destination of Girard's wealth. William Lloyd Garrison's *Liberator* posed the issue sharply: "We have not the smallest portion of encomium to bestow . . . Notwithstanding he had millions of dollars to disburse, he had neither the humanity nor the principle to break the fetters of his poor slaves . . . Execrable conduct!" And to the charge that Girard's wealth was based in part on slave labor, the *Christian Herald* added its voice: "We are not informed what part of his immense wealth was obtained from the products of his Slaves; but it appears that while his thoughts were turned towards the termination of all earthly things, he claimed the right to retain the blacks in bondage, and even after twenty years more of degrading servitude they and their offspring are to be sold, and the proceeds applied to adorn the city of New Orleans!" On the day of retribution neither "difference of complexion nor disparity of wealth" would avert the sentence the "oppressor" would receive. Consideration of the source of Girard's wealth led these newspapers to condemn him. For the present, however, acceptance and approval were the keynotes; the issue of the origin of wealth lay still in the future.

Elsewhere in New England — in tiny coastal fishing communities, in bustling trading and commercial centers, in quiet rural villages — newspapers spilled ink lavishly in praise of Girard. Geographical as well as political differences were of no importance; newspaper editors from every corner of the region balloted on Girard and the verdict they returned was unanimous. The same problems that concerned editors elsewhere concerned those of New England, and the latter altered not a line of the familiar Girard portrait. All expressed agreement that inasmuch as the foundation of Girard's fortune lay "in his great industry and frugality . . . the particular transactions by which he first realized great wealth and was enabled to engage in mercantile operations" were unimportant. All praised his unostentatious mode of living, his devotion to work, the fact that he "died with harness on his back." All were agog at the size of his fortune and showed no restraint in speculating either as to its amount or destination. "But to the will — the will!" exclaimed the Portsmouth *State Herald,* impatient at the slowness with which reliable information was received. Above all, the newspapers agreed that in the most vital consideration of all Girard's career had been exemplary — he had been charitable in life and in death it could be said that no other person had ever devoted "such an immense amount of wealth, for the benefit of his fellow man." And prevailing sentiment, moreover, seemed to support Girard even in the religious controversy over his will. The Portland *Family Reader* mollified critics by explaining that Girard had not been motivated by "an unfriendly feeling toward *religion itself*" but by "fear of *sectarian* influence at some future day," and the Windsor *Vermont Chronicle* expressed confidence that instructors specially trained at Andover or Princeton might teach at the college so long as they were not ordained. Other newspapers were less conciliatory toward the sectarians. "Mr. Girard has shown himself a man of sense in prohibiting the clergy from having any control over the College," the *New Hampshire Patriot* observed. At other colleges, "the first thing on receiving a pupil is to cram down his throat the dogmas of a particular sect — send him to revival meetings"; and at Dartmouth "more attention is paid to instilling into the minds of students the principles of orthodoxy and *aristocracy* than any thing else." Girard's students, fortunately, would not be cramped by narrow prejudice.

Analysis of newspapers from states south and west of New England reveals only confirmation and acceptance of the standard portrait of Girard. Regional variations in the method of analyzing his activities and character — like religious and political variations — were striking by their absence. *Niles' Weekly Register* spoke for itself when it announced hopefully that Girard's donations to the city of Philadelphia would "entirely relieve the people of taxes forever," but it spoke for all when it praised his "incorruptible integrity and uniform regularity in business" and summarized his career as "a blessing to *working-men*" and an "example" of "powerful effect on the conduct of other capitalists." In these states, as elsewhere, the area of agreement concerning Girard as banker and philanthropist was wide enough to encompass diverse political viewpoints. To the Columbus *Ohio Monitor,* a Jacksonian paper, Girard's death was "justly a cause of universal regret . . . his liberality, public spirit and enterprise were eminently conspicuous, and his loss will be FELT and deplored . . . by the entire community." In the nation's capital, where political passions, fanned by journalistic partisans of the major parties, burned hot, Duff Green's Whiggish *United States Telegraph* ran a poor second to Frank Blair's *Washington Globe,* published by Jackson's Kitchen Cabinet, in giving tribute to Girard. The *Globe* ranged the "great Mariner and Merchant" alongside Jefferson, "the philosopher

and man of taste," in the galaxy of Democratic heroes. Indeed, it went
even further. To the "cockney remark" of that "bantling of the American
aristocracy," the Whig editor of the New York *American,* that he would
publish Girard's will only because of the curiosity about it, the *Globe*
retorted with asperity: "Mr. King, the Editor of the American . . . considers it a *'queer'* thing that any man should pick up the orphans of
the country to educate, when his millions might have been so much
better bestowed in swelling the magnificence of some pompous pink of
'good society.' Why did not Mr. Girard think of making Charles King a
King indeed?" In such fashion did Jackson's intimates speak of the man
who was known to be one of the largest investors in the "monster" they
were preparing to destroy, the Bank of the United States.[23]

The flavor of the discussion concerning Girard was not of a brew of
recent manufacture; it was of an aged and respected vintage. In 1695
Cotton Mather had admonished his Boston congregation:

Would a man *Rise* by his Business? I say, then let him *Rise* to his Business.
It was foretold. Prov. 22. 29, *Seest thou a man Diligent in his Business? He
shall stand* before Kings; He shall come to preferment. And it was instanced
by him who foretold it; 1 Kings 11. 28. Solomon, *seeing that the young man
was industrious, he made him a Ruler.* I tell you, with *Diligence,* a man may
do marvellous things. *Young* man, work hard while you are *Young:* You'l reap
the effects of it when you are *Old.* Yea, how can you Ordinarily enjoy any
rest at *Night,* if you have not been well at work in the Day? Let your *Business*
ingross the most of your time.[24]

Mather's exhortation to his audience was more than the expression of
an aspect of his religious faith. It was at once the projection of a secular
as well as religious goal and the revelation of the means by which that
goal could be reached, voluntary acceptance of the obligation to work.
Nearly two centuries later, Mather's moral steam engine was still in good
running order. Thrift, industry, frugality, diligence in labor — these were
still the sparking mechanisms that made the engine turn.[25] Some of its
parts, of course, needed overhauling, and considerable thought was
devoted to clarifying problems which, with Mather, had remained
somewhat obscure. The issue raised by John Wesley — "What way then
can we take, that our money may not sink us into the uttermost Hell?"
— was one of these; and the vast majority of observers agreed with
Wesley that the only salvation lay in the proper uses to which money
was put: "If those who gain all they can, and save all they can, will
likewise give all they can, then the more they gain, the more they will
grow in peace, and the more treasures they will lay up in heaven!" [26]
More precise, too, became the notion that success was a function of
unique individual capacity, of personal effort neither fettered by the
artificial restraints of birth and immunity characteristic of feudalism nor

aided by the governmental franchise and privilege characteristic of mercantilism. In the individualist economics of Ralph Waldo Emerson, it was a fundamental article of faith that "The world is mathematical and has no casualty in all its vast and flowing curve. Success has no more eccentricity than the gingham and muslin we weave in our mills . . . We must reckon success a constitutional trait . . . There is always a reason, *in the man*, for his good or bad fortune, and so in making money." Of this Emerson had no doubt: "Political economy is as good a book wherein to read the life of man . . . as any Bible which has come down to us." [27]

There were some, of course, like Constantine Rafinesque, who felt that the "Besetting National Sin of America" was "Cupidity," the desire to "make money any how, to obtain it fairly or unfairly"; but even he agreed that the important consideration was how money was used, that "spent to better purposes of public or general benefit, it would no doubt command Respect, Esteem, Approbation, and Gratitude." [28] Even such mild reservations, however, were out of tune with the characteristically aggressive, buoyant, and confident expression of the rights of business enterprisers and the high esteem in which they were held. Thomas Hunt sounded the note which echoed back and forth across the land: "To the rich in this world are granted privileges which the poor cannot enjoy. If it be the boast of the gospel, that unto the poor the gospel is preached, yet the rich have the honorable duty to support this gospel, that the poor may enjoy its blessings." Had not the wise men, who provided for the flight into Egypt of the infant Savior, been rich? They had brought gold and frankincense and myrrh. Had not Mary, who anointed Jesus on the day of his burial, been rich? She had brought a costly box of spikenard. Had not Joseph of Arimathea been rich? He had provided a resting place for Jesus. And Abraham, who entertained the strangers — had he not been rich and was he not now in paradise receiving his sons unto his bosom? As it was then so might it be again. "Well, we need not regret that our lots are cast in these latter days," Hunt solaced his readers. "The same honor which these rich and holy men have received, if we do our duty, shall be ours." [29]

Such, then, was the salubrious climate of enterprise in the United States as the first third of the nineteenth century drew to a close. Conflicts there were in society, but all social groups seemed as one in the exalted status they conferred upon businessmen, in the approval they bestowed upon business enterprise, and in the encouragement they offered to the kind of discipline best calculated to advance the interests of a developing capitalist economy. Americans of every religious and political persuasion agreed that "On this soil, every man, under God, may build his own fortunes, and work out and fill up his own earthly destiny. No inherited employment, like his father's name, whether he will or not, clings to him. No hereditary disabilities are heaped upon him, till they crush him to the earth." [30] They drank up the heady draughts of individualism and successful entrepreneurship poured out by the press and reveled in the glow produced by visible confirmation from every quarter that "anyone could be a capitalist, an investor, or a speculator," that cabin boy could become merchant-banker — if only he had the stuff. [31]

If only he had the stuff — this was the keynote. For in a society which was regarded as distributing its blessings equally upon all, distinctions in social status and occupational role were of necessity conceived to be the result of individual differences and not of differential access to opportunity. A society which is not questioned, which is deemed to serve the interests of all, needs no explanation. What needs to be explained, rather, is why each member occupies the position he does in that good society. In this sense, the journalistic interpreters of the career of Stephen Girard, confining themselves almost exclusively to a demonstration of his fitness to perform the functions of the role he occupied and an exhortation to others to model their behavior on his, at once reflected the widespread approval of the existing social structure and stimulated their readers to make its values their own. But the function of the press in sustaining consensus went beyond even this. If character were all and circumstances nothing, if success lay in the subjective factor of personality and not in the objective factor of the nature of the economic environment and man's relation to it, then, just as success was a tribute to the individual who had the qualities requisite for it, so the blame for failure, too, could be attributed to personal, not social, causes. In pronouncing such judgments, journalists, perhaps less consciously than teachers, preachers, and critics, were no less persuasively performing the function of "watchdog of society." [32]

If considerations external to character were irrelevant and if persons of the proper moral fibre to be successful could always be found, what reasons were there for businessmen to lack assurance? When Stephen Girard died, there was mourning for him, to be sure, and his chief clerk notified his agents in distant cities, with "the most painful feelings of distress," to close their accounts. [33] But there were none of the regrets, so characteristic of later decades, that with his death an era had ended, that times and circumstances had so altered that his like would never be seen again. Instead, his friends and associates, with full confidence in themselves and secure in the knowledge that their activities would be understood and supported, petitioned the State Legislature to charter a new bank to take the place of the old Girard Bank and provide the "extensive capital" needed to carry on the business life of the community. [34]

II

John Jacob Astor

On March 29, 1848, Philip Hone confided to his diary that "John Jacob Astor died this morning at eight o'clock, in the eighty-fifth year of his age; sensible to the last, but the material of life exhausted, the machinery worn out, the lamp extinguished for want of oil. Bowed down with bodily infirmity for a long time, he has gone at last, and left reluctantly his unbounded wealth." To Hone, who had known him intimately, Astor had been an empire builder, a merchant prince whose ships, freighted with furs and silks and tea, had sailed the seven seas. "He was the richest man in the United States in productive and available property," Hone wrote, "and this immense, gigantic fortune was the fruit of his own labor, unerring sagacity, and far-seeing penetration. He came to this country at twenty years of age; penniless, friendless, without inheritance, without education, and having no example before him of the art of money-making, but with a determination to be rich, and ability to carry it into effect . . . All he touched turned to gold, and it seemed as if fortune delighted in erecting him a monument of her unerring potency." [1]

Brassy journalist James Gordon Bennett agreed with Whig aristocrat Philip Hone that Astor had been a "modern Croesus," [2] "a self-invented money-making machine," but he dissented none too politely from Hone's verdict that Astor's wealth was the fruit of his own labor. "One half of his immense property," Bennett's *New York Herald* editorialized, "ten millions, at least — belonged to the people of the city of New York . . . The farms and lots of ground which he bought forty, twenty, ten, and five years ago, have all increased in value entirely by the industry of the citizens of New York. Of course, it is as plain as that two and two make four, that one-half of his immense estate, in its actual value, has accrued to him by the industry of the community."

Walt Whitman, writing in the New Orleans *Daily Crescent,* saw in Astor's death an occasion to write neither a treatise on unearned increment nor on the elements of successful entrepreneurship, but an essay on a lonely old man whose wealth could not buy health nor happiness:

> At a very advanced age this very well known personage has at length left that earth on which he had such large possessions. "The rich man also died." It were a trite moral to draw — to go over the oft-said maxims about the vanity of wealth, and its inability to wrestle with death; and we forbear. Wealth is good enough; but unfortunately people don't one-quarter of the time enjoy it, after it comes to them.
>
> For some years past Mr. Astor had been living in a two story brick house in Broadway, New York . . . Somehow, this dwelling always had a cold, cheerless, naked, and uninviting appearance: there were no shutters to the prodigious windows, nor were pleasant faces ever seen at the panes — nor was the warm aspect of family comforts and endearments known there. Ugh! the house gave one something of a chill when passing it, even in summer.
>
> We remember seeing Mr. Astor two winters since, when going down Broadway by this house. A couple of servants were assisting him across the pavement . . . The old gentleman's head seemed completely bent down with age and sickness; he was muffled in furs and entirely unable to help himself. The very groom, a hearty young Irishman, with perhaps not two dollars in his pocket, looked with pity upon the great millionaire! Certainly no man, of the crowds that hurried along that busy promenade, would have accepted the rich capitalist's wealth tied to the condition of being in his shoes.[3]

James Fenimore Cooper was concerned with neither sympathy nor economic theory. On the day of Astor's funeral he wrote to his wife a caustic, double-barreled note aimed at both Astor and Washington Irving:

> Today, J. J. Astor goes to the tomb. It is said that he sent checks of $100,-000 each to several grandchildren a few days before he died, in order to place them at their ease from the start. Irving is an executor, and report says with a legacy of $50,000. What an instinct that man has for gold! He is to be Astor's biographer! Columbus and John Jacob Astor! I dare say Irving will make the last the greatest man.[4]

But the harshest judgment of all was given by T. W. Ward, Boston financier who had known Astor. In a letter to Joshua Bates of Baring Brothers & Company, he wrote: "Mr. Astor is dead & supposed leaves some 15 or 18 millions dollars — six clergymen attended to bury the man whose word by his own acknowledgment should never be taken, nor his promise considered binding unless in writing."[5]

Unbounded admiration at Astor's colossal economic success, doubt that his success was the result of his own efforts and abilities, skepticism as to the value of money-making, scorn for his manner of living, concern with the problem of the proper uses of money, and outright condemnation of his business methods — these were the materials from which were compounded the broad evaluations of Astor's function and status in society. But out of the welter of comment two basic stereotypes of Astor the entrepreneur emerged: the first, lavish in praise of his accomplishments and directly relating his success to personal qualities of wisdom, foresight, and indefatigable application to business affairs; the second, conceding his success as a businessman, doubting that it could be attributed solely to personal virtues, and, on the assumption that money is not the measure of man, emphasizing the meanness and pettiness of Astor's life.

On March 29, 1848, William Cullen Bryant's New York *Evening Post* reported the death that morning of John Jacob Astor. "He was born in a little village near Heidelberg," the paper said, "and came quite a young man to this country, where by the steady application of more than common powers of intellect, he built up a vast fortune, and for many years before his death was the richest man in the United States."

Other New York newspapers, agreeing in the main with the *Evening Post*'s emphasis on Astor's personal abilities, were less restrained in their remarks. The New York *Observer* felt that his achievement in becoming the "richest man in the new world" was "the fruit not of peculiar advantages, but of sagacity and enterprise." His "instructions to his captains were minute and exceedingly particular. He evinced almost as intimate a knowledge of the various markets in which he traded, as though he had been a resident of each respective mart. It has been remarked of him, by one of his intimate friends, that Mr. Astor was capable of commanding an army of 500,000 men . . . At an early age he foresaw the future greatness of this emporium of the Western Continent, and was wont to convert two-thirds of his annual gain into real estate, not one foot of which he ever mortgaged." His business success, the *Observer* implied, was related to his personal habits. "Mr. Astor preserved through life his habit of early to bed and early to rise; he eschewed gambling, was fond of reading, but above all diligent in business. He seldom or never exhibited irritability of temper. He wrote a wretched scrawl, setting spelling and grammar equally at defiance; and yet, the strong, masculine understanding of the man is visible in all of them."

The New York *True Sun* was convinced that Astor as a businessman was an extension of Astor the individual, that the basis of his success lay in certain personal qualities. "There are few men whose biography would prove more instructive or acceptable to the present age, than the life of John Jacob Astor," the *True Sun* stated. "Endowed with an iron memory, and with a lucidity of combination which nothing could confuse, he seemed to possess an instinctive knowledge of every detail that occurred in his vast transactions, without consuming at his counting-house much more than half the time that most merchants feel compelled to bestow upon their concerns. He was always an early riser . . . His mind, it may be presumed, was rarely idle; and it must have been the ease with which he kept so vast a machine in accurate motion, that suggested to one of his early proteges . . . the remark that 'Mr. Astor was capable of commanding an army of 500,000 men' . . . If we esteem him an enterprising merchant who awaits for a year the return of his vessel from Canton or the Pacific, what term shall we apply to the adventurous and self-relying spirit which, regardless of 'the changes and the chances of this mortal life,' organizes and executes a vast and costly project, destined only to mature at the expiration of ten years?"

Endless variations were sounded on the same theme. Even James Gordon Bennett, who had many serious reservations about certain aspects of Astor's career, paid his respects to "the disposition of heart and firmness of purpose, which enabled him to obtain great wealth." And the effusive *Home Journal* attributed his success to "extraordinary sagacity and acuteness" and to "shrewdness and enterprise . . . No man ever excelled him in promptitude of action, and boldness of enterprise, in the various speculations in which he engaged . . . In every transaction of life, this enterprising and fortunate individual has sustained the reputation of strict honor and integrity."

That a chorus of praise should have been sung for John Jacob Astor is not surprising. He was, after all, the richest man in the United States, and in acclaiming him the New York press was hailing an adopted son. But what is perhaps surprising is the similarity of the profiles presented by the publications that praised him, a similarity that extended to the very phrases in which their ideas were expressed. Similar comment, expressions, and imagery appear with such monotonous regularity, indeed, as to create the suspicion that those who used them were all dependent upon the same source of information as to Astor's career.

In 1844, four years before Astor's death, Moses Yale Beach, editor and publisher of the New York *Sun,* compiled a handy guide to the merchant princes of New York City, one that could be used as well by persons seeking credit information concerning potential borrowers as by parents seeking to estimate the dowry of some potential daughter-in-law. Beach's pamphlet, *The Wealth and Biography of the Wealthy Citizens of the City of New York,* proved to be enormously popular. Within two years it had gone through ten editions, and it was revised twice during the next decade.[6] Careful examination indicates that Beach's pamphlet was, in all probability, the source of most of the biographical data concerning Astor that the newspapers reported and, even more, the source of that particular judgment of Astor that viewed his business career as the mirror of his personal life and that found the wellsprings of his business success in his personal qualities. Beach wrote that

John Jacob Astor is classed by those who know him best not only among the richest but also among the truly great men of the world. The talent which in another age, and in another state of society, was exercised in the art of war, is now to a great extent engaged in the peaceful occupations of the counting-room . . . Commerce affords scope for a greater variety of talent, and is a field on which the most gigantic genius, and the most soaring ambition, may expend themselves in unlimited conquests. In this department of human action Astor has displayed a great mind.

Beach commented on Astor's humble origin:

Landing on our shores as a common steerage passenger — a poor uneducated boy — a stranger to the language and the people — he has by the sole aid of his own industry, accumulated fortune scarcely second to that of any individual on the globe, and has executed projects that have become identified with the history of his country, and which will perpetuate his name to the latest age. He was born in July, 1763, in the village of Waldorp, near Heidelberg, in the Duchy of Baden, Germany. His father was a very worthy man and held the office of bailiff. At the age of eighteen young Astor, on the eve of leaving his home for a foreign land, resolved *to be honest and industrious, and never to gamble.*[7]

For Beach's newspaper, the importance of Astor's life lay in the example it provided of "perseverance under difficulties."

The New York *True Sun* embellished Beach's account and informed its readers that "under the shade of a linden-tree, near his native village," Astor had resolved *"to be honest and industrious, and never to gamble."* The New York *Herald* was also interested in Astor's youth. "In the year 1784," Bennett wrote, "he stood on our shores a poor youth, without knowledge of our language or our people . . . His place of birth was the village of Waldorp, near Heidelberg, in the Duchy of Baden, Germany . . . His father, who had good reputation for truthfulness and the leading of a correct life, held the humble but honorable office of bailiff of Waldorp. This worthy man sought with much care to impress on his children those pious views and resolves which he held as the safeguard to worldly happiness and prosperity."

Beach continued his account of Astor's career:

In March, 1784, he landed at Baltimore, a steerage passenger, having sailed from London in November, and been detained by the ice three months . . . The main portion of Mr. Astor's property at this time consisted of seven flutes from his brothers manufactory, at London, which, with a few other articles of merchandize, he sold, and invested the small proceeds in furs, and commenced learning the fur-trade.[8]

Horace Greeley's New York *Tribune* echoed Beach:

John Jacob Astor, when he landed in Baltimore from England, in a merchant ship, on board of which he had been a steerage passenger, in March, 1784, was in his twenty-first year, poor, uneducated, spoke English very imperfectly, and possessed but a few musical instruments, and a very small supply of money . . . He sold a few flutes probably of his brother's manufacture, bought furs, studied the fur trade . . .

Beach's awe-struck statement that Astor's income "on a moderate scale must be, $2,000,000 a year, or $166,000 a month, which is about $41,500 a week; $5,760 a day, $240 an hour, and $4 a minute," [9] was copied word for word by the New York *Observer*. His description of the minute instructions Astor gave to his ship captains was repeated in the *True Sun,* the *Observer,* the *Herald,* and the *Tribune.*

It would, in any case, be of interest to determine the source of much of the material that went into the construction of that stereotype of Astor which claimed to find the secret of his success in his "untiring industry and fidelity," in his "sagacity and gigantic intellect." But what is of special interest in this context is the character of the source of that stereotype. Beach's pamphlet, by his own admission, "originated from figures pencilled by several of our eminent business men, as the ground-work of a series of calculations upon the wealth of certain individuals,. and interesting only to themselves; but conceiving that a more extended and published list would be both interesting and useful to their fellow-citizens, they communicated the idea to the Publisher of The Sun, by whom it was at once taken up . . ." [10] It is reasonably certain, therefore, that material for the lives of the businessmen included in Beach's handbook came from businessmen who wanted it to be presented to "their fellow-citizens," and it is reasonably certain, too, that the material presented and the manner of presentation were such as to lead to the formation of attitudes and opinions deemed desirable by the businessmen themselves. Beach's pamphlet, therefore, takes on the character of an authorized source, a document prepared by persons interested in the creation of particular attitudes with respect to themselves and their activities.

But the existence of an official and favored interpretation by no means precludes the existence of dissenting views. New York newspapers, indeed, dissented with a vengeance and raised broad questions of morality and public policy that agitated editors the country over for months.

Even before Astor's death, as a matter of fact, there were hints of the existence of a certain bifocalism respecting his career, a bifocalism that at the same time conceded his business success and yet doubted that accumulation of wealth should be the purpose of life. William Armstrong, in his *The Aristocracy of New York: Who They Are, and What They Were,* paid respect to Astor for being the fifth richest man alive in 1848, surpassed in wealth only by Baron Rothschild, Louis-Philippe, the Duke of Devonshire, and Sir Robert Peel. But to Armstrong, Astor was also "close and parsimonious," and for all his money was "fast approaching the narrow house appointed for all living, and where the rich man and the beggar lie down alike at last." [11]

But if doubts only were expressed during Astor's lifetime, his death brought forth a flood of derogatory comment. The links which united the concepts of wealth and virtue, wealth and character were in danger of weakening under a concentrated editorial assault.

Horace Greeley, impressed by the revolutionary events of the February days in France and interested in political and economic reform at home, wrote an editorial the day after Astor's death which sounded the notes of moral condemnation and concern with an economic system that permitted such huge accumulations which were to become the two major elements of the chorus of dissent:

"Lay not up for yourselves treasures on earth," . . . and the events of the past month would seem powerfully to inculcate that doctrine, by the force of several very recent examples.

More than sixty years ago, a strong minded young German, with slender finances, and of humble birth and education, crossed the Atlantic to seek a home in America, followed, in a few years, by a bold, yet cautious and shrewd, Frenchman, [Louis-Philippe] who, though nursed in the lap of plenty, and his brain filled with learned lore, had tasted of poverty, and was seeking an asylum from persecution in the land of the free.

The young German adventurer made America his home; his talents and perseverance brought him immense wealth; he is said to have accumulated twenty-five millions of dollars. The Frenchman returned to his native land; hereditary riches awaited him, and, at length, a throne. The German lived just long enough to learn that the French adventurer had escaped from his own capital, unshaven and in disguise, with a five-franc piece in his pocket and that his immense treasures had been confiscated. The richest man in America died on the week in which he received tidings that the richest man in Europe was once more a fugitive and a wanderer, having no home.

Turning to Astor's business career, Greeley, too, praised his "farseeing sagacity," "vigorous intellect," and "promptness and regularity" in business matters; but his compliment that Astor had "adapted his business to the crisis" of 1812 was perhaps a backhanded one. Astor, Greeley took pains to point out, was able to get his furs from Mackinac and Detroit, "through opposing armies and hostile fleets," to Canada and thence to New York City, "and here shipped them *indirectly* for London." He had profited during the War of 1812 in other ways as well. "Mr. Astor lent President Madison's administration some small sums in 1812 or 1813, but in 1814, toward the close of the war, when the banks had ceased to pay specie, and their notes were at thirty to sixty per cent. discount, he concerted with Messrs. Parrish and Girard, went to Philadelphia and Washington, and obtained the bonds of the Federal Government payable, the principal with interest, at six per cent., in specie, for several millions of dollars, at eighty or eighty-two cents. This he paid in the paper of certain banks with which he had connections, which was worth, say, fifty cents in silver for the dollar, and as he received the obligation of the United States for $1 in exchange for eighty-two cents of this depreciated currency, he must have cleared more than a million of dollars in hard money on every two millions of paper thus lent!" [12]

Astor, to be sure, had certain admirable qualities. He "did not play at cards or gamble," he "rose early and went soon to bed," and was "either very good-tempered; or else had great command of his passions." But there was another side to the man: "Although from policy he feasted and caressed the rich and influential, he was a hard man, though less so than his son William B."

Unlike the newspapers which found the source of Astor's wealth to be only in his personal qualities, the *Tribune* found contemporary political and economic policies to have been of material assistance. "The Party called National Reformers express the opinion that land speculators, like Mr. Astor, should be checked in their dealings in the lands and lots of the country by a statute forbidding any man from holding or acquiring hereafter more than 600 or 1,000 acres, or a certain quantity within a city, said statute not to interfere with present holders. Mr. Astor is not to blame for grasping at that which neither he nor his son can enjoy — the law made it right in him to do so. The Nationals are also fond of direct taxation, and are not easily persuaded that it is a wise and just policy in the United States government to protect Mr. Astor's houses, lands, ships, stocks, &c., and yet exact no direct taxes from him according to his income."

"Mr. Astor's successful example," the *Tribune* concluded, "ought to stimulate our youth in a prudent and upright course of dealing. It would, perhaps, have been better if he had possessed less of parsimony in some of his transactions, and it is to be desired that men of his keen and acute intelligence may no longer be permitted to engross millions of acres, and thousands of town lots, nor to find a government at Washington ready to give its bonds for $1 in specie, receiving only forty to fifty cents as an equivalent; but considering his early poverty and defective education, his fine discrimination of character, and great sagacity in choosing the most profitable branches of trade, are circumstances truly surprising."

Where Greeley's *Tribune* was moderate in tone, James Gordon Bennett's *Herald* was bold and forthright. After paying its respects to Astor's "integrity and assiduity," the *Herald* launched its attack:

John Jacob Astor, the great American *millionaire*, has at length joined his kindred dust, and fulfilled his destiny . . . He has been an extraordinary man, and the press of this and other cities will be eager to publish everything connected with him . . . If Mr. Astor was industrious in the accumulation of riches, he was likewise very penurious and niggardly in money matters. What he saved he kept and locked up to the day of his death . . . He was a willing purchaser of mortgages from their needy holders at less than their face; and when they became due he foreclosed them, and purchased the mortgaged property at . . . ruinous prices.

"When the idea first occurred to him of bequeathing funds to establish an extensive public library in New York," the *Herald* stated, "he sent for a mason, and requested him to draw up specifications . . . he inquired what the outlay for the first year would be, and was informed that it would probably be fifteen thousand dollars. 'That will do,' said Mr. Astor, rising from his chair, and placing the specifications in a large trunk, where they have remained from that day to the present."

In filling columns with articles on Astor, the New York press was gratifying the desire of a great many people to learn the facts of his life and, even more, to learn the size of his estate and the details of his will. As soon as Astor's death was announced there had been "a great desire . . . by the public to know what disposition has been made of his immense property," and press accounts of his funeral agree that "crowd after crowd gathered" and "thousands rushed in, until the hall was crowded almost to suffocation." Hope was expressed that "those possessing the requisite information" would "see the necessity of allaying the public excitement" concerning the "absorbing subject" of Astor's will. The publishers of Armstrong's book on the aristocracy of New York took advantage of public curiosity by placing an ad in the *Herald*'s classified section: "John Jacob Astor — A Full and Complete life of this eminent individual, gathered from entirely original sources, and embracing an entire account of his career, is to be found only in the work, called the New York Aristocracy — who they are, and what they were . . . Apply, if by letter post paid, to the New York Publishing Company, No. 88½ Nassau street, in the rear, entrance through the alley."

But popular interest in the amount and distribution of Astor's estate went unsatisfied until April 3, six days after his death, when the New York *Journal of Commerce* announced that it had "examined an abstract" of the will and concluded that the aggregate value of the estate was "less than twenty millions, or less than half the sum we put down the other day." But "either sum is quite out of our small comprehension," the

Journal of Commerce added, "and we presume that with most men, the idea of one million is just about as large an idea, as that of any number of millions." Within twenty-four hours, three New York newspapers reprinted the *Journal of Commerce* article.

Perhaps the most spectacular demonstration of public interest in Astor's death took place on April 5 when the *Herald,* for the first time since Americans had learned of the events in Paris, swept its first page clean of news of the revolution of 1848 and devoted it exclusively to a verbatim transcript of Astor's will. Publication of the will was a journalistic scoop, and James Gordon Bennett made the most of it. "We give in our columns," he said, "an authentic copy of one of the greatest curiosities of the age — the will of John Jacob Astor, disposing of property amounting to about twenty millions of dollars, among his various descendants of the first, second, third, and fourth degrees. This is as valuable a document to them as the famous treaty of the Senate is to the Mexicans — both being worth about twenty millions to the respective parties."

Reading the provisions of the will apparently confirmed all of Bennett's original doubts concerning Astor's personal qualities and, even more, led him, like Greeley, into a discussion of basic economic questions.

The will of John Jacob Astor is a curious document, both in its language, composition and grammar, as well as in its bequests. During the greater portion of the last years of his life, he was the associate and Maecenas of Washington Irving, Mr. Cogswell, Mr. Halleck, and several other literary, philosophical and poetical gentlemen connected with the literary latitude and longitude of New York. The results of their doctrines, their views, their ideas, their talk, appear in the will; and judging from that document, we must say that we don't think too much of their teachings. If we had been an associate of John Jacob Astor . . . we should have given him some instructions in political economy, at least of a very different character from what it appears he has imbibed from those whom he lived among. The first idea we should have put into his head, would have been that *one-half of his immense property — ten millions, at least — belonged to the people of the city of New York.* During the last fifty years of the life of John Jacob Astor, his property has been augmented and increased in value by the aggregate intelligence, industry, enterprise and commerce of New York, fully to the amount of one-half of its value . . . Having established this principle, we would have counselled John Jacob Astor to leave at least the half of his property for the benefit of the city of New York . . . leaving ten millions to be given to his relatives — a sum quite enough for any reasonable persons, of any rank of life in this country. But instead of this, he has only left less than one-half a million for a public library. What a poor, mean and beggarly result from associating with such literary men, philosophers and poets!

We cannot, therefore, pronounce the highest species of eulogy upon the character of the late John Jacob Astor. He has exhibited, at best, but the ingenious powers of a self-invented money-making machine; and the associates, advisers, and counsellors of his later years, seem to have looked no further than to the different pins, cranks and buttons of this machine, without turning it to any permanent benefit to that community from whose industry he obtained one-half the amount of his fortune, in the indirect values added to his estates in the course of years.

Bennett was by no means finished with the subject. He had already stigmatized Astor as tightfisted and stingy, questioned the official stereotype that regarded his fortune as purely the product of his own superior wisdom, and doubted that the true measure of Astor could be taken simply in terms of the wealth he had accumulated without consideration of the purposes to which that wealth was put. Now he broadened the attack by accusing Astor of disregarding basic American principles in the distribution of his wealth:

In reading over this will . . . the conclusion to which the mind is led is the following — that the great purpose of the testator was to leave the bulk of his fortune to his eldest son, William B. Astor, and to get round and evade in some way or other the American law which prohibits primogeniture, or the concentration of the whole of a man's property upon one heir, to the exclusion of the others. This is our American law, and a wise law it is, inasmuch as it prevents the formation of great aristocratic dynasties, which are effected, in England and Germany, by leaving the bulk of the property to the eldest son, while the rest of the family are left in comparative poverty. The great object of the will, is to create an Astor dynasty . . . and to keep up this dynasty by entailing the property upon the regular successors of the individual for ages to come.

No other New York newspaper echoed this argument, but the next charge hurled by Bennett — subsidiary to the main theme — was to have national repercussions:

If the testator had lived ten years longer, it is probable that all, except the eldest son . . . would have been cut off with as small a share as is left to his friend Fitz Greene Halleck, an amount just enough to give that amiable man and sweet poet a supply of segars . . . we should not be astonished to see the other descendants make an attempt to break the will, and produce an equal distribution of the whole property . . . But what would become of the amiable Fitz Greene Halleck and his tremendous annuity in such a case? A dead loss.[13]

Other New York newspapers played variations on the themes sounded by Bennett. The *New-York Organ and Temperance Safeguard,* after a meticulous description of Astor's coffin, was moved to express doubt that accumulation of riches in this world was sufficient to save the soul of the departed in the next: "So a rich man has the advantage of rotting in *velvet, gold,* and *silver* trappings; *silver* headed screws, exquisite needle-work, and *bullion* fringe, while the dust of a poor man must decompose in plain wood! What a compliment to the *immortal spirit* of the departed . . . The entire real and personal estate of Mr. Astor is estimated at eighteen millions. This is much less than was expected, but still too much for any one man."

The *Family Companion,* official publication of the Independent Order of Odd Fellows, agreed that the rich cannot buy salvation: "Mr. Astor was immensely, inordinately wealthy — but in him has been realized, as in all others it has been and must be, the truth of the Divine saying — man brought nothing into this world and can carry nothing out of it." But the Odd Fellows had even more specific objections to Astor's will.

During his lifetime, because of frequent fires that ravaged whole sections of New York City, Astor had insisted that all property pledged to him should be adequately insured against fire by the mortgagors. In managing his property, he made a practice of sending letters to lessees notifying them that their fire insurance policies were about to expire and informing them of the insurance companies on his approved list.[14] The *Family Companion* was bitter because Astor's will expressed no apprecia-tion of the valuable services New York firemen gave him in protecting his vast property. "If Mr. Astor had left the paltry (to him) sum of fifty thousand dollars, how many widows and orphans would have blessed his name — how much happiness would he have conferred — how many crushed hopes would have been raised again." [15]

The *Weekly Yankee* succeeded at once in intimating that wealth alone could not buy salvation, in challenging the notion that economic success was a function solely of personal character, and in emphasizing the crucial importance of matters affecting the distribution of estates:

John Jacob Astor appears not to have had a soaring ambition . . . By con-tributing a portion of his fortune to the good of his fellow men, he would have done something toward sending back into the general account, a portion of the golden stream which he had subtracted from it. Even in Italy and other old countries, where the great men seem to regard the common people as little better than cattle, these public benefactions are not infrequent, but it is too much the case that our wealthy men seem disposed rather to build up and perpetuate an aristocracy like that of the old world, than to contribute of their abundance to the welfare of those who have been less favored by fortune than themselves.

Perceptive observers might have discerned in such remarks the ap-proach of storm clouds, still distant yet ominous by their very existence, that threatened, unless dispersed, to darken the sunny climate in which business enterprise had long basked and flourished. The concept of the identity of wealth and virtue was being challenged by an alternative morality which, skeptical of the value of a life devoted to money-making, afforded something less than wholehearted approval to exclusive concern with business activity. Still more threatening was the emergence of economic doctrine which denied the identity of private striving and public welfare, which held that the activities of businessmen indeed "subtracted" from the "general account." Most dangerous of all, perhaps, was the expression of conviction that success rested upon a broader basis than character alone. If "fortune" was an element to be considered, then failure could not be blamed only on the individual; "luck" put in an appearance, and Cotton Mather's moral dynamo was in danger of running down. Above all, if elements located in social structure rather than in personal character were deemed part of the causal chain leading to success, then a new explanation of failure could be offered: the fault was in society, not personality; and where the fault lay, there must the cure be applied.

Clearly, a considerable body of opinion existed in New York which was markedly at variance with the verdict on Astor that found nothing but praise for his character and that considered his economic success to rest upon the foundation of that character. Quantitatively, expression of this dissenting opinion, at least in its written form, was quite as common as expression of the favorable view. Qualitatively, it differed in certain basic respects. It disagreed that Astor's character and morality could not be questioned; it opposed the view that, in an estimate of the man, it was sufficient only to be concerned with his economic success; it dissented from the opinion that that success rested only upon personal attributes; and it sometimes couched its evaluation of Astor in terms that indicated a relationship between economic success and aspects of the social order which were held to contribute to that success.

So widespread, indeed, was this opinion and so sharp was its attack, that proponents of the favorable view and even some who had participated in the dissent were stung into reply. In answering their critics, these newspapers were forced for the first time to go beyond a mere defense of Astor. Because the dissenters had insisted upon linking questions of economic theory and practice to their discussions of Astor, defense of Astor now included defense of the economic system.

The New York *Journal of Commerce,* frightened by the possible consequences of the attacks on Astor and the reaction to the French Revolution of 1848, a reaction that included huge meetings of sympathy and support, turned to a defense of Astor in particular and the economic system in general:

Liberty. — There are some theories among the French which are quite inconsistent with true liberty, and the general opinion about it in this country. We refer to the notion that government is obliged to provide labor and support for the working classes, and for all the people. In this country, liberty is understood to be the *absence* of government from private affairs: the social doctrine, on the contrary, demands its most minute interference. At the meeting in the Park on Monday afternoon, one of the representatives of the working men, as they are called, presented himself . . . He said the people were rejoicing at the expansion of liberty abroad, and yet in this country there existed a grievous slavery . . . the slavery of labor to capital . . . Then he went on to say that the working men were entitled to have work-houses erected for them by the government at the expense of property, where they should be provided with employment and support . . . Our working men know better than to put themselves into the machinery of such a liberty. What they want is, the liberty to use their hands for themselves, and not for the government, enjoying for themselves and their families the independence and comfort which they have earned, from whoever will pay them best . . . By working for themselves, these slaves to capital become, in our country, to be the masters of capital.

John Jacob Astor's life, to the *Herald,* had represented the negation of the American principle of preventing the formation of aristocratic dynasties by insistence upon the distribution of wealth. His life, to the *Journal of Commerce,* was an illustration of the rich harvests that could be reaped under the American economy:

Who was John Jacob Astor but a penniless German immigrant. What would he have been worth, if instead of working for himself, he had thrown himself upon government provision. Who were most of the capitalists who occupy our up-town palaces, when they began life, but working men? What have they been and what are they now, but working men? Working, many of them, truly, with too slavish a subjection to the love of accumulation. That is all the danger of slavery which exists in the arrangement.

It is only to be expected, the *Journal of Commerce* added, that in Europe, "where the masses have been sacrificed to the few, there should be a strange confusion of ideas among honest men about personal rights. They see through a glass darkly." But in America things were different: "Here, the light is so strong, and the medium so clear, that men may see things truly. They can, at any rate, see that other places are much better for them than a government-work-house. Agrarianism and trades' unions must equally perish here; they are both so obviously opposed to the enterprise and ambition of the men to whom they are addressed." [16]

Horace Greeley's *Tribune,* which had participated in the earliest assault on Astor, attempted to disengage itself from the broader implications of the attack. The *Tribune* was willing to concede that Astor's social vision was narrow: "To pile up such an enormous fortune by trade or speculation, and to use it for the glory of God and the highest good of mankind, are two different things, requiring diverse if not absolutely incompatible characters and faculties. It is a melancholy, insane perversion of a human life to make it mainly subservient to the acquirement of such a fortune." It was unwilling, however, to accept the argument that the rich, of necessity, must have attained their wealth at the expense of others: "Yet we cannot agree with those who openly assume or clearly imply that such an estate could not be honestly amassed . . . that such a fortune must have been made *out* of the earnings of others than the possessor . . . Doubtless many fortunes have been amassed by operations rather injurious than beneficial to the community, such as Monopoly and Forestalling, whether in Land, Provisions, or anything else; but it by no means follows that *all* fortunes have been acquired at the expense of honest poverty." Inventors of devices to prevent steamboat explosions, to soften rock so tunnels could be dug more easily, and to peel wheat, even if they were to reap fortunes from their inventions, were performing socially useful functions and at the expense of no one. Greeley made no defense in his editorial of accumulating wealth through land speculation.

It is perhaps less remarkable that the newspapers of New York City, which for years had been the center of Astor's activity, devoted so much space to his accomplishments than that the press elsewhere in the country did so at a time when the Mexican War, the Revolution of 1848, and an approaching presidential election were competing for the attention of newspaper readers. Interest in Astor's death seems to have been at least as intense outside as within New York. The comments of editorial writers of newspapers outside New York, however, because of their dependence upon the New York press which had already constructed two sharply differentiated evaluations of Astor, consisted largely of additional embellishments on the portraits already drawn. The newspapers of New York City were, therefore, more than merely sources of information for newspapers elsewhere; they raised the questions which served as the starting points for evaluations of Astor the country over.

The content of the articles that appeared in the New England press, for example, and the ideas projected by that content differed little from the stories that had already been printed in the newspapers of New York City.

There was no paucity of newspapers reflecting the favorable stereotype of Astor. For these, Astor was a person of remarkable exploits and "great enterprise," whose vast fortune was built "by the steady application of more than common powers of intellect," "enterprise and integrity." The Exeter *News-Letter* presented a laudatory account of Astor simply by omitting from the New York *Tribune* editorial of March 30, which was the basis of most of its information, those sections in which Greeley had questioned certain of Astor's personal characteristics and had maintained that government fiscal and land policy had contributed to his success. Quoting the "gossip" of the New York correspondent of the New

Orleans *Delta*, the Boston *Evening Gazette* defended Astor against charges that he was "mean; he is not so — he is merely particular. He gives freely; he is most bounteous in his private charity. To his country-men, the Germans, he has been magnificently kind." For these news-papers, at least in the early stages of the discussion, the explanation of Astor's success consisted largely in a demonstration that career was a function of character, that public activities were implicit in private qualities.

As in New York, curiosity in New England concerning Astor's will was great, so great, indeed, that the Boston *Daily Advertiser* felt it neces-sary to comment: "We have no means of satisfying the curiosity . . . except by saying that we believe that Mr. Astor took none of his accumu-lated wealth with him. We are sorry to see people gazing at and wonder-ing about large sums of money; it seems as if they 'lusted after it.'"

Whether or not people lusted after Astor's wealth, the newspapers certainly continued to discuss it, and their discussion was concerned largely with three aspects of Astor's will: the size of the estate, the be-quests for public purposes, and the legacy to Halleck. Estimates of the amount of the estate were continually changing, largely because the New York newspapers were themselves constantly amending their estimates.[17] *Zion's Herald* succinctly summed up the attitude of the pro-Astor press on the question: whatever its size, "still, it is the largest estate that was ever owned in this country." With respect to Astor's bequest of $400,000 to establish a free public library in New York, interest was less intense. The Boston *Atlas* and the Boston *Evening Transcript* viewed it favorably, but the *Liberator* contented itself with the statistical statement: "John Jacob Astor left property to the amount of twenty millions of dollars. For charitable and public purposes, he bequeaths about half a million, or one-fortieth of his estate." Concerning the legacy to Halleck, press comment was less reserved. The *Whig* hoped it was true that "the liberality of William B. Astor" had increased Halleck's annuity to $1,000 per year; and even so staunch a friend of Astor as the *Evening Transcript,* which on March 30 had anticipated that Halleck would "be made comfortable for life," later commented sarcastically that it hoped potential lawsuits to break the will would not deprive Halleck "of his magnificent legacy of $200 a year."

Comment critical of Astor's personal character, as it was expressed in the provisions of the will, as well as of the morality of devoting a life entirely to the pursuit of wealth was especially common in the Boston press. Several journals reprinted in its entirety the New York *Tribune* editorial — "Lay not up for yourselves treasures on earth" — which had agreed that Astor's was a "vigorous intellect" and yet maintained that he had been parsimonious and that, in part at least, his wealth had been gained in a manner that could not be countenanced. The Cambridge *Chronicle* was even more forceful. Under the caption, *A Bad Reputation,* it reprinted a brief note from the New York *Mirror:* Astor's "benevolence did not extend far, and in proportion to his means, we never had a wealthy citizen who did less, in his lifetime, to promote charitable, religious or benevolent objects." To the Boston *Traveller,* the mere accumulation of wealth, even in large amounts, was not necessarily to be applauded. "For more than three score years and ten," the *Traveller* said, Astor had toiled "assiduously . . . to keep up this vast pile of wealth — not a farthing of which he can take with him whither he has been called from his sordid labor." Not even Astor's bequest to establish a public library was virtuous. He might have endowed the library "in his life time — but he would have lost the interest of the money in that case. Posthumous charity demands no self-sacrifice."

The note of moral condemnation struck by so many of the Boston papers received vigorous support from the Concord *Congregational Journal:*

> During his life he was notoriously niggardly and hard in his bargains, though not dishonest. Dr. Spring, at his weekly lecture the evening after the day of Mr. Astor's death, availed himself of the melancholy event to illustrate the truth of the text, "for we brought nothing into the world, and it is certain we shall carry nothing out." "Yesterday," said the preacher . . . "he was worth his 40 millions; today not a farthing." . . . His highest if not exclusive aim was the acquisition of wealth, in which by perseverance and cool judgment he succeeded beyond any other individual in our country. His pleasure was in the acquisition, not the use of money — the most sordid and unworthy passion of which the heart is capable . . . How much more of life he might have enjoyed had he possessed a mere competence, and how much greater would have been the good accomplished by his princely treasures, had he "used them as not abusing them" by freely distributing them to human necessities; and how much dearer and more honored would have been the memory he leaves behind! Nothing is more dangerous to the soul than wealth, though nothing is coveted like that.

The Lawrence *Courier* expressed the notion that the will was the measure of the man, and by that measure found Astor wanting:

> What vast, what incalculable good he might not have done with his money had he been of the same benevolent spirit of some less wealthy persons. He might have established 80,000 families upon ample farms in the western country and thus permanently reserved from want at least 800,000 human beings, and still retained an ample fortune for himself. Now just take hold of this idea: 800,000 human beings! more than any state in the union contained in 1830 — excepting New York, Pennsylvania, and Virginia! Almost as many as all New England contained in 1790 . . . What a river of kindness *might*

have flowed from this man's heart, nourishing, fertilizing, and cheering the hearts and kindly feelings of others! But neither a rill, nor a vapor only such as were poisoned and embittered by the weeds of selfishness, ever flowed from this immense horde of money. All that any one can say of it is, that it is not only a *pity*, but a SHAME.

An even more acid quality was given to the *Courier's* characterization of Astor when it reprinted from the Salem *Gazette* an anecdote concerning Astor and Audubon. Astor had subscribed to Audubon's work on ornithology, had received the book, but had never paid the $1,000 subscription price. Audubon attempted on several occasions to speak to Astor about the debt, but the latter was always "out" to him. Finally Audubon reached him at his home. " 'Ah, Mr. Audubon, so you have come again after your money. Hard times, Mr. Audubon; money scarce!' But just then catching an inquiring look from his son, he changed his tone. — 'However, Mr. Audubon, I suppose we must contrive to let you have some of your money, if possible. William,' he added, calling to his son who had walked into an adjoining parlor, 'have we any money at all in the bank?' 'Yes, father,' replied William B., supposing that he was asked an earnest question, pertinent to what they had been talking about when the ornithologist came, 'we have 220,000 in the bank of New York, 70,000 in the City Bank, 90,000 in the Merchants, 98,400 in the Mechanics, 83,-000 . . .' 'That'll do, that'll do,' exclaimed John Jacob interrupting him; 'it seems that William can give you a check for your money.' "

Comment became so acid as to border on the contemptuous. "Poor man," mourned the Boston *Daily Chronotype*. He had left less than twenty million dollars. "No wonder he could not be more liberal." If it was true that Astor left only $200 to Halleck, the *Post* said, "John Jacob Astor was an &c. He left about $20,000,000." The temperance journal *Excelsior*, commenting on the fact that estimates of the size of Astor's estate were constantly being reduced, seconded the suggestion that "a subscription paper be started" for the relief of the heirs. "The 'upper ten' who have been in the habit of associating with the unfortunate Bill, will of course 'cut his acquaintance,' " it added.

Final summation of the view that condemned Astor's moral code was provided by the *Trumpet and Universalist* in an editorial that virtually equated wealth and immorality:

It is worthwhile sometimes to reflect how little it is in the power of money to do for its possessor. A competency of this world's goods is very pleasant; but beyond that, property is rather a curse than a blessing. It is always a curse, where a good use in not made of it. — Property will not save a man's life; it will not ward off old age; it will not prevent disease; it will not buy a clear conscience, nor a peaceful death-bed. — So far from making men happy in life, it often happens that the rich man is most miserable. It is better to strive to be wise and virtuous, than to strive to be rich. He who strives only to be rich, without regard to the means, is on a slippery foundation. — There are a thousand chances that he will live a miserable life, and die unlamented . . . Health, peace of mind, purity of heart, long life, — the light, the air, the water, are all independent of riches. Let us strive to be good; and if God sees fit to throw riches in our way, let us use them for the best of purposes.

In New England, as well as in New York, evaluations of Astor and methods of analyzing his activities symptomatic of developing strains in the social fabric began to appear. Moral judgment, of course, continued: none of the faculties of "this mighty accumulator," said the Boston *Daily Chronotype,* "except that for weighing pecuniary ends against pecuniary means, expanded with his wealth." And at the end, he had "tumbled into his grave and left his beloved heap behind him." But from Portland, Maine, came what was for New England a new element in the discussion, though one which had earlier been emphasized by James Gordon Bennett. Astor's life and his method of disposing of his fortune, to the *Transcript,* were the antithesis of the American spirit of opposition to dynasties. "No man born under the influence of our free institutions," the *Transcript* said in a reference to Astor's foreign birth, "could be so unmindful of his own fame and so recreant to the Republican Spirit as to dedicate his whole life to the sole object of endowing his eldest son with a more than imperial fortune." And the *Daily Chronotype,* a heretic with respect to the orthodox equation of character and career, was not content with moral judgments alone. That paper was scornful of the view that "every dollar" of Astor's fortune was "the product of his own industry. We doubt whether *forty hundred dollars* of it were the product of his own industry. The other thirty-nine millions nine hundred and ninety odd thousand dollars were the product of his *shrewd* management, aided by the very unshrewd management of the people in legislating to favor the accumulation of capital, and not to favor the comfort, education and elevation of the producing masses. Several millions of it were directly shaved out of Uncle Sam by buying his own bonds at forty or fifty cents on the dollar. But the greater part of his immense estate was amassed by getting hold of city lots when they were cheap as dirt, and holding them till surrounding industry had almost coined them into gold." The *Daily Chronotype* was willing to concede that where "the mass cannot be wise enough to lay up seed corn, tools, capital for the future, there must be close-fisted Astors to do it." But in pointing to the role played by factors external to character — in isolating the importance of legislation and fiscal policy — it had opened Pandora's box. The plaguy insects of social criticism were now let loose. If that criticism was to be forestalled — and if it were not, the consensus which supported enterprise would be threatened — the argument had to be transformed; that which the critics pointed to as miasmic swamps which bred social ills would have to be presented as the fertile soil of social welfare. The *Christian Reflector* made the connection between environment and success — which had earlier been used to criticize Astor — into an instrument of approval for both man and system. Astor's "sagacious promptitude" was but half the story; "boldness in taking advantage of the opportunities" offered by America had also "done its share."

The presentation of dissenting views, at variance with accepted explanations concerning both the characterization of Astor and the relative importance of man as agent and society as setting in the achievement of success, was a function not only of gradual dissolution of the spirit of community and the growth of social fissures,[18] but, as well, of new journalistic developments which reflected these changes. Until early in the 1830's, newspapers, by virtue both of their price and content, appealed largely to the urban commercial and political patriciate. So striking, indeed, did this appear to one observer that he commented: "The commercial part of the community advertise the most, — their interests, therefore, are sure to be advocated . . . The proverb, *'Point d'argent, point de Suisses,'* applies as much to the gentlemen of the press as to the hired soldiers of Helvetia."[19] Businessmen were in fact urged to take advantage of the situation Francis Grund described. "The true merchant will be a liberal but discriminating supporter of the press in his locality," advised the author of *A Practical Treatise on Business.* "He will combine with men like himself to procure the establishment of such a journal as is needed, or the transfer of one already existing into the hands of someone qualified to guide opinion and dispel mental darkness. Such a journal he will liberally and steadily encourage and support by advertising in its columns at good prices, by urging upon other business men the duty of doing likewise, and by soliciting his customers and neighbors to give it their subscriptions." The businessman need not be "a political brawler nor habitual agitator on any subject — there is a better way." By giving "from two to five hundred dollars' worth of advertising per annum" to "an approved and influential journal" in his community, he would "exert a noiseless, unintermitted influence in diminishing the kingdom of darkness, extending the range of virtue, and laying deep and broad the foundations of general and personal prosperity."[20] By the late thirties and forties of the nineteenth century, however, the dominance of such newspapers was being challenged by a new journalistic form, the "penny press," appealing to new strata of readers never before reached by the six-cent dailies. Newspapers, once seen in hotel, tavern, and countinghouse, were now to be found in "every street, lane, and alley" and "almost every porter and drayman, while not engaged in his occupation, may be seen with a paper in his hands." As one contemporary journal summed it up, the "penny papers reach the very depths of the social state and move the mighty waters that lie undisturbed and stagnant below the reach of our daily mammoth sheets." [21] It was largely, though not exclusively, in this new class of newspapers that the voices of dissent were heard.

And the ideas expressed by these voices included condemnation of Astor's greed and lack of generosity; belief in the principle of the stewardship of wealth; conviction that large accumulations of wealth must almost of necessity condemn their possessors to unhappiness and misery; even the argument, which the Boston penny *Investigator* quoted from the Philadelphia penny *Inquirer,* that without "the hands of Astor's employees" his "head would have accomplished nothing."

South and west of New York City interest in Astor's life and will was equally keen. In Cincinnati, metropolis of the West, the issue was sharply joined between those who approved and those who disapproved of the way in which Astor had distributed his money. The *Chronicle,* admitting that "great curiosity has been expressed, in many quarters, to know the will of Mr. Astor," noted "with pleasure" that he had "in the first place, made ample provision for all his relations and their children. This, Mr. Girard did not do. We are glad to see it, because the claims of blood should always be attended to." The *Liberty Hall and Cincinnati Gazette* had the opposite view: "The Will . . . does not conform to the general 'notions' and practice of Americans. Our laws prohibit primogeniture, and the prevailing American sentiment is opposed to the concentration of property upon one heir . . . The Will of Mr. Astor discloses his desire to create a dynasty, by entailing his property, as far as our laws would sanction." A third Cincinnati newspaper, *Cist's Weekly Advertiser,* condemned both Astor and the standards by which he could be considered a great man: "He was industrious, frugal and enterprising, got what he could, and kept what he got. He paid his debts as fast as they became due — doubtless, and as the world estimates worth, was a worthy man, that is, he was worth millions." But in the pursuit of wealth he had "denied himself every indulgence during that portion of life which is capable of rational or intellectual enjoyment, and . . . he has dragged out a miserable existence, a stern and striking lesson of the folly and wretchedness of making the inordinate pursuit of wealth the great object of human life."

From Oregon to Florida, in sleepy Southern bayou towns and in bustling commercial entrepôts, newspaper editors considered the meaning of the life of John Jacob Astor and, in considering, made judgments indicative of new winds of doctrine in the climate of enterprise. The prevailing winds, however, were still fair, and businessmen looking at the weather map could take comfort in a favorable forecast for their activities; they were assured of widespread approval for a life devoted to business enterprise, of esteem and admiration if they should prove successful, and — should they also be charitable — of almost universal respect. The view of Astor which found his life to be one of "perseverance under difficulties," of honesty and industry — even when it inveighed against his manner of distributing his estate — could not but be beneficial to the growth of business enterprise; for the criticism was concerned not with business activity but with philanthropy. Between the lines of Astor's obituaries, perceptive entrepreneurs could read that social disapproval was far more likely to be directed against the way in which wealth was distributed than the way in which it was gained.

But chill winds of disapproval were blowing up. In the Middle Western states of Illinois, Ohio, Indiana, and Iowa, in Florida and Louisiana, Astor was pilloried for his meanness and pettiness. Even more threatening, however, was the growing tendency to cut the links that once had united character and destiny, wealth and virtue. Wealth could no longer be considered, in this view, as evidence that its possessor had lived a life of virtue. On the contrary; "rich men have, indeed, souls generally of a size inversely proportioned to the extent of their affluence." Far out on the Great Plains, in Tahlequah, Oklahoma, the *Cherokee Advocate,* deeply interested in Astor's will, expressed the new view: "Nothing is more easy than to grow rich. It is only to trust nobody, befriend none, to heap interest upon interest, cent upon cent; to destroy all the finer feelings of nature, to be rendered mean, miserable, and despised, for some twenty or thirty years, and riches will come as sure as disease, disappointment, and a miserable death . . . What more than such a thought need occupy a sane mind, to fill and keep it full of unutterable anguish? Life a failure! Probation squandered — ending!! — the soul lost!!!" Nor was there consensus any longer that qualities peculiar to the individual were the sole causes of economic success. Government land and fiscal policy and the general increase of population — all comprehended under the general rubric of "opportunity" — were pointed to as essential elements in Astor's success.

In no section of the United States did newspaper readers obtain impressions of Astor markedly different from those received elsewhere. In the Middle Atlantic states, too, the classical portrait was presented — stern-visaged, sober, frugal, and industrious, Astor the businessman was but an extension of Astor the man. And competing for public attention with the classical portrait was one in which the face of Astor was painted somewhat differently and in which, moreover, material which had been relegated to the background in the classical portrait now stood forth boldly. The conception which determined, at least in part, the nature of this profile was that of the stewardship of wealth; and the criticism which flowed from this conception was directed not toward the processes by which money was made but toward the manner in which it was used. "To desire wealth, to seek for its attainment merely as an end, is, really, ignoble," the Philadelphia *Model American Courier* asserted; "but to desire and strive for it as a means of usefulness in the world, is noble." The widespread distinction that was drawn between how money was made and how it was spent was important, for by directing attention to the latter consideration, it gave assurance that criticism of entrepreneurs would in essence be criticism of their individual qualities and not of the nature of their activities. The Baltimore *Republican and Argus* made the point perfectly plain: "We are not enemies of the rich . . . But this does not prevent us from despising as the meanest of men, the miser who accumulates and aggrandizes a family, and leaves nothing for the people at his death, except a library."

But some newspapers did consider the origins of Astor's wealth and, in doing so, tended to link together the discussion of Astor's specific activities and the environment in which those activities took place in such a way as to imply that the accumulation of wealth was dependent upon considerations external to individual character. The Georgetown *Advocate* spoke out sharply: "Although it is true that every man has a right to dispose of his own property, after his death, by his will, as he may choose, yet, as this is an acquired and not a natural right, a right which society has granted, and which society may, if it pleases, again withdraw, it seems but natural that those who have prospered under this law, should deal liberally with the authority which has granted them the privilege whereby they have been enabled to make their money . . . The time may perhaps come . . . when the public will demand as a right that which is now accepted of as a bounty . . . a law for the taking of a reasonable share for the use of the public from the immense estates of persons, who have accumulated them through the benign operation of the system of laws whose protection they have experienced, may be passed."

And the Philadelphia *Public Ledger* injected a strikingly original note into the discussion by expressing still another theory as to the origin of wealth. The *Public Ledger* began its analysis of Astor by contrasting him with Stephen Girard:

Girard left most of his great fortune to public uses. He had devoted a long life and a powerful mind to the acquisition of wealth, and succeeded abundantly; and leaving a competency to each of his relatives in this, his adopted country, and nothing to his relatives in France, his native country, he bestowed all the rest of his abundant treasures upon the city which has been the field of his enterprise . . . He knew that his wealth had been gathered to his hands, under his directing head, by poor sailors, poor draymen, poor mechanics, poor clerks: that, without their *hands* his *head* would have accomplished nothing. He saw the justice of compensation, and left his wealth for noble benefactions.

But Astor, though he had accumulated millions, left only $400,000 for public purposes. "He had a legal right to leave his fortune according to his own tastes and judgment," the *Public Ledger* stated, "and is responsible for his stewardship, not to us, but to a Tribunal whose justice never errs. If his library is designed for sailors, laborers, mechanics, clerks of merchants and traders, and others who ought to be taught, and who have nothing to spare for buying books, he has done well and deserves praise. If the library is designed for the wealthy and comfortable, who are able to buy books, or for the learned, like a college library, he could have done better, for such portions of society are able to help themselves . . ."

But was Astor under any obligation to give help to the poor? The answer to this question led the *Public Ledger* into a discussion of "fundamental principles":

Among the numerous tenements of the deceased in New York, every one was created by the labor of day-laborers and mechanics, of Irish hod-carriers, and American or other masons, carpenters, blacksmiths, stone-cutters, painters and other artisans. They were paid. True. They were paid punctually, according to their contracts; and they expended their pay in feeding, clothing, and lodging themselves and their families. And did he not expend his capital in building his houses? Yes! They put their labor into daily bread, which is consumed and ended in the earning, and he puts his money into productive property, affording an annual revenue. At the end of life, where are they? Worth nothing. Their labor which was their only capital, has produced daily bread, and nothing more, and is now expended. And where is he? Worth an overgrown fortune, the product of their labor. His money, which was his only capital, has been united with their labor, and has produced a large and permanent fortune for his sole benefit. The money and labor united have produced only daily bread for them, and permanent wealth for him. Upon strict moral principles that is not an equal division of profits; and hence he is morally bound to leave some of his wealth for the permanent benefit of those portions of the community whose toil has been essential to its creation.

That the ideas of the *Public Ledger* received more than local expression is evidenced by the fact that the Baltimore *American,* too, wrestled with the same problem, but from a quite different point of view. The Baltimore *American* was alarmed by a New York *Globe* editorial which had stated that "wealth is the product of labor"; that since Astor "possessed millions of what others had produced, we need not be surprised that a diversity of opinion exists whether the life of Mr. Astor has been a benefit or an injury to mankind"; and that "the more men we have who possess great wealth, the more poverty there exists among the mass." Faced with this assault on Astor from a nonmoral point of view, the

Baltimore *American* was forced to modify the stereotype that his fortune was the product of moral virtues. It conceded that *"wealth is the product of labor,"* but argued for a definition of labor that included mental as well as physical effort: "The most productive element employed in daring enterprise, such as most of the operations by which he laid the foundations of his fortune, is the faculty that conceives, directs and manages the undertaking. Without that all the labor bestowed upon it would produce nothing." In its conclusion, however, that wealth should not be accumulated for "selfish aggrandizement" but for "good and excellent purposes," the *American* was in accord with Astor's critics.

As late as a year after Astor's death, the debate over the issues posed by his manner of living and the method of disposing of his wealth was still being carried on acrimoniously. In 1849 a pamphlet was published in which Astor was accused of having laid the basis of his fortune by giving counterfeit silver coins to Indians in exchange for furs.[22] That same year, Horace Mann gave an address, "A Few Thoughts for a Young Man," before the Boston Mercantile Library Association. "Wealth," Mann said, "so far as it consists in comfortable shelter and food and raiment for *all* mankind; in competence for every bodily want, and in abundance for every mental and spiritual need, is . . . valuable . . . precious." But, he added, "wealth as the means of an idle and voluptuous life; wealth as the fosterer of pride and the petrifier of the human heart; wealth as the iron rod with which to beat the poor into submission to its will, is all the curses of Pandora rolled into one." [23]

It is the "duty" of all, Mann argued, by "diligence in business, abstinence in pleasures, privation even, of everything that does not endanger health," to seek to attain a competence. But seek not, he advised, to attain more than that: "All above a fortune is a misfortune . . . because it makes generosity impossible. There can be no generosity where there is no sacrifice . . . All above a fortune is usually the greatest of misfortunes to children. By taking away the stimulus to effort, and . . . the restraints from indulgence, it takes the muscles out of the limbs, the brain out of the head, and virtue out of the heart . . . Vast fortunes are a misfortune to the State . . . The feudalism of Capital is not a whit less formidable than the feudalism of Force . . . The power of money is as imperial as the power of the sword; and I may as well depend upon another for my head, as for my bread . . . there is no equity in the allotments which assign to one man but a dollar a day with working, while another has an income of a dollar a minute, without working." [24]

The day of a rich man's death is an important one, Mann said, for then is it revealed "whether the man of vast wealth, like Stephen Girard, has welcomed toil, endured privation, borne contumely, while in his secret heart he was nursing the mighty purpose of opening a fountain of blessedness . . . or whether, like John Jacob Astor, he was hoarding wealth for the base love of wealth, hugging to his breast, in his dying hour, the memory of his gold and not of his Redeemer; grasping his riches, till the scythe of death cut off his hands, and he was changed, in the twinkling of an eye, from being one of the richest men that ever lived in this country, to being one of the poorest souls that ever went out of it." [25]

In effect, Mann's advice to young men was that they should not grow up to be like John Jacob Astor. Mann selected him "to point a moral" because he supposed him "to have been the most notorious, the most wealthy, and, considering his vast means, the most miserly, of his class, in this country. Nothing but absolute insanity can be pleaded in palliation of the conduct of a man who was worth nearly or quite twenty millions of dollars, but gave only some half million, or less than a half million, of it for any public object. If men of such vast means will not benefit the world by their *example* while they live, we have a right to make reprisals for their neglect, by using them as a *warning* after they are dead. In the midst of so much poverty and suffering as the world experiences, it has become a high moral and religious duty to create an overwhelming public opinion against both the parsimonies and the squandering of wealth." [26]

Astor's grandson, Charles Astor Bristed, who had inherited from Astor eighty-five town lots, his country estate at Hellgate, and the income and interest on $115,000,[27] replied to Mann.

Bristed took issue with Mann on nearly every count — his characterization of Girard, his description of Astor, his attitude toward wealth. Girard, he said, should be judged not by his will but by his life. "Industry, temperance, veracity, all the *business* virtues" he had; but he was unsocial and "as frugal of the ordinary courtesies of life as of his gold." Moreover, he never "entertained the idea of distinguishing himself in any other walk of life . . ." [28] In contrast to Girard, Astor "aspired to be something more than a mere man of business. Though not a liberally educated man, he enjoyed the society of literary men; though possessing no extraordinary means of political information or training, he saw further into the interests, capacities, and destiny of the country of his adoption, than those who were at the head of the government."

Astor's will was not "in all respects an equitable one," his grandson agreed, nor was his life all that it should have been; but the fault lay with others. "When Mr. Astor found that his efforts for the public benefit were not understood, he did what it would be well if more people did now-a-days — he confined himself to his own business . . ." And as to his will, he had "intended to provide handsomely for all his near relatives, but . . . during the latter years of his life . . . he was imposed upon by lawyers and other designing men." Nor was Mann's scorn at the small bequest for a public library justified. "Words cost nothing," Bristed remarked, "and any man can afford to be liberal of another's property." [29]

Mann's attacks on Astor and on great wealth were reflections of "opinions which are often promulgated in disreputable quarters." [30] Bristed left no doubt as to what he meant:

> Our newspapers, which are generally conducted by average specimens of the people at large, which, collectively, exercise an immense influence on public opinion, and in return, pretend with tolerable truth to be a reflex of that opinion, have, with a few honorable exceptions, a simple *penchant* for abusing rich men . . . If a rich man is in business, of course he is making his money by dishonest practices. If not in business, he must necessarily be idle, and therefore vicious . . . If he gives money for any public object, he is not praised for his liberality, but abused for not giving more . . . If he is in any trouble or affliction, a great shout of joy is set up, and the affair is placarded as much as possible. Now, the gentlemen of the press know pretty well their own pecuniary interests, whatever may be their ignorance on other important points; and with all their horror of rich men, have a knack of filling their pockets comfortably; and they would not be so ready to abuse the wealthy, unless it paid to do it.[31]

Given the degree to which the press had assailed Astor, his grandson's sensitivity is at least understandable.

Such, then, was the discussion aroused by retrospective consideration of the life of John Jacob Astor. It was a discussion which revealed the ideas which served as sources of strength to give courage and conviction to American entrepreneurs and, at the same time, of those counter-currents of thought which were indicative of developing opposition. Certain assumptions — that prestige attaches to the accumulation of wealth and that wealth is the reward of such personal qualities as industry, application, and eminent capacity — appear to have been common to both those who viewed Astor favorably and to most of those who looked upon him with disfavor. The distinction between them lay not in disagreement over the thesis that wealth is the reward of effort and ability. To be sure, the favorable stereotype of Astor, at least at the beginning, regarded his fortune as arising solely from possession of sagacity, diligence, effort, and foresight, while other newspapers doubted that such qualities were the sole basis of his wealth or even that he possessed them to the degree claimed. In both cases, however, the inarticulate assumption was that whether Astor in fact had these qualities, they were the qualities possession of which should be rewarded with wealth. So firmly rooted was this conviction, indeed, that — with the exception of a relatively small number of newspapers, all of them antagonistic to Astor — there was little discussion of the sources of Astor's wealth. Of far more interest than the question of where his money came from was that of where it would go. In making this issue the fulcrum of their discussion, the newspapers were but casting their accounts of Astor's death into the form of a familiar moral issue.[32] As one spokesman of the business class put it: "The *getting* of money, and the proper *use* of money, are distinct subjects, and must not be confounded." The effect of separating these two aspects of the problem was clear; dissent could be expressed in terms antagonistic to businessmen and not to business: "The totally different rules and principles that apply to the *getting* and to the *using* of money, are the rock on which the theorists split . . . They pour out the vials of their indignation on the getting of money, when it should fall upon the improper use of money . . . The wrong, in my opinion, does not consist in the organization of society, nor in the fact that some men have obtained more than their share of the world's possessions, provided they got them legally, honestly, and honorably, but in the fact that they have not properly used what they rightfully obtained."[33] So essential was this distinction, indeed, that it was recognized as a vital factor in the defense of property. A legal representative of Boston business interests minced no words in emphasizing the importance of the problem. He had often felt, he said, that

the aggregation of immense wealth at one end of the scale, and the increasing amount of hopeless poverty at the other, did involve an element of peril to wealth itself, and that the moment the rich men forget the duties of property, the moment that they cease to bridge this interval between themselves and the poor by the perpetual exercise of sympathy, and by the constant recognition of a common humanity and a common brotherhood, then their wealth would be in danger of falling upon the mercy of the merciless . . . It is only in the moral element, flowing from Christianity and humanity, that a corrective is to be found to the danger which always threatens a country in which, while the rich are growing richer, the poor are growing poorer.[34]

Small wonder, then, that in an age in which formal treatises in will-writing for businessmen were prepared,[35] the authors of a popular guide to the wealthy men of Massachusetts meticulously counted over the 1,496 persons worth more than a quarter of a million dollars to determine the 375 "ascertained to be more or less Benevolent."[36]

If the distinction between getting and spending was one which served the business community by defending it against the sins of some of its members, other phases of the journalistic discussion of Astor's death were no less calculated to surround business enterprise with an aura of approval. Those newspapers which emphasized Astor's steady ascent from fur-beater to merchant-capitalist, an ascent based upon his industry, perseverance, and temperance, were reflecting the widely held conception of the world as an orderly universe in which the key to success was merit and merit was ever rewarded. The worthy man of business could congratulate himself on being a member of the only authentically American aristocracy: "The rich are our aristocracy . . . It is no derogation . . . that it rests upon money. Money is something substantial. Every body knows that and feels it. Birth is a mere idea, which grows every day more and more intangible." [37] The verdict on Astor was equally plain: "His badge of distinction was his possession of a vast amount of what, in the estimation of the great majority, effectually 'makes the man.'" [38] And how had Astor and other wealthy businessmen gained this respected status? On this point the newspapers were sharply split. Those who viewed Astor's career with approval found the answer to lie in his character and in arguing thus they were simultaneously eliciting approval for business enterprise and cultivating the moral discipline essential for its growth. If the able are always rewarded, then, even though there will always be the necessity for "different professions, for rich men and poor men, for teachers and pupils, for men to plow and men to execute, masters and servants," each man will rise to his proper level and society will be spared the criticism of the discontented. "We should make the impression on all, that labor is honorable, and that he who *cheerfully* plunges into labor and sustains his part well, is deserving of respect. All the distinctions in our country are but for a day. Those who are at the head of society to-day may be at the foot in a few years; and those who are low now, may, in their children, be greatly exalted." [39] So spoke the preacher, and the teacher said Amen:

The principal causes of the rapid growth of national opulence are moral rather than physical . . . Neither theoretically nor practically, in this country, is there any obstacle to any individual's becoming rich, if he will, and almost to any amount that he will . . . How is it possible, indeed, that the poor should be arrayed in hostility against the rich, when . . . the son of an Irish coachman becomes the governor of a State, and the grandson of a *millionaire* dies a pauper? The consequent of the whole is an unceasing energy and activity in the pursuit of wealth, which accomplish greater wonders than all the modern inventions of science, which actually generate enthusiasm of character . . . The hope of rising in the world is the chief motive for the accumulation of capital. [40]

"The hope of rising in the world" — Cotton Mather's moral dynamo, with slight modifications — was still in good running order. The Phi Beta Kappa orator spoke advisedly when he told his audience of Brown University students about to embark on business careers to "Go forth into the world trustful, but fearless . . . Thine own arm is the demi-god." [41]

Such was the line of defense erected against that body of opinion which held that Astor was not an unmalleable man, that he had been tempered on the forge of society, and that, in evaluating the product, the nature of the tool which had fashioned it would have to be considered.

The defense was a powerful one, aided by press, school, and church. "The unequal distribution of wealth," said the Reverend Jonathan Mayhew Wainwright, summing up its position, "we believe to be not only an unalterable consequence of the nature of man, and the state of being in which he is placed, but also the only system by which his happiness and improvement can be promoted in this state of being . . . Once touch the rights of property, let it be felt that men are imperilled and harassed in their efforts to obtain it, that its possession is insecure, and that portions of it may be taken from them by unequal taxation, and you immediately stop enterprise, and with enterprise the progress of knowledge, and with the progress of knowledge that also of virtue — and then where is the happiness of such a community?" [42]

Astor would have been pleased had he known that the Reverend Mr. Wainwright who preached that sermon was the Reverend Mr. Wainwright, soon to be Bishop, who officiated at his funeral services. [43]

III

Cornelius Vanderbilt

On October 11, 1897, Senator Chauncey M. Depew spoke at Vanderbilt University on the occasion of the unveiling of a statue of its benefactor. It was a fitting occasion for a discourse on the significance of the man's life and Senator Depew, the preëminent orator of the day, made the most of it. "The American Commonwealth is built upon the individual," he said. "It recognizes neither classes nor masses . . . We have thus become a nation of self-made men. We live under just and equal laws and all avenues for a career are open . . . Freedom of opportunity and preservation of the results of forecast, industry, thrift and honesty have made the United States the most prosperous and wealthy country in the world. Commodore Vanderbilt is a conspicuous example of the products and possibilities of our free and elastic conditions . . . He neither asked nor gave quarter. The same country, the same laws, the same open avenues, the same opportunities which he had before him are equally before every other man . . . He was not the creation of luck nor chance nor circumstances." [1] What was the real object of the orator's encomium — Commodore Vanderbilt or the "free and elastic" conditions of American society which made a Vanderbilt possible?

Twenty years earlier, Depew had participated in the writing of another eulogy on Vanderbilt. That, too, was a summation of his career, but Depew and his colleagues were less equivocal then in indicating the real object of their praise. On January 5, 1877, the day after the death of Vanderbilt, the boards of directors of all the railroad companies in which the Commodore had had substantial interests jointly adopted a resolution in honor of the man "who stood as the nation's foremost representative of public enterprise and material progress." A "true man, a sincere friend, a devoted husband and father, a liberal employer, an extraordinary genius of affairs, and a citizen of high public spirit," his career had been "a dazzling success . . . Nor was this glittering success due to any early adventitious advantages. He was essentially the creator, not the creature, of the circumstances which he molded to his purposes . . . Beginning in an humble position, with apparently little scope of action and small promise of opportunity, he rose, by his genius, his indomitable energy, and his clear forecast, to the control of vast enterprises . . . In a period of crafty devices for sinister ends he taught the way of success through legitimate means . . . As a citizen, he was true to the honor and welfare of his country . . . If his patriotism was thus substantial, his philanthropy was equally generous and effective." [2]

Clearly, the primary interest of Depew in 1897 had not been the major concern of him and his associates in 1877. At the end of the century, he seems to have discussed Vanderbilt almost as though he were a testimonial to the opportunities afforded by the unique qualities of American society. But as the century was entering its fourth quarter, he seems — in a mood highly reminiscent of discussions of earlier entrepreneurs — to have been concerned essentially with demonstrating the validity of the ancient equation of character and destiny. And yet if it is true that the problems of business behavior which interested observers in 1877 were not the same as those which were of pressing concern later, neither is it true that they were identical with those which had earlier been at the center of discussion. The resolution which was adopted by Vanderbilt's business associates looked in two directions. In its concern with the identity of virtue and success, it reëmphasized one of the basic tenets of the discussion of earlier entrepreneurs. But in its concern with the nonbusiness activities of businessmen — with the businessman as father, as husband, as citizen, as patriot — and in its hint that "opportunity" is something which lies outside the mind and character of the businessman, it looked forward to what were later to become fundamental items of discussion. The decades of the seventies and eighties had their own problems and molders of opinion formulated their own solutions to those problems. If those solutions seem reminiscent of others, it is testimony to the persistent effort to apply once satisfactory answers to changing problems. If they seem unlike others, it is testimony to the victory of new facts over old categories of thought.

That consideration of the meaning of Vanderbilt's life would pose new problems was indicated long before his death. His activities stretched back over decades and his importance as the leading American transportation entrepreneur meant that he had long occupied a position of public prominence.

The comment of Mark Twain, as early as 1869, was an indication of the questions that would have to be answered:

How my heart goes out in sympathy to you! how I do pity you, Commodore Vanderbilt! Most men have at least a few friends . . . but you seem to be the idol of only a crawling swarm of small souls, who love to glorify your most flagrant unworthiness in print; or praise your vast possessions worshippingly; or sing of your unimportant private habits and sayings and doings, as if your millions gave them dignity . . . Now, have you ever thought clearly over your newspaper reputation? . . . One day one of your subjects comes out with a column or two detailing your rise from penury to affluence, and praising you as if you were the last and noblest work of God, but unconsciously telling how exquisitely mean a man has to be in order to achieve what you have achieved . . . Next, a subject of yours prints a long article to show how, in some shrewd, underhanded way, you have "come it" over the public with some Erie Dodge or other, and added another million or so to your greasy greenbacks; and behold! *he* praises you, and never hints that unmoral practices, in so prominent a place as you occupy, are a damning example to the rising commercial generation — more, a damning thing to the whole nation, while there are insects like your subjects to make virtues of them in print . . . All I wish to urge you now, is that you crush out your native instincts and go and do something *worthy* of praise . . . Do this, I beseech you, else through your example we shall shortly have in our midst five hundred Vanderbilts, which God forbid. Go, now, please go, and do one worthy act. Go, boldly, proudly, nobly, and give four dollars to some great public charity . . . Do not be deceived into the notion that everything you do or say is wonderful, simply because those ones who publish you so much make it appear so . . . pray do not be deceived by the laudation you receive; more of it belongs to your millions than to you.[3]

Mark Twain's animadversions could perhaps be shrugged off, for his barbed wit spared none. But when such a conservative as E. L. Godkin, editor of *The Nation*, poured vials of wrath on Vanderbilt, that, indeed, was cause for alarm. "When a gentleman's hand is discovered to be pretty regularly in the general pocket, he will inevitably find himself the subject of public remarks" — thus did Godkin begin his ironic description of the "Vanderbilt Memorial Bronze" which was erected in 1869 at the Hudson River Railroad Depot in St. John's Park in New York City:

There is the image of the humble boat, in which, in the years when he was poor but honest, he carried passengers from the Battery over to Staten Island. There, near it, under a head of steam that she never knew in life, is one of the vessels of the Pacific Mail line, in which, in later years, he transported many more passengers, with much less comfort and much less safety, from this city to the Isthmus and California. There, also, may be seen the vessel which he so magnificently gave the Federal Government when the rebellion broke out, and when it was rather more unprofitable to keep a vessel in her dock than it was to give her away to anybody who would take her. There, too, are the figures of bee-hives, which ingeniously typify the industry and devotion to business of a man who never served the country at large, nor the State, nor the city, in any public office; nor ever spent the time which is money in advancing the cause of any charity; nor in promoting education, which the self-made man may despise; nor in fostering the arts, which can always wait. There are the railroads and the river boats, which are witnesses to an energy and a luminous sagacity which before now have bought whole legislatures, debauched courts, crushed out rivals, richer or poorer, as the unmoral, unsentimental forces of nature grind down whatever opposes their blind force . . . In short, there, in the glory of brass, are portrayed . . . the trophies of a lineal successor of the medieval baron that we read about, who may have been illiterate indeed; and who was not humanitarian; and not finished in his morals; and not, for his manners, the delight of the refined society of his neighborhood; nor yet beloved by his dependents; but who knew how to take advantage of lines of travel; who had a keen eye for roads, and had the heart and hand to levy contributions on all who passed his way.[4]

The businessman as robber baron, crude, heartless, swooping down from his mountain fastness to take tribute from unprotected travelers — this was a new image of the entrepreneur, one which was equally denunciatory of his business activities and his private life, which hitherto had never been considered relevant to discussions of business behavior. To answer the new questions and to explain the entrepreneur in terms of the changing conditions of American society was the major task of the defenders of enterprise. What, then, in the view of this sector of the press, were the themes to be emphasized?

"The death of any man of extraordinary wealth is sure to arrest the general attention. Whether the public shares in his riches or not, the capitalist is a public character." So editorialized the New York *Tribune* on January 5, 1877, and the remark is to be understood not only as a factual statement of the reaction to the railroad magnate's death but as the herald of a new departure in journalistic explanations of entrepreneurial behavior. New York newspapers had for months been anticipating the Commodore's death and when the event came they were well prepared. On the morning of January 5, long articles appeared on their front pages describing in meticulous detail the scene in Vanderbilt's home the previous evening — the children and the wife gathered by the bedside, the Reverend Charles Deems reading prayers, the doctors standing helplessly at the side of the room, the rapidly sinking Commodore requesting that hymns be sung, and his last words, "That is a good prayer." Such concern with private aspects of the life of a businessman — the closeness of the family circle, the degree of his religious devotion — was, for the newspapers, a new feature in the discussion of businessmen, but it was accompanied by manifestations of interest in the size and distribution of the estate that had characterized earlier discussions of entrepreneurs. The transportation king had left an estate estimated to be between eighty-five and one hundred million dollars — surely the largest fortune yet amassed on the American continent — and the newspapers assumed the burden of attempting to explain the secret of Vanderbilt's success. For some, of course, the explanation was couched in traditional terms. "There never was a better illustration of the theory," wrote the New York *Evening Mail*, "that 'our desires are the predictions of our destinies.' The young, hardy, fearless, careful, economical, hard working Staten Island boy who began his career as master of a pirogue, developed into the owner of fleets and railways, by a process as steady, continuous, and unbroken, as that by which the tall monarchs of the forest rise above their fellows. From first to last," the *Evening Mail* concluded, "his life was one of hard work, steady achievement and unfaltering determination of purpose."

The New York *Herald* had little to add, except to emphasize the valuable results that could be achieved by emulation of the qualities Vanderbilt had exhibited. "The life of a man who, without a single special advantage of any kind, distanced every one in callings where the shrewdest of intellects are engaged, deserves more attention, in public and in private, than feeble moralizings and doleful retrospects ever amounted to. Energy, application, painstaking patience and persistence, made the dead Commodore what he was, and they constitute a set of virtues of which the best man alive might be proud . . . Great enterprises, benevolences and reforms languish everywhere to-day because there is not behind them the intensified manliness by which Cornelius Vanderbilt compelled victory." The formal phrases of the classical theme that destiny flows from character studded the columns of the New York press. "Commodore Vanderbilt belonged to that stoical class of millionaires who are not enervated by wealth. He always adhered to that industrious discipline, that routine of herculean labor which contributed to his first successes. His business was his amusement, and his amusements were part of his business" — this was the verdict of the *Evening Telegram*. "The lesson to be learned from the life of Vanderbilt is simple and impressive," wrote James Gordon Bennett's *Herald*. "Courage in the performance of duty enabled this man to become one of the kings of the earth . . . He had no advantages in his battle — no political, social, educational aid. It was one honest, sturdy, fearless man against the world, and in the end the man won . . . He was simple and direct in his ways, knowing his mind all the time, and ever going to his purpose like a ball from a cannon. In time the world came to his feet." Belief that the causes of economic success lay deeply embedded in the structure of character, that emulation of the qualities exhibited by the successful would lead others to the same goal, that disgrace lay only in lack of ambition and aspiration — the time-tested rhetoric that provided at once an explanation of entrepreneurial behavior and a spur to action was still operative.

But was it any longer a sufficient explanation? Was it true that Vanderbilt had "had no advantages in his battle"? At least as early as 1848 there were those who looked skeptically at the notion that character was all, scene nothing. And during Vanderbilt's own lifetime doubts had been expressed concerning the degree to which he had embodied such virtues, whether possession of the requisite virtues was sufficient to explain the attainment of financial success, and even whether economic success could be considered prima-facie evidence of a good life. Now, for some at least, doubt became certainty and presumption became proof.

How came Vanderbilt by his hundred millions? asked the *Irish World*. "Did he *create* it? NO. Sharp practice — in plain words, swindling — abstracted these millions from labor. With one hand he took in thousands under false pretences and with the other he paid out to his pick-and-shovel white slaves *ninety cents* a day! Bribery and corruption, too, co-operated in the work . . . Society itself is to blame. There are fifty thousand men in New York now chained in enforced idleness — rotting away right under the blighting shadow of Vanderbilt's golden pyramid. Peter Cooper looks abroad upon the sad scene and asks the gamblers and wire-pullers: 'What is government — the agent of Society — good for if it is unable or unwilling to remedy this state of things?' 'Nonsense!' say the Vanderbilts. 'Government is established to protect our property!' Very well! Then the Vanderbilts, for whom it would seem, the government exists, ought to support the government. Put a graduating tax upon towering riches, and you will, in time have no Vanderbilts in society. What would be the result? A more equal division of wealth, a higher tone of morals in business circles, and a happier state of society generally."

If the activities of businessmen like Vanderbilt are detrimental to the best interests of society, if those activities are made possible by the policies of a government which itself is a creature of society, then elimination of the evil requires changes not in individual character but in social structure. Ominous as these words were, penetrating deeply into the armor that had protected society by denying any relation between environment and success, they were but the first count of a long indictment.

Now the attack was carried directly against Vanderbilt himself, in complete denial of the accepted notion that a man of wealth must also be a man to be respected. "His early education was scanty, and he had few of the requirements of culture," wrote Godkin in *The Nation;* "his language was always illiterate and often profane. In his business transactions he was overreaching and exacting, often availing himself of questionable practices; his standard of honor was one which had little regard for his adversary . . . He carried the system of watering stock to an extent which was almost without precedent . . . He was a kind of man whose like we should be sorry to see many of — the typical result of strong character developed by energy and perseverance to the highest point of business success, but softened by no aesthetic taste and tempered by no other refinement than that which is innate in every brave and determined man."

The denunciation of the means by which he had accumulated his wealth was matched by similar denunciation of the means by which he distributed it. Vanderbilt — like John Jacob Astor II and A. T. Stewart, two other New York millionaires who had recently died — was attempting to create a new style in the distribution of estates, the *Galaxy* charged. "The John Jacob, the Cornelius, the Alexander of the past has been blessed with the vision of his millions multiplying as he would have them multiply, and haply has dreamed of accomplishing by his own foresight an entail which he could not create under the laws . . . 'Magnificence is the decency of the rich,' but little magnificence marked the lives of those three rich New Yorkers. Unprecedented and incredible thing in America, neither Stewart nor Vanderbilt left one poor dollar of his fifty or sixty millions to any municipal or charitable purpose. Filled with his posthumous business plans, neither cared for New York as Girard cared for Philadelphia and Hopkins for Baltimore."

But the antagonistic sector of the press did more than implicate society in the practices of the entrepreneur and accuse the entrepreneur of immorality in the manner of his gaining riches and of lack of charity in their distribution. It also proceeded to strip him of the sanction once afforded by the identification of wealth and virtue. Preaching from the pulpit of Plymouth Church on January 5, Henry Ward Beecher hurled anathemas at the railroad king: "Looking at his commercial life, few have equalled, none have surpassed him, but there it stops." Referring to the recent disaster at Ashtabula, Ohio, in which hundreds were killed when a train on one of Vanderbilt's railroad lines plummeted through a trestle to the rocky gorge below, Beecher compared the lives of Vanderbilt and Philip Bliss, a well-known hymn writer who was killed in the crash. "Within a few days another man died, not surrounded by friends and physicians and nurses; not with his name mentioned from day to day in the papers, and the thermometer of his life recorded as in the weather department; he died a death of most unutterable horror . . . Whatever could be done by bruising and burning and drowning was done, and there Mr. Bliss died, a man whose whole life was devoted to softening and ennobling the hearts of men . . . He held no such place as Vanderbilt, and it is not right to compare the two, except to say that it seems to me Mr. Bliss has done a far grander work, he has opened the door for souls, he has caused love to blossom, he has brought something of the spirit of heaven down to earth, he has been a tongue of the Lord." Lyman Abbott took the floor to protest against Beecher's characterization of Vanderbilt. Only yesterday, he said, he had been told by Dr. Deems that Vanderbilt liked *Pilgrim's Progress* and had a particular fondness for certain hymns. Beecher replied: "I am glad he liked the hymns, but if he had sung them thirty years ago it would have made a great difference. He did not sing hymns as long as he could get about. We don't want to give God the fag end of our lives." [5] The editor of *Harper's* accepted Beecher's view. Vanderbilt "did not sing hymns as long as he could get about. It is true of many more of us than the Commodore. But it is pleasant to think of those who do: of the men and women, who, having no ear for music, are yet singing hymns all the time; of lives that, poor and obscure and lonely, are as sweet and inspiring as the loftiest hymn."

In the face of such accusations, the ancient doctrines that the visible signs of wealth were evidence of the invisible gift of grace, that a life devoted to indefatigable pursuit of gain was a noble calling, needed modification.

According to this dissenting view, society was not an organic unity but was composed of disparate parts which were frequently in conflict. To begin with, the criticism of Vanderbilt as a man was such as to separate him from others. The older and more favorable view, that which insisted on the relation between character and destiny, had, to be sure, emphasized individual uniqueness, but in extolling the virtues of the successful and in presenting the successful entrepreneur as a man to be imitated, it offered a method by which the diverse elements in society could be united, the method of emulation. But the new criticism, dwelling upon Vanderbilt's illiteracy, profanity, crudeness, and lack of charity, not only invidiously separated him from mankind as it was but from mankind as it hoped to be; no longer could the qualities of the entrepreneur serve as guides to action. Even that, however, was not the end of the matter. If the entrepreneur's career were simply the outward manifestation of inner qualities, then the characteristics he exhibited could be considered merely as personal quirks, criticism could logically be directed only against him, and society, by virtue of its lack of involvement, would be spared a menacing attack. But the fact is that the new criticism did connect society to Vanderbilt as businessman. If the argument of these critics were accepted, then the results of Vanderbilt's business activities — unequal division of wealth, and the low moral tone that characterized the Erie Railroad scandals — would be found to be rooted as much in the system as in the man. The old image of society as a harmonious unity in which the prosperity of all was assured by the attempt of each to gain prosperity for himself, in which merit always received its just reward, now faced competition from a new view which found society to be lacking in harmony. How, then, was the challenge implicit in this new view handled in such a way as to allay the threat of disunity and give reassurance to the leaders of business enterprise that they still retained widespread approval?

Leslie's Illustrated Newspaper stated the issue clearly:

. . . a rich man's death increases, for the moment, the general interest in his possessions. The public have got the idea that it is, or ought to be, a residuary legatee of all millionaires, and it feels, for the moment, deeply hurt if it does not get a hospital, or a library, or a college. It would almost seem that all of us are communists at heart, and secretly believe that property is robbery . . . Such an interpretation, carried to its extreme, would sap the foundations of social prosperity and of national wealth.

If the view that property is equivalent to theft was destructive of "social prosperity" and, similarly, if antagonistic interpretations of the activities of businessmen led to rifts and cleavages in society, then, clearly, new doctrine was needed to restore the notion of harmony. This, indeed, was what was done, by switching emphasis away from the erstwhile test of the value to society of a businessman — the degree to which he put his money to public uses — to a new standard of judgment, the degree to which his very business activities contributed to social welfare. By this new standard, it mattered little whether the businessman was also philanthropic.

Leslie's Illustrated Newspaper made the point bluntly: "Sometimes a benefactor scrimps and strains his family to devote vast sums to whimsical charities. The charity of a Peabody or a Peter Cooper is grand, but Mr. Vanderbilt, despite his patriarchal family gave away more money than either. An Astor, a Stewart, a Vanderbilt is a blessing in another sense; for each gives honorable, remunerative and permanent employment to an army of men and women. This is a greater service, the political economist will bear witness, than much despised and showy benevolence."

The Public could hardly have been more specific:

By some the usual lamentations are uttered because no large bequests were made to benevolent objects. Whatever Cornelius Vanderbilt acquired he did not owe to public favor, and he had a very clear right to use it as he deemed best. If he believed that $60 million would be better employed in building up, maintaining and defending against all competition, the great railway which now forms the main artery of the commerce of this city, it is at least possible that he thereby established a more useful benevolent institution than any other which his money could have founded. It is better . . . to permanently promote the industry, commerce and prosperity of a great state and city, thereby giving millions of workers a better chance to earn a living, than to found any number of hospitals.

Other New York publications, considering the alternate methods of contributing to the welfare of society by philanthropy or by business activity, agreed that the benefits afforded through providing employment and services were by far the greater. "For his subjects, the public," said the editor of *Harper's*, "his reign was beneficent. Railway management in New York had never known such precision and railway travellers such comfort and convenience, as he introduced." The *Daily Bulletin* denied the charge that Vanderbilt had been lacking in "public spirit," that "the city of New York, which enabled him to accumulate his immense wealth . . . never received any particular benefit from him . . . The development of an efficient system of transportation, which has enabled this port to [become] the leading city of the continent, was certainly the manifestation of a public spirit of the highest order . . . It was never his plan to put away money in a chest, nor yet simply to invest it, but rather, in the fullest sense of the word, to *use* it. Consequently, it is said, he employed more men, directly and indirectly, than any other man in the land." Probably no other citizen of New York, *The Independent* reported, had "left a profounder feeling of regret at his loss, or a livelier sense of the obligations he had laid the community under by his long life of active labor in promoting the means by which the commerce of the city and, in fact, of the whole state, was carried on . . . Whatever the wealth which he has left to his family may be, whether a hundred millions or only eighty or ninety millions, it is but a small percentage of the wealth which others have gained through his means." The benefits of posthumous charity, editorialized the *Evening Express*, are not to be compared with those of business enterprise. Vanderbilt gave to charitable causes, "but most of all gave employment to thousands of mechanics and tens of thousands of laborers by the creation of works on sea and land of great public utility." What else had Vanderbilt done? "This is none of our business and none of the public's business."

So fundamental was this new idea that it was abstracted from the context of discussion of Vanderbilt and erected into an enduring principle. "He worked for himself," wrote the New York *Sun*, "but in so doing he served the public as well as himself — as every powerful individuality must always do." To the New York *Evening Mail*, Vanderbilt's success was an illustration of the divine plan of the universe: "It is the part of the Providence that overrules all human efforts and events, that such incarnations of energy and enterprise as Mr. Vanderbilt *must* serve the public uses, whether they want to do it or not. The organization of such a magnificent business machine [benefits], directly or indirectly, many millions of people — in fact all the world." The effectiveness of the argument in diverting criticism from entrepreneurs was revealed when one newspaper commented, "Men work more wisely than they know, and the making of money cannot go on without promoting the progress of society and multiplying its good opportunities. This being true, it is hardly necessary for us to enter into any nice criticism of Mr. Vanderbilt's personal character. There was much in it which it was impossible not to admire. Of that which was not altogether admirable, let us here say nothing."

Such, then, was the argument which denied the charge that business activity of the scale carried on by Vanderbilt must necessarily be detrimental to the interests of society, which negated the once crucial test that the measure of a businessman was to be found in his will, which restored in part the unity of a society that critics insisted was not united at all. But defenders of the social order had more than one string to their bow, and they proceeded systematically to answer the other charges in the indictment.

The opposition press had insisted that Vanderbilt was not like other men, that the qualities he possessed were not only different from theirs but less admirable. His defenders now set to work to demonstrate that, except for his money, he was a man like other men. For the first time, therefore, consideration of the nonbusiness activities of businessmen became germane to the evaluation of their status in society.

Other men loved and married. So, too, had Vanderbilt. "Mr. Vanderbilt was always an affectionate man. He lost his heart before he attained his majority. In 1813, at nineteen years of age, he was married to Miss Sophia Johnson, the excellent lady with whom he lived fifty-five years." Other men were solicitous of their mothers and good providers for their children. So, too, was Vanderbilt. When reminded by his mother of his promise to retire at the age of forty, he replied that although he was worth $400,000 he would never retire, "that he was just under way, and his children were growing up; that there was to be a large family, established in many branches; and that to them, to the public, and to God he believed he owed it to work much longer; but that he did not intend that she should ever work again." Other men ate, drank, smoked, worked, played, met with their friends, worshipped; no less did Vanderbilt. "The Commodore had an excellent constitution. He dressed plainly and wore white cravats. He was a good liver, but not a high one . . . He drank wine sparingly, but was fond of his cigar to the last . . . The Commodore's favorite amusement was card-playing, and he had a great fondness for horses . . . He had three friends among ministers, and he seemed to enjoy their society more than that of most men." He was neither more nor less educated than the majority of men; "like others, he had his friendships"; he was patriotic, as his gift of a warship to the Union during the Civil War demonstrated; he liked good food and drink, but not so much as to be distinguished for his capacities; despite his great wealth "his home was always plainly furnished"; like most men, he was unostentatious in the manner of his worship, but of his religious faith and zeal there could be no doubt. Even the manner of his burial — plain, simple, devoid of all pomp, but attended by two hundred employees of the New York Central Railroad as mourners — attested to the fact that he was but one among many. "He was certainly not a vulgar rich man," the *Evening Telegram* stated. "In no legitimate sense could the term *parvenu* be applied to him. If he rose from the ranks of the people, it was not to affect a disdain for them." Only in his business success was Vanderbilt different from others; as to the rest, he was indistinguishable from his brothers. "Turning from Mr. Vanderbilt as a colossal railroad genius to Mr. Vanderbilt as a man and a citizen, we are confronted with many peculiar traits of character that are distinctively American." [6]

Such concern with the nonbusiness activities of the entrepreneur, the description of him as a man who, like other men, embodied a multiplicity of roles, was a new feature of journalistic discussion of businessmen. The dissidents had proclaimed the rich entrepreneur to be a man almost generically different from others. If the defense had proceeded in the traditional manner, with emphasis exclusively upon those unique characteristics which had led to Vanderbilt's success, surely the result would have been confirmation of the accusation. What, after all, did the New England textile worker, the Southern tenant farmer, the clerk in the village dry goods store feel in common with a man discussed by friends as well as enemies entirely in terms of his enormous wealth? But the new mode of presentation offered possibilities for identification. It was only with respect to his wealth that Vanderbilt was different; all else he had in common with his countrymen, for they were all Americans. By placing the discussion of the entrepreneur in a new context, one which countered the personal qualities which led to his success with emphasis on the roles he had in common with all men, a method was achieved whereby identity between the many and the few could be maintained and the unity of society reaffirmed.

By now the very business activities of the businessman, not alone his philanthropy, had been asserted as socially useful and the businessman had been presented as one with mankind. It remained only to relate him to society in such a way as to imply that only under the peculiar advantages of the American scene could such success be attained.

What elements of the American setting contributed to business success, the press was not quite certain; exact definitions were to come later. But that there was some quality in the environment which was essential, many newspapers were sure. All were in agreement that Vanderbilt had been a "Carlylean hero," one of "those aboriginal facts that cannot be disposed of," a Napoleon of business; and agreement was equally complete that from early boyhood he possessed the qualities necessary for the attainment of great wealth. There was, to be sure, some dispute as to how fully he conformed to the approved model of achievement. By most newspapers he was portrayed as having begun his career in bleak and miserable poverty. But others were not quite as certain. "His father was a well-to-do agriculturist, not possessed of any considerable fortune, indeed, but owing no debts and owning his land," reported the New York *Times.* The *Herald,* knowing not what to say, said everything. Under the headline "How the Poor Boatman's Son Became a Millionaire," it remarked that Vanderbilt's father had been a "farm owner," a "speculator," owner of "a superior boat, one much better than any that was owned by his neighbors"; and that his mother possessed savings of "$3,000 at least, all in brightest gold; and how much more . . . the world will never discover . . . From the very beginning he was independent." But whether he began poor or only less rich than he was later to become, the search for the explanation of his successful career took newspapers beyond the limits of the old character-career ratio. Was it the opportunity offered by the time and place in which he lived that was material to consideration of his success? Some thought so. Vanderbilt's "remarkable career was due" as well to "the exceptional circumstances of the time in which he lived" as to "the original vigor of his nature" and "the wisdom of its direction." It had been "the flush times of the present century, partly by accident and partly by . . . superior sagacity," that had enabled him to make his money. "The railroad and the telegraph have evoked a new order of genius; and the development of corporate action consequent upon the utilization of these new machines of progress, has invited the efforts of the best organizing minds." The new age called for certain qualities and Vanderbilt had them — bold, able to devise "revolutionary measures," inventive, he was quick "to discover new paths and prompt to push out into them." [7]

But was the character of the times the only element external to Vanderbilt himself that was essential to an understanding of the man? Was there not something even more fundamental than this?

The New York *Graphic* felt that there was: "His vast power and property were the legitimate results of the old democratic notion that everybody should be allowed to do anything short of direct robbery or murder without let or hindrance from the Government . . . It was the individual on the make . . . He belongs to the system." And the editorial, unique for its time, of the New York *Evening Telegram* was a harbinger of the future: "His life is more important to us than his death, because it is a typical career, illustrating one of the principles by means of which a man may make progress in a country like the United States . . . Taking his career as a whole we must accept it as representative of a certain very important phase of American life — that phase which consists in pursuing wealth, not with the miser's palm of avarice, but as an exponent of power, as the reward of endeavor, as a giant lever that moves the world."

Thus did the press of New York City answer the accusers — by insisting that the activities of Vanderbilt were in conformity with the best interests of society, by identifying him with the people, and by making the first tentative gropings toward identification of business success with both the economic system and the nation. This was indeed more than an explanation and defense of Vanderbilt; it was a justification of a social order.

In the Middle West and in the South, however, caught up in the rising tide of agrarian discontent, criticism seemed especially concentrated. From Wisconsin came the voice of the Greenbacker, merging scorn for Vanderbilt and dissatisfaction with the economic system:

Cornelius Vanderbilt is dead. He was one of the wealthiest men in America. What more can be said of him? Nothing that shows benefit to mankind . . . That he is dead cannot change our convictions with regard to his life . . . we pronounce Cornelius Vanderbilt a blight to a wise civilization, and a reproach to the character of our country. That a free government, professedly founded on the equal rights of man, can so legislate, as to make it possible for one man to accumulate so much of what other people earned is its reproach. Cornelius Vanderbilt was an extortioner and "grabber" . . . He was selfish, hard and unrelenting to his kind. We have no spite to bear for Mr. Vanderbilt, nor for anyone. We have a testimony to bear against a system, that in this country, makes it possible for the outgrowth of such character. So long as we legislate for the benefit of men like Vanderbilt, ruin and crime will come to our people. Such characters are warts on the body politic, whose roots are nourished from the gains of productive labor . . . The example of the life of Cornelius Vanderbilt, is evil, inasmuch as it awakens a desire in the young for an amount of wealth that should rightfully belong to no one man. It fosters wrong notions of honor, and blinds the soul to the enlightenment that should come from the teaching of conscience. Let us do away with the practises that have been engrafted upon our Republic from the decaying tree of British aristocracy, by which alone it is made possible for Vanderbilts to be created among us.[8]

This was no rifle shot of criticism aimed only at the entrepreneur; it was a shotgun blast aimed at the man and at the system that was thought to have produced him. Other newspapers picked up the range and began firing.

From Georgia:

He who was the head and front of a great monopoly has finally succumbed to a monopoly greater than he . . . How Wall street trembled as the fact became patent that Vanderbilt was no more.

From Illinois:

It is fortunate for mankind that mankind is mortal, and that nature wisely provided that Vanderbilt should not live eighty years longer; for in that time, judging from the rate of his actual achievement, there would scarcely be a railroad or a water-route in all America that would not be absorbed and consolidated by the great monopolist.

From Ohio:

He has no God, save to swear by; profane to a proverb, and yet he has a God to serve — Mammon is his name. He is hungering and thirsting with greed . . . A hundred men are in his service; hard work, light pay, with liberal profanity . . . Workmen are cheapened; pay is withheld; the browbeating power of the capitalist is displayed. No man gets as much work done for the same money as this tyrannical Vanderbilt. No wonder he succeeds . . . "rule or ruin," "serve me or be crushed" . . . Other moguls were but the subjects of the railway autocrat, who, like the beast in the Revelation, came up out of the sea . . . The Commodore will be canonized by the press, and especially by Deems, the preacher, to whom he gave a life-lease of a church, being moved thereto by his wife. While all these platitudes are in circulation, it is still more important that truth should be spoken . . .

From California:

He was largely engaged in undertakings in which the public had deep interest, and yet we can remember no undertaking of his which was not founded upon the abstract idea of gain to himself, irrespective of the comfort and good of others. If he broke a monopoly it was only with the idea of squeezing more money from it and not of relieving the oppressed. There are thousands of witnesses in this State, whose silent testimony is that they have nothing to thank him for.[9]

But the bill of particulars against Vanderbilt was not yet complete. His activities had been castigated as detrimental to the interests of the people and the economic system itself had been implicated in those activities. Now he was put beyond the pale of humanity.

He lacked true religious faith and charity:

If we sum up the case of this rich man . . . it presents little for us to envy; a life devoted to successful speculation, purified by few scruples of conscience, destitute of the finer enjoyments of those who have sought self-culture and self-conquest, without God, except as His name was taken in vain, and closed with not adequate assurance of happiness in the world to come; who would not prefer the poverty and obscurity of the Christian, cheered by the smiles of the Heavenly Father.

His coldness and brutality were sufficient to offset his great accomplishment in piling up more wealth than that possessed even by the people of eight whole states of the Union:

He did not leave his home with his worldly goods and chattels tied up in a handkerchief, nor was he conspicuous in early life as a pious teacher in Sunday school, and a regular attendant upon church socials. In this respect he does not offer the slightest opportunity to be built up as a model and pattern for the average American boy to follow after. He was a domineering young bully of exceedingly limited education . . . In every relation in life he has been hard and cold, and frequently needlessly cruel. He has, domineered over those who have served him, and crushed out those who have opposed him. His children have not been treated any better than the rest of mankind, and there is not, it is believed, much love lost all around.[10]

In every really important respect Vanderbilt was to be scorned, not admired. He had been an ignorant youth and he died an ignorant old man; he "had no manners, and mashed his way to fortune"; he "was very careless of the rights of others so long as he kept technically within the law." Contempt for Vanderbilt filled the pages of such newspapers. Was this man who had risen from "ferryman of Staten Island to the dictatorship of Wall Street," really a worthy person? Hardly; he was nothing more than a tax dodger.[11] Was he deserving of the tributes lavished on him? The St. Louis *Globe-Democrat* replied: "How much money is required to entitle a corpse to the honor which was paid to the dead Vanderbilt, though he had never come within reach of a similar honor while living? . . . Shall there be a different scale of plutocratic honors for each city, or shall no city but New York be permitted to publicly proclaim its worship of the Golden Calf by paying municipal honors to those who had no other claim to them but sordidly acquired wealth? Somebody ought to write a politeness-book on this subject."

The condemnation of the man, tinctured with criticism of the system that had produced him, was comprehensive; but the refutation was no less broad, defending the man against his detractors and the system against its critics. From every part of the nation a chorus of voices was lifted asserting the worth of the man, emphasizing that he was but one among many, reaffirming the value of a society that could produce such as he, and holding forth the shining promise that his career was a pattern that others could follow.

In Tennessee, beneficiary of Vanderbilt's largest single philanthropic venture, his endowment of Vanderbilt University, action was taken which illustrated virtually every phase of the refutation. Do the acts of business-men necessarily create cleavages in society? Clearly not. "One thought especially forced itself on the mind of" Dr. J. Berrien Lindsley, a speaker at the citizens' memorial mass meeting held in Nashville the day after Vanderbilt's death; "that was the great debt of gratitude due from the poor to those who had amassed large fortunes, thereby enabling them to endow hospitals and universities. Such men act as saving banks for the whole race." [12] Judge James Whitworth, another speaker at the same event, reinforced the point. "There is a feeling among the masses to look with envy and suspicion on those who acquire large wealth; but such feeling is wrong, and had its origin in a false estimate of the charac-ter of such men as Mr. Vanderbilt. He rose from the humbler ranks of society by honest effort and perseverance . . . He was . . . wise and liberal . . . broad-minded and philanthropic." [13] Had Vanderbilt served his country well? Mr. Goodwin, speaking in support of a resolution of mourning proposed in the State Legislature, thought so: "In the late war he was devoted to the stars and stripes, and gave his means freely to that cause; but when the smoke and dust of the battle had passed away he looked over this Southern land and saw us in need, and he came to our relief." [14] Did America itself contribute to his success and, if so, could other Americans emulate his career? Representative Smith answered the question: "He has illustrated what this fine government of ours is capable of doing, and what a man in this great and free country of ours may do for himself." [15] Could those who sought to follow Vanderbilt receive assurance that they would pay no penalty for having devoted their lives to business, that their goal was a noble one? Methodist Bishop McTyeire, in his sermon at the memorial service held at Vanderbilt University, gave that assurance: "His benefactions . . . were a means of grace to himself . . . O that men of wealth could learn its best uses, and oftener taste the luxury of doing good! O that they know what a *means of grace* to them-selves it may be made as well as of mercy to others!" [16]

Out of this basic melody the nation's press wove an intricate harmonic pattern. Vehemently denied was the assertion that Vanderbilt's business activities profited none but himself, that business enterprise was good for the entrepreneur but not for the country. "History will do justice to him," wrote the Boston *Daily Advertiser.* "During his lifetime he was often exposed to misrepresentation and abuse. Doubtless, in the sharp struggle to obtain and retain the place and power he held by right of ownership and leadership, he did many things which seemed to be and which were hard, arbitrary, and not sufficiently regardful of the rights and feelings of others. But with blame for his sins of commission and omission we must mix praise for the very great service he rendered in the development of business, and for an example quite exceptional of thorough and systematic anticipation of business to come, and of preparation for it. Commodore Vanderbilt has practically illustrated the truth of the trite maxim, which we all profess to believe, although few of us act upon it, that they best serve themselves who best serve the public. He has completely disproved the popular theory of the unwisdom of the 'one-man power' . . . He served the public and the company faithfully, and had the reward of such success as no predecessor or contemporary could boast of having achieved."

Other newspapers were even more explicit in repudiating the notion that private gain and public service were incompatible and in reinforcing the concept that business enterprise itself, not merely philanthropy, was the true test of social utility. "His deeds of charity cannot be bounded by such magnificent gifts as that of the university established by him," the Washington *National Republican* declared. "They found a greater scope in the employment he gave to honest labor in presenting his vast undertakings. New York may well mourn the loss of a man who in amassing a colossal fortune for himself made her the greatest commercial city in the New World." The Cleveland *Plain Dealer* echoed: "The Vanderbilts of society are the promoters of a practical activity that indirectly benefits the community as a whole. The man who is constantly pushing forward enterprises which furnish employment in a large degree . . . is a public spirited man in the best sense." The Providence *Journal* succinctly summed up the case: "He was in a material sense a public benefactor in that he worked intelligently and earnestly to increase the wealth of the community, and to utilize the means and resources of the community . . . In the general panorama of life and national growth, such men are as necessary as coal and iron."

Having disposed of the accusation that business enterprise profits only the entrepreneur, the non-New York press proceeded to refute the charge that Vanderbilt, simply because he was a businessman, was different from other men. Did he not, like others, love his family, enjoy the solid satisfactions of life, throw off the cares of business when he could? The Washington *National Republican* thought so:

In his private life the Commodore was always distinguished by three things — overwhelming affection for his family and his friends, hatred of ostentation and love of solid comfort . . . he was in private life governed by his affection, nor did age take from him the sweet-smiling look of his boyhood . . . The Commodore ate sparingly and never took wine, but insisted that the little he did eat should be good and well prepared . . . He retired early . . . He was a good strong talker himself . . . His stories were noted for their sharp, pithy sentences, and they were as pointed as needles. He was given to the inculcating of sound business principles in all persons whom he cared for . . . A tremendous worker half of his life, he had short business hours in his old age . . . He was a good liver but not a high one.

Charitable he was even to his enemies: "Although, in his giant speculations, he would ruin half a dozen brokers at a single blow, he would often put some of them on their feet again, after the crash, and was never known to desert a friend . . . In the course of his long and active life he has alleviated much distress, and given a great deal of money in public and private charity." Like other men, he, too, had his favorite hobbies, his favorite foods. Whist and riding were his chief recreations. "The old gentleman carried into his use of horses and his driving on the road just the same characteristics which he displayed in business. He would drive along the middle of the road and intimate to people that they must get out of the way." As for food, "woodcock, Spanish mackerel, and venison were favorite dishes, and Burgundy and Veuve Cliquot were his choice wines; but he was too discreet to become the victim of dyspepsia or gout." He read no more than most men, his language was that of the man-in-the-street, he was neither zealot nor backslider in his religious faith, and, like all good citizens, he loved his country deeply. He was both the one among many and the many in one, for while his life stood out like a towering beacon it was also the incarnation of "all the possibilities and capabilities of the American character." This man, whose qualities were peculiarly his own yet somehow common to all, whose career had been a triumphal procession — surely his "life could serve as an example to most of our youth . . . Such a record is honorable and worthy of emulation." [17]

But could a man even of Vanderbilt's qualities have attained such success at some other time, in some other place? That part of the press which considered the question doubted that he could have. He "lived in a great period for making money," said the San Francisco *Daily Morning Call,* and others confirmed the statement. It was a time when men could "carve out opportunities" for themselves, and if one vein petered out, one could easily "seize upon some other equally valuable source of wealth." Vanderbilt's career was asserted to have been not only characteristic of the time in which he lived, but of the country in which he lived as well. National character and personal character were of course identical in this case. No one "possessed the national attribute of 'push' to a greater degree . . . he was a fine specimen of the true American." But if his inner qualities had been molded by his environment, so had his outward career. "The life of this important personage has been characteristically American . . . Its record is that of a progress in two-thirds of a century from humble, if not extreme, poverty to fabulous wealth by means of extraordinary business talent, phenomenal shrewdness, exceptional energy, and an unfailing capacity and willingness to seize any opportunity." From the verdict of one Midwestern newspaper — "He is one of the most conspicuous examples of an American self made man" — all Americans could take hope, and, in hoping for themselves, give sanction to those who had already attained what they yet sought.[18]

One day, Petroleum V. Nasby tells us, a poor country boy came to crave a second boon of Abou Ben Adhem, the seer of New Jersey. The magician had already made him a politician, but he was not satisfied.

"I see men wield with money a power which I cannot with the arts of a politician, and they seem to find in that a happiness which I cannot in my pursuits. Great Abou, make me a money-king like Dan-il-droo, or Ja-Goold, or Stoo-art, or Tomscot, or any of those mighty men." And again the young man changed: his eyes turned to a cold gray; his head became narrower and long, his lips thin and bloodless, and his fingers long and constantly clasping at something.

Abou explained the transformation:

"Any grovelling worm in worldly dust, any puller and hauler of the worldly muck-rake who knows enough to realize that a hundred cents make a dollar, and who, at the same time, is too infernally mean to spend any part of it, may become as rich as Croesus, if he don't starve to death too soon. To amass shekels, all that is necessary is to live like a beggar, and write the word 'grub' in your hat, if indeed you allow yourself the luxury of a hat. You must, however, go through the process of eliminating from your nature everything in the shape of love, charity, mercy, tenderness, liberality, warmth, geniality, taste, and all desire for enjoyment of any kind . . . The love of money is a tape-worm — it feeds on the body that carries it." [19]

But Nasby was, after all, a humorist, and men may have laughed with him without believing him.

What, though, of more sensitive observers than the lusty Nasby?

> Look up the land, look down the land —
> The poor, the poor, the poor they stand
> Wedged by the pressing of Trade's hand
> Against an inward-opening door
> That pressure tightens evermore . . .
> Does business mean, Die you — live, I?
> Then "Trade is trade" but sings a lie;
> 'Tis only war grown miserly.
> If business is battle, name it so . . .[20]

This was a literary man, however, and doubtless there were many who read the lament of the poet but did not weep with him.[21]

But if in certain quarters of society only chill winds of dissatisfaction blew, in others tornadoes of dissent were ripping people loose from their ideological moorings. In the face of the business practices of the day, could one still believe that the pristine virtues of thrift, industry, and frugality alone would yield success? Conservative E. L. Godkin thought not: "The practise of these old-fashioned virtues will not bring success now as it once did. In the present state of society, a man who relies on them solely, as his ancestors did, is pretty sure to be left behind in the race." [22] Godkin, it may be argued, was a learned and perceptive man, one who could see where others floundered in darkness. But the fact is that the doctrine which he declared to be outmoded was becoming a target of derision precisely among those at whom it was especially aimed: the poor, the uneducated, the young. Charles Loring Brace, director of the New York Children's Aid Society, tells a revealing story. One day, while directing some visitors through the Newsboy's Lodging House he asked for one of the orphan boys to step forth and demonstrate what he had learned. "Paddy" stepped up on a chair, motioned for quiet, and began an oration:

"Bummers," said he, "snoozers, and citizens, I've come down here among ye to talk to yer a little! Me and my friend Brace have come to see how ye's gittin' along, and to advise yer. You fellers what stands at the shops with yer noses over the railin', smellin' ov the roast beef and the hash — you fellers who's got no home — think of it how we are to encourage ye. (Derisive laughter! Ha-ha's, and various ironical kinds of applause.) I say, bummers — for you're *all* bummers (in a tone of kind patronage). *I was a bummer once* (great laughter) — I hate to see you spendin' your money on penny ice-creams and bad cigars. Why don't you save your money? You feller without no boots, how would you like a new pair, eh? (Laughter from all the boys but the one addressed.) Well, I hope you may get 'em, but I rayther think you won't. I have hopes for you all. I want you to grow up to be rich men — citizens, Government men, lawyers, generals, and influence men . . . Now boys (with mock solemnity), be good, mind yer manners, copy me, and see what you'll become." [23]

Could even the most obtuse miss the irony and, behind the irony, the threat: "You haven't any idea of what ye may be yet, if you will only take a bit of my advice. How do you know but, if you are honest, and good, and industerous, you may get so much up in the ranks that you won't call a general or a judge your boss. And you'll have servants of all kinds to tend you, to put you to bed when you are sleepy, and to spoon down your vittles when you are gettin' your grub. Oh, boys! won't that be great! Only think — to have a feller to open your mouth, and put great slices of punkin pie and apple dumplings into it . . . and the best of it will be that if 'tis good to-day, 'twill be better to-morrow." [24]

Clearly the America of 1877 was not that of 1831 or 1848. The broad consensus which gave sanction to business enterprise, which helped create the discipline necessary for its development by infusing into the minds of the members of society the attitudes which guaranteed that their responses would be the appropriate ones[25] — this consensus was dissolving. The old formulas could not withstand the shock of slums and depressions, of rural farmer protests and urban labor strife, especially when advocates of change pointed to business enterprise itself as the cause of the blight they felt was spreading across the land.[26] "The system must be wrong which breeds the perpetual dissensions between employers and employees, so familiar with us to-day, say the more thoughtful working-men." [27] Business enterprise itself was the cause of this alienation:

In any organism . . . all parts are united in a harmony of processes and powers . . . if we look at any sample of human society, in its economic, civic, social relations — say the society of the United States — we are struck with the awkwardness with which its parts go together, the multiplicity of the non-adjustments and mal-adjustments it everywhere contains . . . If we look at society as it offers itself with us, we see that there is a constant tendency to disintegration. Men are failing to find a place in it; are failing to render a service, and so to secure a reward. The tramp is a completely disorganized element; the workman who is drifting from man to man, from place to place, to find work, is a partially disorganized one . . . It is with this unorganized material that society, as an organization, is contending. It is this alien matter that throws it into convulsions. Not till these men find a permanent and fitting place in society can society be at rest with them.[28]

Old loyalties, in short, were being broken, old identities, denied; and if consensus were to be maintained, "the standards of goodness which formerly obtained" [29] would have to be revised.

That the defenders of business enterprise were alarmed at these symptoms of disapproval and cleavage is evident. Referring to the decision of the Supreme Court in the Granger cases, Justice Stephen J. Field wrote to David A. Wells: "I think that the doctrine announced by the majority of the Court practically destroys the guarantees of the Constitution intended for the protection of the rights of private property." [30]

"It is time," said one leading religious journal, "that culture, refinement, and the spirit of unity, order, and progress should combine against the ignorance, jealousy, hatred, and lust of the laboring classes; for the vices of the land inhere in these classes." [31] Could any who read the words of one of America's pioneer social workers hold back a shudder of fear:

It has been common, since the recent terrible Communistic outbreak in Paris, to assume that France alone is exposed to such horror; but, in the judgment of one who has been familiar with our "dangerous classes" for twenty years, there are just the same explosive social elements beneath the surface of New York as of Paris. There are thousands on thousands in New York who have no assignable home . . . there are other thousands, poor, hard-pressed, and depending for daily bread on the day's earnings, swarming in tenement-houses, who behold the gilded rewards of toil all about them, but are never permitted to touch them. All these great masses of destitute, miserable, and criminal persons believe that for ages the rich have had all the good things of life, while to them have been left the evil things. *Capital to them is the tyrant.* Let but Law lift its hand from them for a season, or let the civilizing influences of American life fail to reach them, and, if the opportunity offered, we should see an explosion from this class which might leave this city in ashes and blood . . .[32]

In discussing Vanderbilt in a way in which it had not discussed Girard and Astor — in emphasizing the relation of man to system, in describing the nonbusiness activities of the entrepreneur, in insisting that the businessman's activities were at least as beneficial to society as posthumous philanthropy — the press was at once recognizing the existence of new problems and attempting to answer them. But the press was not alone in this. Bench, pulpit, and school joined in the defense of business enterprise and utilized methods similar to those of the press.

Indeed, the very cornerstone of the conservative economic position — the notion that in America no obstacles stand in the way of economic achievement — became even Supreme Court doctrine, a test of judicial correctness as well as of economic desirability: "The 'theory upon which our political institutions rest' prescribes that 'in the pursuit of happiness all avocations, all honors, all positions are alike open to everyone.' " [33] Nor was one of the leading legal minds of the period reluctant to admit the existence of alienation and the need to defend that which was threatened:

Socialism, Communism, and Anarchism are rampant throughout the civilized world. The state is called on to protect the weak against the shrewdness of the stronger . . . Contemplating these extraordinary demands of the great army of discontents and their apparent power . . . the conservative classes stand in constant fear of the advent of an absolutism more tyrannical, more unreasoning than any before experienced by man, the absolutism of a democratic majority. The principal object of the present work is to demonstrate by a detailed discussion of the constitutional limitations upon the police powers in the United States that . . . democratic absolutism is impossible in this country . . . If the author succeeds in any measure in his attempt to waken the public mind to a full appreciation of the power of constitutional limitations to protect private rights against the radical experimentation of social reformers, he will feel that he has been amply requited for his labors in the cause of social order and personal liberty.[34]

No less were educators involved in "pointing out the duty of the school to counteract challenge to the established order." [35] From the Mc-Guffey Readers in the grade schools, uniting the interests of all groups, giving moral sanction to the quest for wealth, [36] to the more sophisticated texts of the colleges, the lesson to be learned was the same: "Each human being . . . is naturally able to become a Capitalist; economic laws present no obstacles to all men becoming rich." [37] More and more, educators, like journalists, turned their attention to the discussion of systems and to the "social sciences as a means by which schools might inculcate respect for law and order, and suspicion for the doctrines of socialism and anarchism." [38]

But of all social institutions the church was possibly the one most deeply involved in discussion of the new problems presented in the era following the Civil War. What role was the minister expected to play in the discussion of these problems? According to Joseph Tuckerman, it was a role not substantially different from that being played by judge, teacher, and journalist, the role of mediator, of pacifier. The minister has, he said,

daily opportunities . . . of calling forth the kindly affections of the poor towards the rich; giving to them Christian views of the connection which God has instituted between all human interests and human duties; and of inculcating the principles which will secure fidelity in duty, even in the poorest and lowest of all the employments of life. And he has . . . opportunities . . . of giving to the rich a knowledge of poverty and of the poor, which is not otherwise to be attained . . . Let this ministry be continued, and wisely appointed, and it will do more, I believe, than can be done by any other agency, for making the rich and the poor advantageously known to each other; and, through the knowledge and feelings which it may extend of their intimate relation to each other as God's children, and of the inseparable connection which exists between all their various interests, for the excitement and maintenance of a mutual Christian sympathy and feeling of brotherhood between them . . . This ministry . . . may bind the employed to the employer by stronger ties than any pecuniary compensation could form. And in various ways . . . it may be made one at least of the strongest bonds of moral conviction which can be found, between the great classes of the rich and the poor. And on what other, I ask, than moral bonds, is any reliance to be placed in the great exigencies of human society? Above all, under a government like ours, what may not be feared from an extent of pauperism, like that which exists in the old world? What may not be feared from a division and hostility among us of the classes of society . . . ? [39]

Business enterprisers could take satisfaction from the words of Tuckerman, for the effect of his argument was to make of religion a medium of communications which would bind social groups together by explaining to each its need for the other. But from other ministers of the gospel even more enduring satisfaction could be obtained, for the identification of business enterprise and religion became so complete that the vocabulary of the one was applied with equal ease to the discussion of the other. "Men who have tried it," said the *Congregationalist,* "have confidently declared that there is no sleeping partner in any business who can begin to compare with the Almighty." [40] "No!" Rudyard Kipling heard a minister answer to some disputed question about the Judgment. "I tell you God doesn't do business that way." [41]

In every respect the portrayal of Vanderbilt by that large part of the press which viewed him favorably conformed to the broader currents of thought that permeated nearly all phases of American intellectual life.[42] The discussion in these newspapers of Vanderbilt's character and career, of the degree to which his countrymen could claim that their character was like his, of the extent to which nation and economic system could be said to have contributed to his career — all of this led to the possibility of forming a new set of values which embodied approval of both man and system.[43] These new values, by inducing individuals in lower social levels to identify not with their peers but with those in higher ranks whom they hoped ultimately to join, by holding out the promise that the same system which had aided the successful would also aid them, encouraged the kind of behavior which welded society together and supported the activities of business enterprisers.[44] Long before he became a buccaneering business leader, Jay Gould exhibited awareness of the social function that could be performed by portraying a man as Vanderbilt had been portrayed:

. . . a careful study of history, by showing the height to which man as an intellectual being is capable of elevating himself in the scale of usefulness and moral worth, teaches that the virtues of a good man are held in sacred emulation by his countrymen for ages succeeding, long after the scythe of time has gathered the earthly remains of the actor to the silent grave.[45]

The funeral oration of Vanderbilt's pastor, Dr. Deems, made quite clear that eulogy for the behavior of the dead was one form of directing the behavior of the living:

I will not talk of the dead, but to the living. Living men have no time to think of death. Their lives are too busy. The Holy Ghost says true religion is "work, work," by abounding in good work. Be busy in good to humanity and devote no time to the thoughts of death. The Lord will attend to that as he attended to our birth. Some people say we must all die, and therefore they argue that we ought to spend our lives in preparing to die. This is not true of the Christian religion; not one bit of it. True religion is to go forward with life and hold well in the reins, but don't stop the chariot. Our friend was of this belief, and his life abounded in works and good deeds.[46]

This was not only a hymn to the departed entrepreneur but a hallelujah to living enterprise.

IV

J. P. Morgan

"*I, John Pierpont Morgan . . .* commit my soul into the hands of my Saviour, in full confidence that having redeemed it and washed it in His most precious blood He will present it faultless before the throne of my Heavenly Father."

So began the last will and testament of the great J. Pierpont Morgan, and the poet — thinking he had found in these words a clue to understanding of the man's career — was moved to song:

> When all were silent and the gloom
> Grew thick, the dead man rose. The mask
> Slipped. Loath to tarry in the room
> He glanced not at the agate casque,
>
> Nor at his tapestries, his scrolls,
> The ransom of a hundred kings.
> For he that conquers life, his soul's
> Wraith is not chained to mundane things.
>
> His cane with slow, deliberate care
> Swinging, along the street moved he,
> Until he reached the Golden Stair
> That only dead men's eyes may see.
>
> Of newly dead a spirit host
> Made low obeisance when he came.
> Though some be saved and some be lost,
> He was the Master of the Game
>
> In life and death. A grunt, a nod,
> Thanked them. They nudged each other's sides
> For each was fettered to the sod
> By some earth memory. A bride's

Caress. A lad's clean limbs. The sheen
  In a child's face. A battle won.
A crime. A dream. What might have been —
  August, untroubled he passed on.

He puffed at his cigar. The spheres
  Made music. Then the ceaseless drone
Of prayer went up. By myriad tiers
  Encircled rose the Holy Throne.

With no uncertainty of fate
  He brushed aside the angel throng
And strode through the emblazoned gate
  Into the Heaven of the Strong.[1]

Thus did the great financier enter into heaven, as serenely confident of his success in the next world as he had been of his operations in this. And yet, so the poet suggests, the very confidence which had contributed so largely to his success in both worlds set him apart from the rest of humanity and, even as he stepped across the threshold of heaven, made of him something less than a man. Even the damned had their tokens of humanity, dreams and memories, hopes and regrets; but Morgan strode into heaven with a cane and a cigar.

Others, however, denied the accusation:

A giant frame, an iron will
A mind that sped as lightning speeds,
Clearing a way for wits less keen —
A man whose words were deeds.
Simple, sincere, accessible
To all that sought; but woe betide
Him who before those piercing eyes
Faltered, evaded, lied!
And yet those eyes, so quick to blaze
And sear, were no less quick to bless;
For strength and courage, in great hearts,
Mate still with tenderness.
Honest, for honesty's own sake —
Loyal, for so his soul was made —
With one swift glance he chose his ground,
And held it unafraid.
Keen to acquire, to spend, to give,
Ardent in all things, small in none,
He joyed and sorrowed, lived and loved,
And toiled till his work was done.[2]

This, indeed, was a man among men, greater than others, to be sure, but only because he possessed common characteristics to an uncommon degree. In such fashion did the poets enter the lists to engage in a controversy which, nonexistent during discussion of the earliest entrepreneurs and relevant for the first time in the period following the Civil War, emerged with the death of J. Pierpont Morgan as a major criterion for the evaluation of businessmen. On what grounds did that part of the press which was antagonistic to the financier consign him to the outer fringes of humanity; and what were the means by which the majority of the press which viewed him favorably restored him to humanity and thereby reaffirmed the unity and harmony of the social order?

Few of the elements which newspapers deemed relevant to consideration of entrepreneurial careers on the occasion of Morgan's death had not been at least implied on the occasion of Vanderbilt's, but if the ingredients were old, the proportions of their mixture were new. The ancient and honorable equation of character and career, so characteristic of those periods of American history when nothing seemed seriously to challenge business enterprise, was now almost an afterthought brought in to buttress a conclusion based largely on other considerations. On the other hand, the ideas that the very business activities of the business enterpriser are valuable to society, that he partakes of the same human qualities as even the most ordinary members of society, that the nature of the social order itself contributes materially to his success — ideas which first made their appearance at the time of Vanderbilt — emerged to a new peak of prominence.

What impressions of Morgan, what stimuli to thought was the reader of a large metropolitan newspaper favorable to the financier's activities likely to receive from its articles and editorials?

"J. P. Morgan Dies In Rome; Almost Unconscious For Five Days" ran the banner headline over the Associated Press dispatch from Rome in the April 1, 1913, issue of the New York *Tribune*, and eight full newspaper pages of articles followed. But for perhaps the first time the major item of interest was not the size of the rich man's estate nor the manner of its distribution. Dominating the first page of that issue of the *Tribune* was a large drawing of Morgan by Boardman Robinson entitled "A Titan." Elsewhere on that page were the articles which explained why Morgan deserved that appellation, and in none of these was wealth a major consideration. "Gibbons Praises Morgan," "Taft Calls Morgan One of Our Greatest Men," ran the headlines, and the articles that followed made clear why it was that "no more general, or even higher, tribute to the character, integrity and usefulness of one of America's foremost citizens has ever been paid by the voices of the men that lead in every walk of life." The *Tribune* was somewhat less comprehensive than it claimed to be in gathering testimonials from leaders "in every walk of life" — farm leaders and labor leaders were conspicuously absent — but the statements of the lawyers, churchmen, and financiers who were represented provide at least some evidence of those aspects of Morgan's character and career which such persons felt it important to emphasize. "His patriotism and his unflagging work of upbuilding the business and best interests of the country has been of the highest order," said George F. Baker, president of the First National Bank of New York and a close associate of Morgan, "and his career of service to the world has been most extraordinary." Patriotism and service were the elements emphasized by Baker and, following him, by the leaders of the financial community. Frank A. Vanderlip, president of the National City Bank, stated: "No man has ever been more closely or more honorably or more patriotically identified with the growth and progress of this country than he."

"In my opinion he was the greatest man this country or the world has ever known," said investment banker James Seligman; and investment banker Jules Bache repeated: "In the death of Mr. Morgan the United States has lost one of the most potent factors for progress of his epoch." If Morgan's essential quality had been that of service to all, to the nation as a whole, then truly he deserved the encomium of President Mahon of the New York Stock Exchange: "His death is a loss to the country at large."

Not until page four did the *Tribune* discuss Morgan's business activities, his rise to prominence with the marketing in England of Vanderbilt's New York Central Railroad securities, the organization of the United States Steel Corporation, the part he played in the consolidation of once competitive railway lines. In its discussion of Morgan as a businessman, the *Tribune* conformed in part to the age-old stereotype of the man who reached the pinnacle of success from the lowest levels of economic life, in part to the new model of the entrepreneur which laid stress on his nonbusiness activities. Morgan's early life had not been characterized by poverty; indeed he had inherited millions from his banker father. The obvious discrepancy between the fact and the stereotype required the *Tribune* to devise a formula which would permit the fact to be recognized and yet allow the stereotype to retain its utility. Despite the fact that he had "no traditions of the steerage," the *Tribune* maintained, "in him were the qualities of the self-made man, and by his own efforts he traversed relatively as many rounds of the ladder as did many other financiers who began with nothing." In his nonbusiness activities he exhibited the same fundamental patriotism as he did in his business life. "Morgan Intensely Patriotic Afloat As Well As On Shore" read the headline whose article revealed that both his yachts had been built in the United States and that "he loved the flag." But if as yachtsman, as art collector, and as connoisseur of rare books he was somewhat beyond the reach of ordinary men, he was like them in his love of the simple pleasures: "He was fond of a good dinner, good wines, and big black cigars, but enjoyed all in moderation."

Ten additional articles, taking up three full newspaper pages, emphasized the importance of Morgan's art collection, asserted that his death was a tremendous loss to the nation's charitable organizations, revealed that his death would cause no change in the policy of his banking house because his son would be his "worthy successor," claimed that his firm was "a rather democratic institution," and insinuated that his death had been caused by the rough interrogation he had received at the hands of the Pujo money-trust investigating committee shortly before his departure for Europe.

Concluding its first day's comments on the death of Morgan, the *Tribune* editorialized:

Nobody will deny to J. Pierpont Morgan the title of a great American . . . His name was known the world over and the weight it carried was due to personal achievement rather than to any accident of station, fortune or public favor. It was not in his stars but in himself that he achieved greatness . . . In the common and narrower sense of the word he was not a self-made man at all . . . But Morgan rose superior to the often relaxing environment of great wealth. He was as eager as any yet-to-be-made financiers starting at the foot of the ladder to test his powers and exhaust his last ounce of energy . . . In the broader sense he was always a man self-made and still in the making, and his superb energy and intellectual resources easily put him in the front rank of those who do things in the largest way, not so much for self-profit as for the sheer pleasure of doing them . . . In recent years attempts have been made to influence popular opinion against Mr. Morgan by picturing him as the sinister creator of a "money trust." It is an entirely unjust view of his activities as a financier to regard him as the selfish creator of the concentration of credit . . . The conditions which made this possible were not of his creation. The situation called for a man of his sort and he merely responded to the call . . . To inspire confidence was the keynote of Mr. Morgan's career . . . He left great riches, but he also left a good name more priceless than riches. He was a leader of his day whom both his fellow citizens and the world at large have long recognized as a representative American.

Belief that high status attained through personal achievement was worthier than similar status ascribed through birth or bestowed by others, that the banker was motivated not by the quest for profits but by sheer love of the "game" and the will to serve, and explicit identification of the financier as an "American" — these were the basic ideas projected by the *Tribune*'s image of Morgan. Such an argument was more than simply a denial of the accusations that Morgan had been greedy and that his business activities had been detrimental to the interests of the country. By explicitly identifying the financier with the nation and its people, it placed those who had a less favorable view of Morgan in the awkward position of apparent hostility to the country as well as to the man. The implication was that no one would express animosity toward a man so patriotic and so typical of all that was best in the American character unless he were also hostile toward that which the man represented.

The concern exhibited by such a newspaper as the New York *Tribune* with defense of a living society as well as of a dead entrepreneur was no mere matter of rhetoric. It was the product of a situation in which certain elements of a society which in the very year of Morgan's death was being rent by strikes in the textile mills of the East, the garment factories of New York, the coal fields of West Virginia and Colorado, the copper mines of Michigan, and the railroads of the West, were themselves challenging the desirability of a system which, in their view, produced men like Morgan. At a time when the spokesmen of business enterprise were formulating their defense more and more in terms that dealt with the noneconomic activities of businessmen, the opponents of such enterprise tended more and more to mold their arguments into an attack on the businessman's business activities and on the social conditions which made them possible.

Only a small part of the group which was antagonistic toward Morgan avowed total repudiation of the society of which he was a member. The Socialist New York *Call*, however, was one:

J. P. Morgan was the mightiest figure in international finance. Up to the time of his death he was the leader of the financial interests in this city and country and of international bankers. In this country he stood supreme in the world of money . . . and through the occupation of the leadership of the chain of banks actually controlled the economic destinies of the nation. It was generally conceded that he was the motive power behind the political government of the country, and it is well known that before his sway monarchs made obeisance . . . He was the very typification of capitalism, in all its cruel remorselessness. He never scrupled as to the methods concerned when it was a question of crushing a competitor, and to the intensification of his wealth and power every other consideration took a position in the background.

Had Morgan really been patriotic? Hardly; he had been a draft-dodger during the Civil War, and "his first recorded transaction of any note" — the sale of allegedly worthless rifles to the Union Army — "premeditatedly consigned great numbers of his fellow men to . . . destruction." [3]

Had Morgan really been unconcerned with profits? "He was not above exploiting the most cherished sentiments for his own commercial aggrandizement," the *Call* observed.

Was it true that he had been generous to his employees? "He bore organized labor an animosity that was intense," the *Call* charged. "It sought to restrict his profits; therefore, it had to be annihilated."

But the real concern of the Socialist newspaper was not with the man but with what he symbolized: "There does not seem to be any aching void to fill because Mr. Morgan has departed from earth . . . Up until the last moment he was represented as working indefatigably for the welfare and stability of society . . . and the reader of these effusions was given the impression that the loss of this overshadowing figure would prove an unmitigated and irremediable disaster." Yet nothing of the kind had happened, the newspaper stated, because the "Morgan represented by the press" had been "an allegory — almost a myth . . . Morgan was no more the controller and director of . . . great social and industrial forces than the simple-minded old Pope is the director and controller of the great Catholic Church, or than the driveling, weak-minded, half-insane Czar is the real 'autocrat of all the Russias.' There was power there, not in the individual, but in the system that he typified. He passes; it remains." But so, too, did socialism remain, the *Call* asserted, and "if Morgan is remembered at all, it will be for the part he played in making it possible and assisting, though unconsciously, in its realization. Outside of this, history has no place for him and mankind no reason for remembrance."

Others, too, who were not Socialists, agreed with the verdict of the *Call*, that newspaper reported, but for very different reasons. Evaluating "his career from the Christian standpoint," the Reverend Dr. George Chalmers Richmond of St. John's Episcopal Church in Philadelphia preached a sermon on the subject, "Has J. P. Morgan gone to heaven? If not, why not?" Morgan had not gone to heaven, the churchman asserted, because he had been neither Christian nor democrat. "Mr. Morgan was not a great Christian and always paid more attention to art than to our missionary work on earth. His belief in foreign missions arose from a desire to see our business interests prosper in the East and not at all from a great love for common humanity . . . Mr. Morgan did not believe in the equality of man or in giving the common people their many liberties. He believed not in free speech . . . If it caused his death to testify before the Pujo Investigating Committee, then I hope more of his type will be called to testify . . . God knew just when to take Mr. Morgan out of this present world, and send him on to another state of existence."

Why did the press persist in pouring praise on Morgan, asked the New York *Daily People,* official publication of the Socialist Labor Party, when at the time of his death he had long ceased to perform any essential function? "As he, his mission being performed, could die 'at the throttle of the engine' without the engine being the worse for it, so with the

Capitalist class. Its mission is performed . . . To deliver this object lesson was J. P. Morgan's main mission. It took his death to perform the task . . . The Socialist Movement gratefully acknowledges its obligation to J. P. Morgan for having died."

Those sections of the labor movement which were under the influence of socialist ideology, like the Industrial Workers of the World, viewed Morgan's life in much the same way.

Morgan had earned the thanks only of his own class, said the IWW newspaper, *Solidarity*, but "despite his arrogant and brutal oppression of the working class," he had one quality deserving of universal praise, the quality of "daring imagination. Observing the tendency of the times toward large combinations of capital, he headed this tendency and developed it in a manner profitable to himself and allies." But Morgan's very success was his downfall. "At the same time, Morgan was, unconsciously, doing another, and altogether different, kind of work. He was helping to organize large combinations of labor — to organize the working class in industry in a manner that has made ITS imagination more daring than ever before. It has caused the workers to become aware that, in the last analysis, it is upon their co-operative labor . . . that society and its welfare depend. The workers are beginning to perceive in every large industrial strike, that society is paralyzed when they stop work, though it goes right on when Morgan, with all his financial genius dies . . . Let us praise Morgan, then, for having helped to create a society in which labor is united . . . not only for the profit of capital, but also for its own emancipation. The technical unity of labor has made possible the social unity of the race."

That Morgan was of significance only as a symbol of a particular kind of society and that the evils of the man were those of the society were the major points emphasized by the radical sector of the labor press. The journal of the Western Federation of Miners left no doubt that, for his critics, the view which regarded the entrepreneur essentially as a symbol of a social order might act as a powerful solvent of the consensus which sanctioned the growth of business enterprise. "Another czar will take his place," said the *Miner's Magazine*, "and the successor of Morgan will be just as brutal in the exaction of profit as the man who formerly wielded the money scepter of America. Sometime the people will overthrow the hellish system that breeds a billionaire and a tramp."

Not all the antagonists of Morgan, of course, not even among the trade union press, indicted an entire society along with the man. Such critics directed their attention in part to the qualities of the man, in part to those particular aspects of the social system which they felt made possible his less desirable activities. They expressed none of the sense of inevitability that characterized the discussion of the Socialist critics of society, nor did their demand for reform envision so complete a change in the structure of society. "Where is he?" asked the *United Mine Workers' Journal* of Morgan, and contrasted the statement of the Reverend George Chalmers Richmond that Morgan had "not gone to heaven, he would be very unhappy up among the angels" with that of Professor Jesse B. Carter, director of the American Academy in Rome: "Two weeks ago Mr. Morgan was seated in a pew at our Easter service, unconsciously adding himself to the long list of the great, beginning with Charlemagne, who worshipped on Easter day in the Eternal City. From this Easter service Mr. Morgan has passed to the Eternal City of God." In order to solve the problem of Morgan's whereabouts, the *United Mine Workers' Journal* suggested, "an investigation committee should be appointed with the power to summon J. P. Morgan to testify in his behalf. The court may hold its session in the moon." The Duluth *Labor World,* less facetious, was more critical:

What are the works which this man has built? A system so powerful that it has been able to do what would a few years ago have been thought impossible. The power to give value to paper back of which there has not been real wealth; the power to make or mar fortunes of other men; a greater power over the products of industry than the very captains of industry themselves possessed. A sinister power it has been, so independent that it could be exercised for good or evil. More and more the man has come to be feared. And his power has been dangerous in this . . . it has dealt with money, with the organization of finance to produce certain results; it has done that which cannot but be dangerous, concentrated power in a very few hands.

Thoroughly repudiated was the notion that Morgan's career had been of service to his countrymen. Certainly the employee of "the steel trust," laboring in the mills "twelve hours a day, seven days in the week, year in and year out, for the lowest wage for which his services could be secured" had no reason to feel grateful to the man. His name had "not been known for philanthropy," nor had his "genius . . . been used in the service of patriotism or of his fellow men." Thus far, the criticism of this more moderate section of the labor press had been in accord with that of the Socialists, but the distinction between them was sharply drawn on the issue of the remedy to be applied to the disease which both recognized. For the Socialists, society had been at fault and society would have to be reorganized. For the less radical labor critics, the essential lesson of Morgan's life was that excessive power in the hands of one person was dangerous and would have to be curbed. It was not the system but the man who was at fault. "Already we are convinced that there must not be another Morgan," concluded the *Labor World.* "The people will overthrow the hellish system," the Socialists had concluded.

However much the dissenters differed with respect to the prescription needed by the ailing patient, the fact that they agreed that the patient was ill and that the sickness was caused by prevailing modes of business enterprise was cause for concern among entrepreneurs anxious for acquiescence and approval. Opposition to Morgan was symptomatic of conflicting criteria of social desirability and such conflicting criteria, especially when linked to the kind of analysis which insisted that changes, however limited in scope, be made in the conditions in which enterprise was flourishing, portended the possibility of even more drastic action to limit and restrict the activities of entrepreneurs.

From north, south, east, and west came voices critical of Morgan, to be sure, but focusing their attention on the social conditions which they felt had brought him to power and on the reforms needed to curb that power.

The New York *World,* flushed with enthusiasm at the recent success at the polls of Woodrow Wilson and the New Freedom, was confident that Morgan "was the last of his line . . . Never again will conditions of government make it possible for any financier to bestride the country like a Colossus." For the *World,* Morgan's career had rested on his alliance with the government; after "the triumph of Hannaism in 1896 this country was given over to Wall street to be exploited like a conquered province. The welfare of Wall street was made the national welfare . . . In all of Mr. Morgan's great operations he worked in partnership with government." But now the New Freedom had triumphed and conditions of government had changed. "The Morgan empire is one that the satraps cannot govern and will not be permitted to govern. In time little will remain except the feeling of bewilderment that a self-ruling people should ever have allowed one man to wield so much power for good or evil over their prosperity and general welfare, however much ability and strength and genius that man possessed."

Preoccupation with the problem of power, exemplified by the trusts in whose organization Morgan had been a dominant figure, mingled with scorn for his apparent lack of charity and human warmth, were the hallmarks of journalistic criticism of Morgan.

From the region of the Rocky Mountains came the bitter denunciation:

To him the gratification of ambition was paramount, and he cared little how it was accomplished . . . No great philanthropy is stone-marked with the name of Morgan . . . The time server, the sycophant and the idolator of dollar power will chant their te deums for him for a brief period, until a new pillar is installed in the Morgan space . . . But the many who felt in their souls the iron of his ceaseless and relentless foraging, who winced and suffered and fell before its voracity and arrogance, they, too, will stand in the market places and proclaim to a listening world their estimate of his record and his works . . . Friend and foe alike will pay tribute to the cold genius of the man; to his energy; his power for concentration; his disregard for ideals; his contempt for precedent; his pity for ethics; his disdain of principles and his scorn for the higher moralities of commercial life.[4]

From the Great Plains came even more menacing criticism:

We verily believe that J. Pierpont Morgan has done more harm in the world than any man who ever lived in it. It was Morgan who started the idea that the trust is an economic necessity . . . The enslavement of labor, the crushing of individual initiative, the blighting of womanhood, the premature aging of children, these are the awful sidelights thrown on the terrible journey of this modern juggernaut — crushing, craunching, and destroying all who tried to resist it . . . It will be a weary fight for the American people to get from under the continuing burden which J. P. Morgan has left upon them . . . If Morgan had left every dollar of his estate to the American people, he could not, by such act, have undone a hundredth part of the damage he has worked upon our people . . . Let those covet his millions who will but give us for envy the man whose wife and children greet him with smiles at the end of an honest day's labor, and upon whose grave in the end shall fall the unfeigned tears of those he brothered, and loved and helped.[5]

From Middle West and South came similar comment. "One difference between Robin Hood and Morgan," said the Chicago *Day Book,* "was that good old Robin robbed the rich and gave to the poor. Morgan played no favorites."

"To be perfectly frank," the Mobile *Register* remarked, "we begin to fear this great power, in any one man's hands. The mere possession of it makes its possessor unscrupulous. Let us say that Mr. Morgan was trusted . . . yet see the powerful banking man at work, note the combinations, the deals, the lifting here, the leveling down there, the dominating of commerce, the partitioning of trade territory, the aggrandizing of some seaports, the closing of others, the virtual dictatorship exercised over every new enterprise demanding the employment of considerable capital or entering a field already apportioned to some Morgan interest — are we not right in saying that we must view such a man and such a situation with the feeling of alarm lest what is meant be not simply the crushing of individual enterprise but eventually the submerging of public freedom? . . . We believe that in Mr. Morgan we have seen the culmination and flower of a system that will be reformed or be done away with."

The judgments expressed by some of the more sophisticated magazines served only to confirm the fundamental conclusions already reached by the sector of the daily press antagonistic to Morgan. Morgan was to be understood as the creation of his environment, the creature of the era of trusts and business consolidations; but the reforms of the New Freedom and of Progressivism would break the stranglehold he and his kind had imposed upon the nation's economy and rid the people of the tyranny of the money-power. "The world was his table; gigantic enterprises were his pawns; monopoly power was the winner's portion," wrote *La Follette's Weekly*. "Morgan's almost unbroken succession of winnings cannot be attributed wholly to genius; the rules of the game were enforced or set aside according to his need. With government as his silent partner, with his fiat regarded above the law, what may not a man accomplish! . . . When the history of the period since the Civil War is written, the 'House of Morgan' will stand out conspicuously as a monument to the grim individualism of the masters of capital at whose head for many years stood the silent, determined figure of Morgan."

"The passing away of such leaders as Mr. Morgan . . . marks the end of an epoch," wrote Walter Hines Page. "In spite of the constructive work and the masterful leadership of Mr. Morgan and of his great deeds in the era that we are now passing out of, a revision of the currency and banking laws, if a wise revision be made, will prevent any other such career, even if another such strong personality were to arise. The possession of such great power — or the possibility of its possession — does not fit into the American scheme of life or business."

Buoyant confidence that, fortunately, there would be no successor to Morgan was a pervasive theme of the opposition press. "Mr. Morgan was, more than anything else, a product of his environment; and the Wall Street environment of the future is going to be decidedly changed as compared with that of the past," *Moody's Magazine* predicted. The country would be the better for it, because it had been his "firm and financial group . . . rather than the community, state or nation which profited by his great ability. He was not a builder of industries or a creator of wealth, or an inventor of new commercial or productive methods, through which the sum total of the wealth of the world is augmented. His work, when compared with that . . . of any of the great inventors . . . pales into insignificance."

"It is a nearly extinct race, these billionaires," the *California Outlook* exulted, "and there will never be another generation of them."

But other critics were less sanguine that the race of billionaires had indeed passed; "fundamental conditions," they felt, had not yet changed sufficiently for that. "We do not blame great financiers who had taken advantage of our toleration of trustifying robberies," the Lewiston, Maine, *Journal* commented, "so much as we blame those political leaders, and the masses who misled by party emblems have played into their hands, creating such tariffs as the Aldrich trust-promoting law, and accentuating the resources of those who got rich without perspiration and without aspiration . . . The economic warfare between poor and rich . . . has been such as to forebode, in the near future, another social and political revolution which may or may not be as serious as that which was the price paid for the emancipation of the slave . . . The segregation of what would be public wealth, in the hands of a few, must be remedied by processes of taxation, if not by processes of revolution."

"Morgan's power was not in himself," the *Progressive Woman* remarked. "It was centered in the present social system which he personified. His power he acquired because the industrial order of today placed him in a position to exploit the working class and crush competition . . . But now a new clamor is being heard everywhere around the world. It is the voice of labor demanding that it alone is the rightful heir to all wealth . . . This declaration of labor is found in the international Socialist movement, and it is the presage of a social order in which the means of life will be used for the enrichment of the workers themselves."

Walt Whitman's friend Horace Traubel proposed to show that Morgan's personal character was molded by the nature of capitalist enterprise:

The masters of money die. The servants of men are immortal . . . He was a brute. His code was barbarous. He put us all under tribute. He walked over rather than round the humanities. He was endowed rather with tooth and claw than with forgiveness and reciprocity . . . My eyes see past his literal body to what he stood for. I am not satisfied when he is discredited and dismissed . . . He was a certain civilization. What the power of wealth stood for: he was that. He was stocks, bonds, banks, railroads, trusts, financiering, chicanery, profit. He was success. The victory was over innocence. The crown was won through force . . . If we had to present the statistics of an era in a person why is he not eminently the logical summing up of the problem? . . . When you say God bless you miss him. But when you say God damn you reach him at once . . . He was not malign. But he was not quite man . . . You can't consider him as an individual. As mister so and so. He was horribly impersonal. He was the shadow of his time . . . He was not the thief in the night but the thief in the day doing your work and my work in a thief age . . . We put his age away in the hole in the ground with him. Now we can pass across the frontier unburdened. What will come after the dollars? The same thing that came before the dollars. Folks. Men women children.[6]

Such, surely, was the ultimate threat to that complex of ideas which for so long had provided a climate of security and approbation for business enterprise. Totally repudiated was the notion that either posthumous philanthropy or business activity itself was beneficial to society; and the acceptance of enterprise which stemmed from the belief that social welfare was attained through the individual's attempt to achieve personal economic success was in danger of dissolution by the corrosive idea that the welfare of all would be attained only through reconstruction of the social order. Whether the dissenting view, as with the Socialists, envisioned a complete reorganization of society or, as with the Wilsonians and Progressives, reform in the structure of government and curbs on the power of business, it was characterized throughout, as the Chicago *Tribune* put it, by emphasis on the relationship of "the economic facts to the welfare of the average man, to his political, social, and material condition," and by "profound public concern and hostility" toward "the Money Power." Criticism of such kind, the newspaper felt, was something new in America. "Thus, Mr. Morgan, much against his will, found himself taken not as a private individual whose business was his own affair, but as a public man, a force, the representative of a system of government, a ruler whose activities and powers were potent for the good or ill of man, and, therefore, to be criticised and controlled. To the previous generation he would have been a very rich, public spirited, and gifted citizen, to be envied and honored. To this he was everything good or evil, from a selfish oppressor to a benevolent autocrat." That successive generations should have such startlingly contrasting judgments of business enterprise was evidence of the far-reaching changes that had taken place in the American economy and, correspondingly, of divergent views regarding the desirability of those changes. If confidence in business enterprisers were to be maintained and, even more, if faith were to be maintained in society itself, then their defenders would have to provide a convincing demonstration that business was less private enterprise than it was public service; that the entrepreneur was less a man of unique qualities than a man like other men; that the system which allowed one man to achieve high status through effort would permit any man to do so; and that whatever faults were associated with the entrepreneur were really the responsibility of the "times" in which he lived and not, therefore, necessary consequences of business enterprise itself. Such a demonstration would be, of course, more than praise of a man. It would be recognition that Morgan had "stood forth as the defender" of finance "in the war that is being made on wealth throughout the world," and a defense against the "world-wide rising tide of questioning of the rights of capital and capitalists." [7]

The concept of private enterprise as public service was the foundation of this argument.

"Wonderful Development of U.S. Due to J. P. Morgan" read the headline in the Atlanta *Georgian,* and the article beneath it summarized the position of newspapers the country over:

To Morgan, more than to any other man, is due the credit for the wonderful development of the United States in the last generation . . . Morgan was always unique in that he always worked on the constructive side of business and made more money for other people than he did for himself. Money-making was to him only an incident in business. He delighted in great productive enterprises just as an artist delights in a great canvas. When he looked at the stock market he did not see figures. The ticker tape was to him a panorama of rushing trains and steamships and roaring factories . . . The world . . . need not worry as to the future, for Morgan and Company will remain at the helm.

"Mr. Morgan's genius was entirely constructive," said the Chicago *Record-Herald*. "He believed in building up, not in tearing down and profiting by others' misfortunes." If Morgan had been nothing more than an operator in the stock market the country would have had little regard for him. But the fact was that he had been "the molder of the railroad history of the nation, the man who gave character to broad financial operations, the man who financed the nation itself and who first opened the doors for American participation in world financial undertakings." It was these services in the interest of others that gave Morgan "proportions that undoubtedly will give him a permanent place among the men who upbuilt the nation. For the making of the nation was not a process confined to those who bore the pioneer tasks of statesmanship and of constructive effort. The nation is still in the making, and J. P. Morgan was one of the molding influences in epochs of its career." Had Morgan not saved the nation during the panic of 1907? "With banks crumbling to pieces on every hand, with credits gone and panic running riot, Morgan took charge. Into his protecting arms he invited the bulls, and the bears, and the lambs — all altogether, and no favorites, and he rode the storm to safety." [8]

Because he had "done much for the financial, industrial and commercial stability of the country, and aided in creating conditions that have made the United States the richest and most prosperous nation that ever existed," Morgan was clearly entitled to be called a patriot. The most potent factor "in the matter of upbuilding personal respect among the rank and file of American citizenship, has been the fact that J. P. Morgan was always an intensely patriotic American, and was literally regarded as the nation's bulwark against panics." The function that could be performed by discussing business activities in terms of patriotism was evident. "We Americans permit our politicians to inculcate in us a distrust of our men of big business." Yet "Mr. Morgan was a better American than many men who loudly give lip-service to their country . . . America is further advanced that Mr. Morgan lived, for he accelerated the growth of this country." [9] Successful business enterprise had already been attributed, at least in part, to the unique advantages offered by American society. The identification was now made even more complete and the climate of enterprise more favorable by giving it the sanction of patriotism.

Once the harmony of society had been affirmed by demonstrating the indispensability and desirability of business enterprise, the press sought to reinforce that sense of harmony by asserting that in all respects save that of his wealth Morgan was like other Americans.

"Ultimately it will be recorded," said the Louisville *Courier-Journal,* that although "he was a human being with a large capacity for dealing with fiscal affairs," his main characteristic was that he had "much the same proportion of those virtues and faults which appertain to other human beings." Indeed, though few had realized it during his lifetime and so had failed to do him justice, he was in all essential qualities a man like others: "J. P. Morgan came into the hearts of men when he died . . . When the massive man, who was to so many millions of people the tremendous symbol of wealth and of privilege more powerful than wealth, closed his eyes forever, those who vaguely had feared, and perhaps hated, him, now observed him, it might be said, for the first time, as a person, a man, a father, a husband, a friend, a companion, an acquaintance . . ." There was in Morgan the man a bit of every man. "Religion, education, art, literature, charity, help and, following them as if of lesser importance, property, wealth, enterprise, and speculation, as well as the manlier sports of sea and shore, entered within the range of his Jovian genius, and his manifold work and play . . . Productively great, influentially great, and intuitively wise, he was personally unaffected and simple to a degree hard to associate with the contemplation of him as a concrete king of the world forces and the world opportunities of the age in which he lived."

"The character of this man was complete," said another newspaper. "His word on art was supreme . . . He interested himself in medicine . . . He was strong in church affairs . . . He was personally honest, of course; personally a good citizen, a charitable man, a helper in worthy movements, a clean character in the usual moral sense." He had no need for "the services of that modern instrument of publicity, the press agent," for he was really a simple man. "Beneath the rugged exterior of Mr. Morgan beat a heart of warm sympathy and understanding for his fellow men . . . of friendship and . . . sympathetic regard for mankind in all walks of life." The simple virtues he had in common with all humanity, but in his case virtue was more than its own reward: "The world pays tribute to the human qualities which made possible the acquirement of the tremendous fortune he leaves, but more important gave him his limitless influence in the world of finance." [10]

But, the press asked, on what foundation were based the qualities which Morgan had in common with others? Were these qualities the common property of all humanity or had they been bestowed more discriminatingly? The answer was forthright. They rested on the "Americanism that has wrought grandly in varying precincts of endeavor." He had been a "great American," "a colossal American," and both his business success and the qualities he exhibited in his nonbusiness activities, his "large ideas and large purposes," were to be attributed to that factor. "Morgan was typically an American," said one Middle Western newspaper, "the product of American institutions and the opportunities fostered by them. So also were his ideas and ideals sprung from the country that gave him birth." [11]

This, truly, was a mirror for Americans, but a very special kind of mirror, one which reflected a double image; for, at the same glance, it permitted men to see themselves as they were and as they hoped to be.

But two additional elements were necessary to make of Morgan's career a demonstration of the superior opportunities offered by the economic system prevailing in the United States. Business enterprise had already been asserted to be socially useful and desirable, and Morgan himself had been portrayed, except for his extraordinary wealth, as an ordinary man. It now remained to deny that his career was in any sense the product of unique personal advantages, his success anything but merit rewarded, and to relate personal career and social system in such a way as to prove that others might have similar careers.

"It will be found," wrote the *Deseret Evening News,* "that although he was born rich, yet his success in building upon the foundation laid was due to his rare natural gifts, and the moral qualities without which no success is possible." That he had been wealthy from birth had not affected his career, the Springfield *Republican* insisted: "Mr. Morgan's life was a romance of individual achievement, in its outline not unlike other careers in this country." Indeed, possession of such vast wealth by inheritance had been a positive disadvantage. "Unlike many of the men of great wealth in this country," said the New York *Times,* "Mr. Morgan . . . did not have the incentive of poverty to spur him on in the early stages of his career. He was not born poor. On the contrary he was heir to a fortune . . . When J. P. Morgan went into business here in the early '60's there was open to him a career entirely honorable and very comfortable, that would have carried him to an inconsequential old age and an unhistoric grave. He did not choose this career, but rather chose to work as few men have worked in the last half century."

That Morgan successfully overcame the handicap of having been born rich, that his career conformed to the model of aspiration, was not only a tribute to him personally but evidence of the continuing validity of the notion that effort alone is crowned with success. "Contrary to the rule that has prevailed among our captains of industry, J. Pierpont Morgan was not a 'self-made man,'" wrote the Sioux City *Journal.* "He was of wealthy parentage — a handicap to commercial success, as all biographers agree. If they are right about this Mr. Morgan must be given additional credit." This, indeed, was "the greatest marvel of his epochal career" — "that he did not choose to follow the primrose path where most rich men's offspring are wont to wander into the vale of insignificance." The lesson was obvious. Even as between rich and poor, "no man's opportunity is greater than another's." [12]

And no man's opportunity was greater than another's because opportunity itself was conceived to lie in the environment which was the same for all. So far as Morgan himself was concerned, "his matchless career was the product of the unprecedented financial and commercial age in which he lived." The "exceptional opportunities" of the time in which he lived, the "individualistic atmosphere of the third quarter of the nineteenth century," had made possible his career.[13] Uniqueness of time and place was the factor to be taken into consideration. "In truth," wrote the Montgomery *Advertiser,* "perhaps no other country and no other era furnished such opportunities for a financial genius as were furnished in America in the era of rapidly made fortunes of the past fifty years."

Critics of Morgan, too, had considered him in relation to the time and place in which he lived, but they had insisted that his defects were those of the system of which he was a part. The defenders of Morgan succeeded in transforming the argument. They used it not only to demonstrate the relationship between Morgan's success and the opportunities offered by the system, but to explain that his faults were not inherent in the system he represented. If "judged by his times," by "the characteristics of the age in which he lived," these newspapers said, it would be seen that "he reflected only the business morality and methods of his time." If his "general course" had been "ruthless," if his "conscience" lacked "tender scruples," it was because "his operations were conducted along the line of the general business code." [14] If such were the case, the critics of business enterprise might well be mollified, for its evils were to be traced not to business enterprise itself but to those who made the codes by which it was conducted.

All the people of the nation, irrespective of distinctions of wealth and status, plunged into mourning at the death of the great financier — the respect and approval from which such visible evidences of regret emanated were the ingredients of the kind of consensus sought by the pro-Morgan press. "Rich And Poor Mourn Death of Morgan" — the headline in one of these newspapers — may or may not have been a reflection of the whole truth; but it was an expression of the wish.

The higher priced magazines agreed with the less expensive newspapers that the elements of Morgan's life to be emphasized were that service to all was inherent in the very nature of business enterprise, that nonbusiness activities were fully as important as business in arriving at an estimate of the businessman, that Morgan was to be doubly applauded for having overcome the disadvantage of being a rich man's son, and that in every respect he was a patriotic American.

"A great banker — the greatest of his or perhaps any time," wrote George Harvey, editor of *Harper's Weekly*, about Morgan:

A matchless upbuilder of properties, who never encouraged or profited from destructive performance.

A faithful trustee of billions, ever conscious of his tremendous responsibilities . . .

A man of amazing comprehension and extraordinary insight, possessing a capacity to foresee events which amounted almost to genius.

An optimist full of faith in his country and his fellow-man.

A most human lover of humanity who never in his long life rejected an appeal for aid to the helpless and suffering.

A Christian, staunch, devoted, and untiring in fidelity to Christianity as he understood it.

A generous but shy giver.

A proud and sensitive but extremely modest man.

A citizen of the highest integrity and staunchest fidelity.

Above all, a true patriot, the most distinctive and most vivid embodiment of the spirit of his time — a lover of power, but not of money; a great, a very great American . . .

It is a gratifying thought that he died serene in the hope and belief that in his last days he had come to be known for what he was, and that he held the affection no less than the admiration of his fellow-citizens . . .

"That nation is strongest and best in which the rich wisely spend and the poor wisely save," said the *Review of Reviews:* "Mr. Morgan . . . gave a fine example of beneficent spending of his own money, while, by his financial operations, he did much to make savings and investments safer and more numerous." That Morgan had acted so wisely was indeed a tribute to him, for he "had the disadvantage of being born rich . . . To be a rich man's son is a fearful handicap. Sympathize with the poor, always; but the present-day talk about the dreadfulness of poverty is mostly sentimental twaddle . . . Poverty is the diploma of ambition . . . Success, in this country, at least, has had its hardiest growth in the soil of poverty." Like other men, then, he was under the obligation from birth to hew his own way, and his successful career was evidence not of any special advantages he may have had but of the universal approval he had won: "Morgan was as truly chosen by the people as President Wilson is. He did not obtain his power by conquest. He did not arrogate it to himself by any assertion of brute strength. It came to him by what may truly be called the suffrage of the people . . . He could not compel their confidence. He had no monopoly in international commerce. He had no letters patent on credit. He possessed no divine right of sovereignty. The secret of his power is no secret at all. It simply was confidence in his leadership. That's all."

To demonstrate that Morgan deserved the confidence of all Americans, that to an overwhelming degree he had that confidence, and that those who refused it were somehow not good Americans was the primary concern of the magazines.

"Confessedly he stood at the head of the business life of the country," the *Independent* observed. "But he did not thereby incur the jealousy of rivals or the enmity of the ranks of labor . . . All thought well of him as a fair man, whose aims were for the general good." Had not even such dissimilar Americans as John D. Rockefeller and Secretary of State William Jennings Bryan paid tribute to Morgan? "It was a fine and patriotic thing to do," said Rockefeller of Morgan's loan of twenty-five million dollars to help stop the panic of 1907, "especially when you remember that Mr. Morgan is not a very rich man." [15] And Bryan's action in ordering the American ambassador in Rome to offer the embassy as a place for funeral services was applauded by the press: "No matter how much Mr. Bryan and many of the rest of us may have been opposed to Mr. Morgan and his financial methods and system, we recognized in him a great man. While enriching himself and his associates he had also done much for his country . . . Mr. Bryan took the proper course, that of a true American." [16]

Against those, like Vice-President Marshall, who continued to look askance at Morgan and even intimated the desirability of legislation limiting the size of estates that might be transferred upon death, the speech of George Harvey before the American Bankers Association suggested a possible line of defense. "To a larger degree than is given to most men" Morgan "possessed what Carlyle pronounced the greatest need of the world — a public soul." Of Morgan, he continued, it could genuinely be said that his every waking hour was a demonstration of the famous verse:

> "Breathes there the man, with soul so dead,
>   Who never to himself hath said
>   This is my own, my native land!"

Since Morgan's patriotism was above reproach, the taint of lack of patriotism must fall upon his critics. "Perhaps some historian will record that in the early years of the twentieth century the United States maintained for its protection a small standing army and Mr. J. P. Morgan," *Life* asserted. "People who didn't like the Army didn't like Mr. Morgan."

But what of the business community itself? How did it view Morgan's career and in what respects did its estimate differ from that of groups less closely identified with business enterprise?

The organs of the business community, like the press in general, rested their favorable verdict on Morgan on the fact that his business activities had contributed to the welfare of the nation. "In the death of J. P. Morgan, America lost one of the gigantic figures of its history," wrote the *Engineering and Mining Journal*, "a figure of the quality of Bismarck and Rhodes. He rendered extraordinary and enormous services to the nation as a financier and as a builder of railway and industrial enterprises. He stood ever for construction, never for destruction. He wielded great power, more financial power than any one man ever wielded before him, but he wielded it for good." Somewhat more willing, perhaps, than other media of opinion to endorse fully Morgan's work of consolidating great business enterprises — "he brought order out of confusion . . . he forced co-operation where there was antagonism and distrust" — the business press interpreted such activities as having been in the public interest. "The generations to come will appreciate, even more than does the present one, the everlasting service which this man rendered to the United States when it was first striving to be recognized as a world power," said one such journal, "when it was in need of a leader in commerce and industry." Friend and foe alike recognized Morgan's services to his country: "Here was a man his countrymen were proud of — even those who were opposed to the economic principles which he upheld and in a large measure personified . . . Even those editors who violently attack this system have been as sincerely appreciative of his character and work as those who upheld his doctrines." Judged by the standard of what he had "achieved for the world's good," Morgan's place was "a very exalted one. No one has ever done more for the growth and development of the country. No single individual can be truthfully declared to have done as much." That the "Pujo Money Trust Committee and its counsel" were "directly responsible . . . for removing forever from his sphere of usefulness on earth the individual who more than any other man of his time contributed to the industrial advance of the United States" was the major count in the indictment of that body.[17] Morgan's career, concluded *The Market World and Chronicle*, was a demonstration of the greater good to be derived from private rather than from government control of the economy:

A democracy . . . must have leadership, and this leadership must have authority. But the more this leadership can be made to inhere in plain private citizens, into whose hands it comes by reason of their genius and character, the better for the democracy as a whole. Government itself is essentially incapable of any but stupid and inefficient leadership. Its best function is to play the part of umpire, holding the scales even between the community and those who, under the guise of leading, would exploit. But when a true leader is discovered . . . then no harm but only good comes from giving him, for the brief span of his life, the largest scope.

In but one respect did the discussion of Morgan in the business press differ materially from that in the daily press. For the latter, analysis of Morgan's career provided an opportunity for reaffirmation of the notion that honor is due only to those who succeed by their own merits; as they phrased it, Morgan had overcome the disadvantage of having been born rich. But in the business press such emphasis was entirely lacking. Indeed, his inherited wealth and the opportunities he received by virtue of his father's position as a banker were deemed to be positive advantages. As *Bradstreet's* put it, "The career just ended was fortunate in its commencement, Mr. Morgan's early education in affairs having been obtained in the best of schools, that of a merchant banking house doing an international business."

"Favorable circumstances of birth and early education contributed some share of this man's success," said the *Bankers Magazine,* and other journals agreed: "J. P. Morgan was at the head of [financial affairs] in this country by virtue first of his superior mentality and second of the advantages which he possessed at the outset of his career, for he was born of a wealthy banker family."

"He owed a great deal to the prestige and funds of his father." The audience which read the journals of business, of course, was not that to which the editorials of the daily press were directed. Men who had already achieved substantial careers needed no convincing that they lived in a desirable society. They knew it. And knowing it, they could rise in tribute, as did the members of the American Iron and Steel Institute, to one of their fellows who had achieved unparalleled distinction; for in honoring him, they were pledging their continued faith in a society which not only respected achievement but made it possible. [18]

"I speak," wrote Frederick Townsend Martin only two years before Morgan's death, "as a rich man. I speak as a representative of the class of which I write, and to which in particular I address myself. We can no longer blind ourselves with idle phrases or drug our consciences with the outworn boast that the workingman of America is to-day the highest paid artisan in the world. We know those lying figures well." [19]

The white-hot light of social criticism had fallen on the rich, Martin wrote, and many were disturbed and angered by what they saw:

. . . the attitude of the people at large toward the rich has been changed indeed. I remember, even in my own lifetime, a period when the people of this country looked up with admiration and respect to their wealthy classes

. . . [a period] in which the wealth of the nation was well distributed and had not been gathered together into the hands of the few by means of the exploitation of the masses.

To-day how great the change!

When the nineteenth century closed, America worshipped great wealth. It sanctified its possessors. It deified the hundred-millionaire. In five years' time America has learned to hate great wealth. Plutocracy is disgorging, but public opinion is relentless . . .

In the midst of the peace and calm of high prosperity we hear the rumble of the thunder of war. We read in the papers that a great manufacturing city of the Middle West has chosen a Socialist mayor . . . an anti-corporation campaign in Denver has broken to atoms the organized power of both the great political parties which, for generations, we have used as pawns in mightier games than theirs . . . Public clamor and disapprobation greet the plan of one of the richest of men to incorporate his charities in order that they may be more efficient. The people refuse absolutely to believe that there is no ulterior project behind the incorporation.

These are incidents of warfare, not of peace.[20]

Martin's vision of imminent chaos may have been hysterical, but that there was some cause for alarm even the most sober would have agreed. If J. P. Morgan had chosen to walk east but a few minutes' distance from his office at Broad and Wall streets, he would have entered upon a different world. There, in Sanitary District A of New York's Eleventh Ward, teemed the densest population anywhere in the world, 986.4 persons per acre for thirty-two acres. The Josefstadt in Prague, the most slum-ridden area in Europe, had only 485.4 persons per acre, and even the most densely populated city in Asia — Bombay with 759.66 persons per acre — was less crowded.[21] At the turn of the century, one observer reported, 14 per cent of the families in Morgan's own borough of Manhattan were evicted each year from their homes; 18 per cent of the population were continually on relief; and every year one person in ten who died was buried in potter's field. Even in prosperous years, he continued, nearly half the families in the United States were totally propertyless, four million Americans were public paupers, two million workers were unemployed from four to six months each year, and nearly two million child laborers wore out their bodies in mine and mill.[22]

This was the acid that was eating at the complex of ideas and attitudes which for so long had provided sanction and security to business enterprise. By the first decade of the twentieth century, Socialist critic Charles Edward Russell asserted, "The avenues of fortune-making in commerce had been walled across. Equal opportunity for all had become a myth . . . The truth is, then, that under the conditions produced by Business in its present stage of evolution, the chief and almost the only prospect before the young man in America to-day is the prospect of spending his life as somebody's hired man." [23] Economist Richard T. Ely agreed: "If you tell a single concrete workingman on the Baltimore and Ohio Railroad that he may yet be the president of the company, it is not demonstrable that you have told him what is not true, although it is within bounds to say that he is far more likely to be killed by a stroke of lightning; but it can be mathematically proved that by no amount of diligence, thrift, and intelligence can one out of a thousand employés attain that position. The number of those who can rise to the top of industrial society relatively diminishes because production is carried on on an increasingly large scale." [24] The fact that people in increasing numbers were turning their backs on old gods to follow new idols was the cause of an intensified effort to reaffirm old values and loyalties, one critic commented. The "continual output" of ideas "from pulpit, sanctum, forum, and college chair" attempted to create conviction that "conditions, while not perfect, either are reasonably near to perfection, or, if evil, are not to be corrected except by individual regeneration. We learn of the irrationality or the moral obliquity of discontent; the viciousness or fanaticism of impertinent persons who seek to change things; the virtues of obedience; the obligation of toil (specifically directed to those who are doing most of the world's work, for the profit of others), and of the worth, benevolence, and indispensability of our magnates." This was not a faith which stemmed from the experience of all and served the needs of all. It was "an expression of class feeling . . . the defence of class interests. It is counsel that makes for the acquiescence of the lower orders and the increased security of the upper . . . This counsel of endeavor, promulgated by the few who have striven and 'succeeded,' is thus a social sedative of great efficacy." [25]

That the defenders of business enterprise were well aware of the existence of such hostility is evident. "The hostility to large fortunes does not diminish with time and events," J. Lawrence Laughlin wrote. "To say that a man is a millionaire is to many equivalent to saying that he is an enemy of society, reaping where he has not sown . . . Yet, as we look back a century, there was not, at least in the United States, any such antagonism between rich and poor." [26] And it is equally evident that the defenders of enterprise, alarmed at the disintegration of the consensus of which they approved, saw the need for positive action if enterprise itself were not to be placed in jeopardy. The unity of enterprisers themselves, through the formation of employers' organizations, was not enough.[27] Especially needed was realization that all alike were united in a great society in which, though each labored in his own field for himself, yet the fruits of his labor were shared by all. "So we start out in our dealings with the public under a heavy handicap," said E. K.

Hall, vice-president of the American Telephone and Telegraph Company and a pioneer in the development of corporate public relations:

They do not know us, they misunderstand us, they mistrust us, and there is a continued tendency to believe that our intentions toward them are not fair . . . This general attitude of the public mind is, as I believe, not only a serious danger to the property of the business but it is in my judgment the only serious danger confronting the company, because the natural tendency of such hostility, founded as it is on misunderstanding, prejudice, and distrust is, under slight incentive, to crystallize at any time into adverse legislation.[28]

To create identity where there was division, to find public virtues in private acts, was the need.[29] "Wealth . . . is a sociological blessing, not a sociological danger," declared *The Outlook*.[30] To unite "the workman and the capitalist in one and the same person" was the prescription offered by steelmaster Andrew Carnegie.[31] But how was this sense of identity and unity to be achieved?

The president of Dartmouth College provided a method:

What I have to say is in the nature of some reflections upon "the mind of the wage earner," an expression which I borrow from the opening sentence of the recent work by John Mitchell on Organized Labor: "The average wage earner has made up his mind that he must remain a wage earner" . . . It is, I think, the most serious statement which has been made of late concerning the social life of the country; for it purports to be the statement of a mental fact. If "the average wage earner has made up his mind that he must remain a wage earner," we have a new type of solidarity, new at least to this country. No other man among us has made up his mind to accept his condition . . . The fact of the great number of wage earners signifies nothing in a social sense, unless they have made up their mind to some conclusion which separates them from the community at large or the body politic . . .

What can be done to so affect "the mind of the wage earner" that it will not work toward that kind of solidarity which will be of injury to him and to society? . . .

I am convinced that the interpretation put upon the mind of the wage earner, if it represents a present fact, ought to suggest a duty toward the mind of labor. That duty is to give it freedom, breadth, expansion, to incorporate it into the common mind of aspiration and hope, the American type of mind.[32]

To incorporate their readers "into the American type of mind," first by identifying Morgan with the symbols of Americanism and then by identifying all men with Morgan, was the function performed by that section of the press which sought to defend business enterprise against the onslaughts of its critics. "Society," said Frederick Townsend Martin, referring to the wealthy and socially prominent, "was forced in its own defence to begin the study of wealth and poverty";[33] and that defense consisted primarily of the presentation of a series of identifications. Morgan the financier was identified by the press with a society in which the gates of opportunity stood open for all, with the objects for which men reserved their deepest loyalties — church, family, and country — and with the thousand and one little things that mark the ordinary lives of ordinary people. Some intimates of Morgan, in less widely circulated publications, may have denied that the portrait presented by the press — Morgan as one man among many — was accurate. "He was handicapped by a lack of knowledge of the country he lived to serve," said the Reverend W. S. Rainsford, rector of the church at which Morgan worshiped. "He did not know the man in the street, the man on the farm, or in the mine or factory. How should he? He never read himself into their lives, and he never met them." [34] But the press, blanketing the nation from ocean to ocean, couched its discussion of him in terms fully in accord with prevailing doctrines that "Godliness is in league with riches," that business "is really the most respectable and useful human activity," that "every man who accumulates a surplus, finally accumulates, also, a disposition to help the weak," and that "the chances for business success" in this "country for any young man are not wanting." [35] Dipping into the "slogans, symbols, and ideas in the general cultural heritage," newspaper editors, like the new school of novelists, linked businessmen to humanity by discussing them "as sons, husbands, and fathers," by "including . . . deeply personal aspects . . . of their lives"; like educators, they "advocated the ideal of a classless society and the ideal of co-operation between economic groups"; like scholars, they affirmed the desirability of the economic system by asserting that "the nonpersonal factors conditioning the process of fortune accumulation attain an ever-increasing influence in affecting the size of the individual's gain"; and like the philosophical supporters of business enterprise they linked capitalism to democracy itself.[36] Above all, they affirmed the unity of business enterprise and patriotism. "The system is at fault," cried Morgan's critics; "He loved and built America," his defenders replied. Thus were the goals of business enterprise given the status of universality and business success, at first conceived to be the salvation of the individual, transformed into the salvation of society itself.[37]

Doubtless there were those who, after reading the discussion of Morgan, would have agreed with the sardonic Ambrose Bierce that an epitaph is "an inscription on a tomb, showing that virtues acquired by death have a retroactive effect" and that a eulogy is "praise of a person who has either the advantages of wealth and power, or the consideration to be dead." [38] But no doubt the majority considered Morgan's life in more affirmative fashion. "Let the young aspirant turn to biography," the leading American apostle of success had said.[39] "Every great and good life is rich in necessary warning, in hopeful promise." "How wonderful is the influence of a hero," said Andrew Carnegie — and who had a better right to speak? [40]

The press, in presenting Morgan as it did, was not quite a mirror reflecting without passion the scenes which passed before it. As early as 1886, Augustus A. Levey, commenting on the changing nature of the press, had concluded:

. . . these writers' sole purposes are to defend positions which they have been instructed to take up. This must be done in the firmest words, with the greatest vigor, and always with such an assumption of authority as to forbid the suspicion that there are arguments to be urged in opposition. It is evident that no subject upon which there must be a conflict of opinion can thus be readily discussed in newspapers . . . The working-men find the journals out of sympathy with their aims and aspirations, and have learnt to regard them as helplessly subservient to what they call "capitalism." [41]

It could hardly have been otherwise, since the same "trend from individual to collective enterprise that marked American business after the Civil War was as apparent in journalism as in oil, steel, or railroads though at a lower rate. By the 1890's city papers came to be published by large corporations for the financial benefit of stockholders and directors. They became primarily profit-making enterprises rather than vehicles of private opinion. And their advertising revenue by 1890 was their most important source of revenue. Thus journalism took its place in the ranks of Big Business." [42] The relationship between press and business became even more intimate. George Harvey, for example, the author of some of the most extravagant editorials in praise of Morgan, had for years done public relations work for Thomas Fortune Ryan and Harry Payne Whitney, promoters and financiers; and the Morgan firm itself, especially through Thomas W. Lamont and George Perkins, two of its partners, had invested heavily in newspapers and magazines.[43] Under the circumstances, interpretation of such a news event as the death of a great entrepreneur became "instrumental to [the] kind of program for the public good" that the majority of the press advocated, and rapidly growing wire services guaranteed that that interpretation would be uniform and widespread.[44] Some were skeptical as to the truth of what they read, believing, with Bierce, that an editor is one "who approaches greatness on his belly so that he may not be commanded to turn and be kicked . . ."

In Morgan's praise you smite the resounding wire,
And sing hosannas to great Havemeyer! [45]

That such a response was widespread may be doubted. "Politicians and soap-box haranguers" might present men of "power and prosperity" as "gross giants and predatory monsters called the 'Milk Trust' or the 'Traction Interests'"; but the overwhelming number of newspapers, whose audience was numbered in the millions, translated, as publicist Ivy Lee phrased it, "dollars and cents and stocks and dividends into terms of humanity, and so succeeded in presenting the businessman as a man to be loved and not as a magnate to be feared." [46]

The press, in a word, was in agreement with Morgan's colleagues. For them, too, he had "combined and embodied the American ideals of enterprise and integrity"; had been "moved . . . not to accumulate but to do"; had taken "from no man, but . . . acquired a great fortune by making the prosperity of many"; had "not become rich by making others poorer"; had had a "pure, high, unselfish character." [47] For such persons, the study of the life of "one so distinctly the product of both our faith and our institutions" had a particular value, for it could be used to hurl back the challenge of alien thought: "In the midst of pretension and ignorance in high places, at a time when . . . every system of signals is set flying to attract notice, it is comforting to turn, as a relief, to consideration of some of the characteristics of an ingrained American." [48]

"I declare my judgment as being that J. P. Morgan will rank in the history of this Republic as one of the greatest men God has yet raised up to serve it," said the rector of Trinity Parish. "I give praise to God for all the grace given to him. Here now on this Street I call all men who hear me to dedicate themselves as did Jesus Christ, each in his measure, to serving God by blessing men." [49]

The people who heard the voice of the Reverend William Wilkinson were hardly those most in need of convincing, for he spoke at the corner of Broad and Wall streets, the heart of the financial district, in the shadow cast by the House of Morgan. But, though many new converts may not have been made, those already devout, as they hurried back to their banking offices at the end of the noon lunch hour, had at least the assurance that the business enterpriser was in the service of God and country. So, too, had the press argued, and thereby bestowed upon the entrepreneur new sanctions of religion and patriotism with which to make him the focal point of a new consensus.

V

John D. Rockefeller

A great responsibility rests upon newspapers . . . There is an ethical duty they owe to the community which I sometimes feel they regard too lightly. These stories about my wealth, for instance. They have a bad effect on a class of people with whom it is becoming difficult to deal, and when I say this I am not forgetting that a great responsibility rests upon wealth. But the stress which is laid in those stories arouses hatred and envy not against the individual only but against organized society . . . It is the general trend I have in mind, which is arraying the masses against the classes.[1]

So spoke John D. Rockefeller in 1907, thirty years before his death. If the indictment of the press was warranted at that time, it was clearly inappropriate in 1937, for then the press, far from arousing "hatred and envy" against both man and society, so thoroughly identified the man with the economy that nourished him that it approved the one by giving sanction to the other.

"John D. Rockefeller, senior, who earned more money than any man who ever lived, died today at the age of 97," said the United Press, and with that sentence it began its obituary which was to be printed by newspapers throughout the nation.

His wealth had purchased for him comfort, luxuries, power, and the esteem of his fellow men . . . Mr. Rockefeller was all things to all men — a titan among business men; a fatherly old man to members of his family; a benefactor to the lame, the halt, and the blind. But here in Ormond Beach he was "Neighbor John" . . . Years ago Mr. Rockefeller retired from business, weary of coining money that rolled into his vaults faster than he could spend it . . . His trucks were on the main street of every crossroad town in the United States; his oil caravans plodded the Arabian deserts; his tankers fed oil to South America; his oil barrels rolled into doorways in Chicago and along jungle trails in Africa. And everything he touched turned to gold. So he turned away from the accumulation of money and began to give it away . . . He was attacked as few men have been attacked, for avarice, ruthlessness, and commercial brutality. He made the benevolence of the world's greatest philanthropists shrink to insignificance when he became the world's most generous giver.

But what was this most remarkable of men — "titan among business men" and "the world's most generous giver" — really like? Was his life adequately summarized in his public acts, or was there not a private life which, when understood, would reveal that all along there had been beneath the symbol of gigantic enterprise a man to be measured in terms of the common attributes of humanity? The United Press thought that there was: "Throughout his life, a life marked by asceticism, abstemious living, conservative conduct, there ran a strain of intense religious faith . . . As he declined in business activity, so he appeared before the world to have mellowed in philosophy . . . His tastes, his hobbies, his desires were few. He retired at 10 P.M. and rose at 6:30 A.M. He ate sparingly, lived frugally. He never went to the theater; never tasted wine. He carried his age gracefully, kindly. His face, corrugated by wrinkles, retained a shy smile to the last."

Such was the image of Rockefeller projected by the United Press — magnificent in the scale both of his enterprise and his philanthropy, successful in having overcome animosity aroused by his business methods, and, despite the complexity of his operations, simple and unaffected.

But what of the other great American news service, the Associated Press?

"John D. Rockefeller spent the first half of his life making money and the last half giving it away," that organization explained:

> His career described an almost perfect arc. At the age of 16, he began with nothing . . . By the time he had reached middle age he had amassed what many persons believed to be the largest fortune ever controlled by a private individual in the history of the world . . . With him began the real development of big business and the era of the so-called "swollen fortunes."

His business activities, the Associated Press reported, "whether justly or unjustly" had led many to consider Rockefeller as "a money grabber, a ruthless monopolist who crushed his competitors, or swallowed them up in his determination to dominate the oil business." But time and understanding corrected the earlier impression, and "the world knew him in his later years as he wished it to know him, as a kindly old gentleman who gave dimes to children and untold millions to education, to the relief of human suffering, and to religion. Mr. Rockefeller's story is of the kind that is dear to the American people — the poor boy who rose to riches through hard work and determination."

Individual differences between the two dominant press services there were, but uniformity, not diversity, was the striking characteristic of their evaluations of the oil man's career. If the Associated Press and the United Press were competing in the sale of a product, they were competitors in conformity, for, excepting the brand name, the commodities they sold were almost indistinguishable.[2] Similarity of appraisal was indeed the keynote, acknowledged *Editor and Publisher:*

. . . it must be admitted, without a grudge, that Ivy Ledbetter Lee did a swell job of press-agentry in not only removing the stigma of commercial pirate that the old gentleman wore for so many years, but actually substituting for it a saintly halo. No editorial that we have read referred in biting terms to the manner in which the rapacious oil man of sixty and seventy years ago amassed his fortune. The Ida Tarbell note of thirty years ago was completely missing . . . He [Rockefeller] paid little attention to newspaper comment, until the Colorado mine massacre turned the big Eastern papers loose at him and invested 26 Broadway with a howling mob of protesting pickets. Then the suave Lee entered the picture, gave the Rockefeller press relationships the guise of candor, played no favorites and succeeded, it must be admitted, in more than once turning merited public anger toward approval.

The trade journal of the newspaper industry not only testified to the uniformity with which the press regarded Rockefeller but advanced an explanation for that uniformity. Still, dissent there was, though with few exceptions it was not to be found in the daily press.

Far more even than in the case of Morgan, criticism of Rockefeller was in reality criticism of the economic system and was, therefore, largely confined to that ever-decreasing section of the press which explicitly avowed its repudiation of that system.

"John D is Dead — But the Trust Goes On," exclaimed the Communist *Daily Worker,* and its editorial permitted of no uncertainty that in the minds of those for whom it spoke business enterprise itself was under attack:

The death of John D. Rockefeller, Sr., marked the passing of the first of the Big Trust Barons and the most definite symbol of plutocratic wealth in the United States for more than a half century. Though he is gone from the earth, the giant trust that the elder Rockefeller founded lives to plague the people. Great as were the bequests of the Rockefellers, more potent still is the wealth they amassed out of the exploitation not only of labor and the farmers but by the destruction of their middle class competitors. The history of the Standard Oil Company, which is the biography of the deceased Mr. Rockefeller, is the most sordid story of corruption, of capital concentration, and its finance-capital phase in the history of the United States.

Again and again the identification of Rockefeller with capitalism and with evils attributed to that system was repeated:

Behind the official eulogies of the newspaper hirelings, the press services and the editors, who long ago became his respectful servitors, fearful of his tremendous power and relentless punishment, there is a long life which epitomizes the brutality, corruption, efficiency, greediness, and cunning of industrial capitalism rising to finance capitalism. He is dead. But the monstrous power which he created . . . lives on with its grip reaching deep into the lives of the American people.

What of the argument that Rockefeller had concretely demonstrated the possibility of rising under this economic system from poverty to immense wealth? "The eulogists sing his praises as one who rose from small beginnings, knowing how to use his independence and initiative," the *Daily Worker* said. "But they refrain from mentioning that . . . under conditions of capitalist exploitation, he pitilessly crushed the initiative and independence of millions of Americans from whom he drew his profits and upon whose backs he climbed upward."

What of the argument that Rockefeller's great philanthropies were not only evidence of his humanity but, even more, of the fact that under this economic system all alike, even the most humble and downtrodden, benefit from profitable enterprise? "The Rockefeller philanthropy is the well-spent insurance which is intended to safeguard the whole structure from attack. It is the social insurance of huge monopoly capitalists who have learned that it pays to throw some crumbs to charity in order to protect the main loot."

What of the argument that Rockefeller was really a simple, kindly man whose business activities were of benefit to the whole nation? "The Rockefellers have always thrived on panic and misfortune." Had they not purchased cheaply huge blocks of shares in 1929 when the stock market crashed? "He always hated labor." Were not the charred bodies of women and children, burned by agents of Rockefeller's Colorado Fuel and Iron Company during the Ludlow Massacre of 1914, evidence of that hatred? "In his money-grubbing soul, he despised the poor." Had he not, during the coal shortage of 1918, sold his own coal at a large profit to the poverty-stricken residents of the community in which his huge New York estate was located? Had he not consistently refused to grant the Labor Day holiday to employees on his estates?

Despite his crimes, the "Al Capone of the oil industry," whose "bloody name" would forever be associated with the memory of Ludlow, was being wafted by the press "to the Baptist heaven he believed in, where entrance for a rich man has been reputed to be more difficult than for a camel to pass through a needle's eye, travelling light, encumbered by his dwindled fortune of only twenty-five million dollars."

For the explicitly radical press, the events of Rockefeller's career were significant only as they illustrated the development of large-scale capitalist enterprise. What Rockefeller may have been like in his private capacity as husband and father, as friend, as churchgoer, was of no consequence for these critics. Not Rockefeller's private roles but his public role as businessman was important, for it was in that capacity that his activities impinged upon the lives of others and lessons could be taught illustrating the relationship between human activity and social system. "All things to all men," the United Press had called Rockefeller; and then had particularized in such a way as not to admit of the possibility of an unfavorable view, for "all things" — when itemized — turned out to be "a titan among business men; a fatherly old man to members of his family; a benefactor to the lame, the halt and the blind." But to the Chicago *People's Press,* speaking for the Workers' Alliance, an organization of workers on emergency relief projects, Rockefeller was "billionaire, killer, philanthropist, libertine, patron of the sciences, labor-hater, churchman, and exploiter alike of workers and competitors." For the great press services, the story of Rockefeller's youth was a model of aspiration, illustrating that in the United States no height was unattainable. For the *People's Press* it was a model of a different kind: "John D . . . was the son of a very religious mother and a father who peddled a fake cancer cure. Religion and graft colored his life from the cradle. At eight he made his first money. It is rumored he still had it at 97." His life had been far from one of service to the people of his country, said that newspaper: "At 22 he faced his first great crisis. His nation was engaged in a great war to determine whether a nation conceived in liberty could long endure. He went in the oil business in 1861 and was rich by 1864. His family, ultra-patriotic, has made money on every war since." But if this was the real Rockefeller, how had he achieved the reputation of "a philanthropist, religious, kindly, devoted to the church, the arts and the sciences?" That reputation, said the *People's Press,* was synthetic, manufactured — "at a magnificent salary" — by publicist Ivy Lee and Harry Emerson Fosdick, pastor of the Rockefeller-endowed Riverside Church.

"He never had the slightest understanding of the fact that great wealth is unearned, that it is taken from the earnings of others," the Milwaukee *Leader* wrote. And although Rockefeller was "an ardent adherent of the Christian religion," he never realized that "great wealth gives one power over the lives and the livelihood of thousands of other human beings. It destroys all the possibilities of human brotherhood in any real sense. This is a part of the system. The individuals are hardly to be blamed for taking advantage of the unbrotherly opportunities which the system affords, but it seems kind of queer that they should not recognize that the system whereby the few roll in wealth and the many are their underlings is anti-Christian, irreligious, and immoral."

Critical attention was focused on analysis of the means by which Rockefeller's fortune had been accumulated, with results far different from those obtained when philanthropy was used as the basic criterion for evaluating the man.

"It is amusing to read the Rockefeller obituaries in the capitalist press with their neat glossing over of the fact that this week they are burying one of the most unconscionable, altogether ruthless, incredibly cruel money-bags that ever took a widow's last share of oil stock or snatched pennies from the lean purse of a workman," the *Socialist Call* stated.

"How did he do it?" asked the *New Leader* of the methods by which Rockefeller had amassed his fortune." "Well, by monopoly, to make a short answer. He did it in exactly the same way as Al Capone tried to do it — and by means just as bloody . . . Absolute ruthlessness characterized the acquisition of the fortune which is great enough to buy nations, and control channels of information." The word "philanthropist" had indeed become associated with Rockefeller's name and he had "died in the odor of sanctity and in the image created by Ivy Lee," but his was not the real philanthropy, said the New York *Weekly People*. That distinction belonged to "the Standard Oil workers, who . . . have been, and still continue to let themselves be, exploited out of the major portion of the wealth they produce."

Most of the newspapers of the labor movement, concerned primarily with either supporting or combating the recently organized Committee for Industrial Organization, did not regard Rockefeller's death of sufficient importance to deserve comment; but those newspapers which did choose to comment cast their remarks in such a fashion as to leave no doubt that their antagonism was directed as much toward business enterprise as toward the entrepreneur himself. For these newspapers, Rockefeller "represented the brutal, ruthless, competitive system that virtually made its own rules in a day when 'anything went'"; he symbolized those "fortune builders who pipe-lined the country's natural resources into their private coffers."[3] Newspapers of the Industrial Workers of the World, the Committee for Industrial Organization, and the American Federation of Labor — at war with each other concerning the methods to be used in achieving the reforms they desired — were united in regarding business enterprise as the thing to be reformed.

Said the IWW's Chicago *Industrial Worker:*

The daily papers lament the passing of Rockefeller with the grief no doubt that a Sultan's harem would bestow on the passing of that worthy . . . Somehow the same papers that hold John D. Rockefeller up as a praiseworthy example, run little filler lines regularly: "Crime Does Not Pay." Naturally it doesn't — but Rockefeller certainly made it pay. That his actions were criminal is not the allegation of a radical; it is the decision of the courts . . . The story of the Rockefeller fortune . . . stinks to high heaven — and it is praised to heaven by a prostitute press. Such are the gods of capitalism!

Said the CIO's *Hosiery Worker:*

It is significant that the same week saw the death of John D. Rockefeller and the unmasking of Henry Fraud of the Fraud Motor Co.[4] Both were benevolent men, according to the legend that has been created about them by kind propagandists. And yet in truth Rockefeller was, and Henry Fraud is, a symbol of the worst, the most vicious, and the most unforgiveable aspects of capitalism . . . Rockefeller is dead and the God's gold (as he called it) which he has hoarded will not suffice to pay his ferry fare across the River Styx.

Said the AFL's Detroit *Labor News:*

Hell must be about half full now.

A great man has died, a fine Christian giver — of dimes.

A piece of silver is a cheap price for a reputation of benevolence. But then, it isn't the gift that counts; it's the spirit of the thing.

The dear old man. He looked like a mummy. The spirit behind his gifts was a fine one . . . of love for his fellow man and respect for his right to live.

(*Eleven thousand miners in Ludlow, Colorado, will answer to that. Three women and fourteen children suffocated in the fire of the Ludlow tent colony will answer to that. Striking miners mowed down by machine guns will answer to that. Ten thousand slave miners crushed by a huge corporation's avarices, forced to live in the slate heaps of the wilderness will answer to that.*)

His road to heaven, bought by churchly gifts, is lined by the accusing fingers of the men he crushed on his climb to fame and fortune. Those millions mean nothing now. Whatever Power we answer to cannot be bought with a dime, or a billion dimes. A majestic window in a church, shedding a rich glow of colors through a high vaulted nave has no weight in the judgment . . .

The years must have been hard on the old man. More than half a century he had to think about his God's ire and his calendar of money sins. The years were hard. He grew from a narrow-eyed, thin and tight-lipped man to a walking, cadaverous, mummy-like, stumbling, frail figure, and all the while he quoted dollar sign scripture.

(*Every hunk of coal that came from Ludlow was blessed — blessed with a workman's horny hand, anointed with a worker's blood and sweat. But evidently the old man's own God had no blessings for the slaves who mined the coal that made the money for the old man to offer his God . . .*)

There are seats for the mighty in heaven. High seats where the rulers of the world sit. There are seats of ignominy for others in hell, and hell is only a little more full now.

The old man has died.

This was not criticism of the individual idiosyncrasies of an entrepreneur; indeed the implication was that such could not be criticized
because in large measure the entrepreneur did not possess full control
over his own activities. Rather was it criticism of the "ruthless lawlessness" characteristic of the "bloodstained and graft-stinking annals of
American Big Business" and of the "bitter poverty and ceaseless unrest"
that were regarded as its fruits.[5]

A mere handful of metropolitan newspapers joined the labor and
radical press in condemnation of Rockefeller; but, while their denunciation was phrased in milder terms, they were hardly less insistent upon
relating entrepreneur and economic system in such a way that an attack
upon one was indicative of dissatisfaction with the other.

"Through all the years of the twentieth century," the Milwaukee
Journal commented, "thoughtful men have been seeking ways to limit
the excesses of an economic system which his success exposed. Long
since we ceased to indict the man — a hard worker, thrifty, 'diligent in
his business,' with no lower standard of ethics than prevailed about him,
with no stain attaching to what we call his 'personal character.' It
became merely childish to attack John D. Rockefeller. Yet the truth
remained that a system of which he was long the crowning exemplar
would, if it persisted, destroy civilization. On the problem which his
unequalled success emphasized, society is still at work."

That the whole complex of social and economic conditions which
contributed toward the accumulation of Rockefeller's fortune needed
reform was a constant theme of these voices of dissent. Commenting on
the way in which Rockefeller's career had been evaluated by the vast
majority of the press, the Negro newspaper, *The Afro-American,*
observed:

That the founder of one of the world's most colossal fortunes amassed it
through the sweat and blood of thousands of underlings is the charge most
frequently hurled, but the fact that his enormous philanthropies during the
last half of his life helped countless thousands of others, may in some measure
be deemed compensatory . . . That is all well and good. But the thing that
strikes home so forcibly is the ironical fact that our economic system permits
one man to gain control of such vast wealth. It doesn't add up right when one
considers the thousands of individuals willing to work but unable to find employment. And while there was but one Rockefeller, there are many lesser
financial giants, who among them control the nation's wealth. Somewhere in
the economic cycle there is need for drastic regulation if these conditions are
to be changed.

"Ruthless expulsion or absorption of competition . . . the use of
railroad rebates, underselling, sabotage, and an arsenal of other devices
of the trust era" were the means by which Rockefeller had made his

money, said the Madison *Capital Times*. But "perhaps the passing of old John D. marks the last of an era when society permitted financial pirateers to cruise on business and industrial seas and prey unmolested upon the weak and plunder the defenseless. Let us hope so. Let us hope that we have entered an era typified by liberalism, lasting recognition and protection of human rights, and a real new deal for the rank and file of mankind."

With condemnation of large-scale business enterprise and demands that it be restrained went denunciation of Rockefeller himself. "He was smart," wrote New York *Post* columnist Cal Tinney. "Complete proof he was smart showed up when he was twenty-two, at which time he refused to join up for the Civil War and, taking seventy-five more years to die, got rich. Was ever better evidence offered that Pacifism Pays?"

"John D. Rockefeller won from life everything except greatness," the Detroit *News* maintained:

Far-flung power he had, vast wealth; notoriety and fame, alike substantial enough to carry his name familiarly to the ends of the world. Nonetheless, he remained to the end of his days what he had been in youth, a collection of narrow habits vitalized in human form. First and last, he lived by the book and the book was small and thin in keeping with the spirit of the man. His wealth never grew large enough to ransom him from littleness. He was a man who never developed . . . The sharp-featured, fragile, remote figure, legendary if not heroic, moved shadowy through the twilight years, murmuring platitudes of morality and religion and the virtues of being poor and working hard. He was America's poor little rich man.

For journals like *New Masses,* John D. Rockefeller was evil because what he represented was evil, and the world would be plagued by others like him until the economic system which had produced him — capitalism itself — should be eliminated. "What an indictment of our civilization," wrote *Common Sense,* "that such a man should . . . be regarded as one of our great public benefactors! But if Cal Coolidge was right in stating that 'the business of this country is Business' then John D., Sr., was more than a benefactor, he was one of our great men. Until another day, let his only creative achievement, his one poem, be his (and capitalism's own) epitaph:

> " 'I was early taught to work as well as play;
> My life has been one long, happy holiday —
> Full of work, and full of play —
> And God was good to me every day.' "

Other journals, however, were less convinced that the evils associated with Rockefeller's career could be written off only when the epitaph of capitalism itself should be written. To these journals, reflecting in a sense the spirit which had recently carried the New Deal to a second smashing victory at the polls, not business enterprise itself but the magnitude to which it had grown was the evil that needed correction. Bigness and the methods by which business became big were the problems. "It is an entirely unnatural and unsafe situation in a republic," *The Nation* observed, "when any individual is permitted to amass such wealth — even if the methods used are beyond reproach. To no man should be given the power which Mr. Rockefeller wielded during his active life." For the *New Republic,* Rockefeller's life was "the perfect laboratory specimen for several outstanding problems of American life." It typified the "multi-millionaire who seeks to give away his money in socially useful ways"; it attested to "the art of the press agent"; but, above all, having been characterized by nothing of real value to the American people but only by "an abnormal talent for acquisitiveness," it exemplified "the forty years' struggle to enforce 'fair competition' by law, a struggle that still goes on and is still far from a satisfactory conclusion." Liberal Catholic and liberal Congregationalist united in scoring the methods by which Rockefeller's particular business had been conducted. "While Mr. Rockefeller deemed himself the steward of God, others, more incisively critical, held that he was, if not the originator, at least the cool, calculating and, usually, successful supporter of some of the worst excesses that have ever disgraced the economic world," wrote Jesuit Father Paul L. Blakely in *America.* "We are proud to remember," observed the Congregationalist *Advance,* "that from a group in our own fellowship, under the leadership of Dr. Washington Gladden, there came the sharpest and most unqualified protest against the social and business ethics and methods . . . the overt acts and dishonesty for which [Rockefeller] was responsible." In this verdict the Cooperative League of the United States concurred: "John D. Rockefeller was as near a perfect example of the ideal of our present monopoly system as we have produced or may produce. He gained his wealth by predatory greed, by ruthless crushing of competitors." As to the desirability of emulation of such a career, the journal was particularly sharp: "There are young men today, doubtless of equal ability, who do not want to pursue a similar course and are turning their backs on the system which produces philanthropy and greed. As a result they will reach old age with the honor of their fellows and the satisfaction of having helped to build a new system which will eliminate the twin curses of poverty and riches."

Clearly the dissenters did not see eye to eye regarding the measures to be taken to reform society, but from the point of view of the defenders of Rockefeller and of business enterprise that disagreement was perhaps of less importance than was the evidence of distrust in the regime of enterprise and of alienation — particularly in the lower ranks of the social order — from the goals and standards which provided its ideological security. For these critics, such goals and standards no longer possessed legitimacy, no longer could serve to exact allegiance; and with allegiance broken, how then could business enterprisers confidently expect the routine of actions and responses that characterized industrial discipline to be maintained? But more than dissent and dissatisfaction lurked in the diatribes of the critics. If the activities of an entrepreneur like Rockefeller were functions of a social organization which was itself the cause of discontent — of poverty and unemployment — then no longer, its critics maintained, did that social organization deserve to be supported and no longer would "young men" fall into rank behind its cultural standards. With sufficient change — and it was at this point that the critics themselves differed — a new and better social organization could be achieved. This was — or could become — more than merely discussion; it was a charter for action. And because the action contemplated restricting the scope and freedom of action of enterprise, its journalistic defenders had to meet the challenge. Loyalties in jeopardy needed reaffirmation, and every new evidence that they were in jeopardy — from sit-down strikes in Flint to New Deal legislation in Washington — added urgency to the task.[6]

Far more than any other single factor, of course, the great depression of the 1930's had shattered the view which regarded business enterprise with optimism and acquiescence. The notice which appeared in the "Swap" column of the Cincinnati *Enquirer* — "Have complete course, 'How to become a success,' will swap for room rent" [7] — was an index of the gap that now yawned between the goals and standards held aloft by business enterprise and popular acceptance of those standards. The prosperous America of the 1920's, one newspaper observed, had been made by men who, as boys, had read Alger and Marden and Thayer. Had the crash of 1929 occurred because someone had bungled the standard formula for success or because the formula itself was no longer applicable? And after the disclosures of the Pecora Committee and the Insull scandal, could it be said any longer that wealth and virtue were synonymous? "What do boys read now . . . Schopenhauer?" sadly queried the New York *Herald-Tribune* in 1932.[8]

But if boys five years later, in 1937, were reading Schopenhauer, it was not because the *Herald-Tribune* felt Horatio Alger to be inappropriate. "Press Recalls Rockefeller As An Alger Hero," read that newspaper's headline, and a seventeen-inch editorial, a full page of pictures, and fifty-three complete columns — fully 21.2 per cent of the editorial space in its issue of May 24, 1937 — were devoted to demonstrating that Rockefeller's career was proof of the continued vitality of the Alger thesis.[9] But it was proof of more than that. To be sure, "Rockefeller Earned Pennies at 7, Dollars at 10, and Millions at 40" — a headline version of the Alger process — but personal success was, in addition, equated with the welfare of society. "Leaders Hail Rockefeller For Help to World," "Entire World Was Aided by Huge Fortune" — the *Herald-Tribune* headlines told the story. Was the achievement his alone, or had the economic system contributed to the benefits he had wrought?

Like Napoleon, with whom he was so often compared, like the elder J. P. Morgan, with whom he divided economic empire thirty or forty years ago, like Henry Ford, whom in certain respects he resembled — he was, of course, a product of his time. He could have done what he did in no other social setting . . . John D. Rockefeller was a great expression of a great age.

Quantitatively, perhaps the most striking characteristic of the editorial defense of Rockefeller was the emphasis placed upon his philanthropy. In this sense, the editorials served merely as a gloss on the press service obituaries which had discussed Rockefeller's career as one in which the oil man had lived two lives, the first devoted to acquisition, the second to distribution.

"The giant had two entities," the New York *Sun* stated. "The first was most vitally manifested from the Civil War down to . . . 1911 . . . And part of his reward . . . was abuse by those who saw only monopoly in vigorous enterprise and only selfishness in American development in a titanic manner. The second phase was Mr. Rockefeller's period of happiness . . . Out of the wealth of his old empire he had created a new one according to the desires of his heart."

"In his irresistible march to domination," wrote the *Arkansas Gazette*, John D. Rockefeller defeated and crushed his opposition . . . His name became a symbol. He was bitterly attacked in his more active and aggressive years and he became the target of action by the government itself. But then he conquered anew . . . To John D. Rockefeller were vouchsafed what other conquerors were denied — long and peaceful years in which to prove his good purposes and good wishes for his fellow men, to endow powerful and effective instruments for humanity's service and win the admiration and affection of the people. There were two John D. Rockefellers. He lived two lives. He conquered two worlds. And so ordered were events that it is benefaction and human service that write his epitaph.

The "unique distinction of his life" had not been the "heights of wealth" he had reached, but "the wide disposal of the gigantic sums which the march of civilization and his own genius combined to accumulate." Newspaper after newspaper supported that conclusion. "For every man and for all the widows and orphans who cried that he was cruelly crushing them," said one, "he was planning to give millions of dollars that would save millions of souls and bodies. He was neither vulture nor hypocrite. He wanted to do good with his money and he did it . . . And so, a faithful steward, he went to make his reckoning." Not only had his money been used for worthy purposes, but the method of its expenditure had been the best of available choices. "John D. Rockefeller Sr. in his life derived a lot of satisfaction in giving away his millions. If he thereby deprived the government of a lot of taxes, he still did not deprive the general public of the benefit of his wealth. And he may have done far more good with his money the way he chose to spend it than if he had let the government spend at least seventy-five per cent of it."

"The Rockefeller Foundation will do more to improve the world, to cure the sick and broken, to rid the world of poverty," snorted columnist Malcolm W. Bingay, "than all the billions of the taxpayers' money spent by bureaucrats at Washington." Small wonder, then, that Rockefeller had died "in the sunshine of . . . public favor." [10] With the conclusion of the Lewiston *Evening Journal,* nearly all newspapers agreed: "After death credit is given for one thing especially — Mr. Rockefeller's philanthropies."

There was in this phase of the discussion at least a suggestion that recognition of the generous uses to which Rockefeller put his money more than compensated for the allegedly unethical means by which he had made it. "The ruthless methods for which he was hated will be seen as a natural element in the fashion of business as it evolved in the 1890's," the Cincinnati *Enquirer* predicted. "His enduring fame will rest, instead, upon the magnitude and wisdom of his philanthropies." A "predatory element was involved" in the acquisition of his fortune and the "big business units resulting were not regarded by everybody as an unmixed blessing," wrote the Washington *Post;* but "the magnitude of his gifts" and his "method of giving do honor to his memory."

"The methods which piled up this huge fortune so fast were wholly indefensible," the Youngstown *Vindicator* commented; but because "Rockefeller was the pioneer of the new philanthropy . . . America on the whole has been less harmed than helped by John D. Rockefeller's long and amazing career."

Selective emphasis was the keynote of the Portland *Press Herald's* editorial: "No one at this time is disposed to review the entire course of Mr. Rockefeller's life and to dwell upon those perhaps debatable methods and transactions by which he became the world's first billionaire. The emphasis is and should be upon his stewardship of that billion dollars, and there can be but one opinion — that he was a power for good." What is the place "history has accorded him?" asked the Memphis *Commercial Appeal.* "It is true that many a crime against the social order was committed in his name during the monopolistic period of thirty and forty years ago. But Mr. Rockefeller goes down to posterity, not merely as the builder of a great fortune, but as one who in the end showed that he loved his neighbor and that he hoped to leave the world a better place in which to live." "Whatever the means by which he became one of America's few billionaires, it must be said for John D. Rockefeller that he has allowed wise men to direct his benefactions," wrote the Baltimore *Sun;* and the *Ohio State Journal* agreed: "However his wealth was won, he gave most of it away." That there were acceptable and unacceptable methods of attaining the goal of great wealth was clearly implied, but equally clear was the implication that in the hierarchy of social values philanthropy stood higher than the modes of acquisition. Money obtained even by unsanctioned means, the press implied, would lose its stigma because of the higher sanction attaching to the uses to which it should be put.

In a sense, therefore, the journalistic defenders of Rockefeller removed the issue of the morality of the means by which he had made his fortune from the area of argument by invoking the higher morality of the use to which he had devoted it. Vindication of the entrepreneur would be even more complete, however, and the relevance of arguments directed toward consideration of the origins of his wealth would be made even more tenuous if only it could be shown that he bore no unique personal responsibility for the sins he had been charged with, that all who lived when he had lived committed the same acts. Shared guilt was not guilt at all; it was the "spirit of the times."

"The students of moral philosophy will examine his record for years," said the Boston *Herald:*

> Some will stigmatize Mr. Rockefeller as an enemy of the society of his day, a monopolist . . . They will apply the higher standards of their own era to the commanding figures who dominated industry when ethics had little place in life, and competition was based on the old principle of devil-take-the-hindmost . . . Mr. Rockefeller, it is fair to say, merely played the game more adroitly than his rivals. He did to them what many of them tried to do to him . . . He lived the life of his time. His personal merits and demerits were similar to those of men who went down before him.

"Rockefeller was a product of the times in which he lived," wrote the Louisville *Courier-Journal.* "Big business was in the making and it did not scruple to throttle opposition. The law of the tooth and claw ruled and success was a survival of the fittest." What had Rockefeller done that his colleagues on the business scene had not also done? "If Rockefeller and his partners employed . . . business methods that might come under the ban today," the Reno *Evening Gazette* observed, "it must be remembered that it was the age of the Hills, the Goulds, the Vanderbilts and others of their kind, and the course of business organization must be judged by the standards that were then prevalent." As the Brooklyn *Daily Eagle* put it: "His methods of marketing, of spying on competitors and of preventing competitors from getting oil to market would be called unfair nowadays. The important thing to remember is that they were not considered so unfair in his own day." No one would defend the ruthless methods employed by Rockefeller and his associates in building the oil trust, that newspaper observed. "Yet they were simply doing, on a large scale, what was being done in all lines of business. It was part of the old American system."

Beginning with a simple description of what they deemed were prevailing business practices during the first half of Rockefeller's life, the newspapers went on to assert that the entrepreneur was guilty of nothing that others had not done, proceeded further to claim that it was only the requirement of survival that forced him to act as he did, and concluded finally in reinterpreting the very practices that had originally been under attack.

First came description of the period: "During the epoch of giantism, the swollen fortunes of a few were merely the logical culmination of what all were trying to do. We were all scrambling for money, and we reasoned that, because a little wealth was good and more was better, the most wealth was best."

Then came description of the man: "Business ruthlessness was a policy of his day forced upon Rockefeller and, there is much evidence to prove, against his own nature . . . so it is unfair to judge him by current standards. Judged by the standards of his own time he's notable only for his wonderful ability and not his ethics which were normal for his period."

Next came reinterpretation of both man and period: "We would not return to those days and those methods. But with the passing years and changing perspective the American people understand that period better, and in his older age they freely and cheerfully gave to John D. Rockefeller the admiration and respect which his character and achievements commanded."

Finally came defense:

Now that the man himself has drawn his final breath, the legend which has been developed around the career of John D. Rockefeller also should die. In many of its aspects it has been a monstrous myth — a vicious libel, created by jealousy and malice, kept current by professional promoters of class strife; its purpose was deliberate traduction, its object a conscious attempt at character assassination. But the pity of it is that the propaganda has succeeded . . . But the facts were simple enough to be understood by an unprejudiced inquirer. Mr. Rockefeller was merely one of a considerable number of captains of industry who, sensibly enough, believed in the principle of organized efficiency . . . His critics complained that his methods were ruthless, forgetting perhaps that the law of mathematics never is sentimentally merciful. To know Mr. Rockefeller, however, was to appreciate both his motives and his policies. He was a rationalist . . . Also, he was by temperament kindly and generous . . . he believed in a personal deity who demands an accounting of every soul. Likewise, he was possessed of infinite faith in humanity.[11]

Emphasis upon the time and place in which Rockefeller had lived served more than to absolve him of any special guilt for the means he had used in acquiring his fortune. Indeed, if that fortune had been placed in the service of mankind — as the majority of the press insisted — then to the degree that it could be demonstrated that special qualities of the American economy and society in the late nineteenth century contributed to the amassing of that fortune, to that degree could that economy and society be considered desirable and departures from them deplored.

The note that only in the America of the post-Civil War period could a Rockefeller have flourished was a consistent theme of the press. "In the early sixties," wrote the San Francisco *Examiner,* "fortune was flying fleet-footed across the land, and men clutched her garments . . . On this virgin field there stepped Rockefeller with his doctrine of combination and with his sure touch of genius put his hand on the basic principle of the oil industry, the control of transportation facilities." Success was more than the outward manifestation of inner qualities. "Nowhere but in America, and never before, could anyone make so much," declared one newspaper. "His time was the happy hunting time of our Robber Barons," said another, the era when "conditions . . . were ripening into great opportunities." "On the Record," the syndicated column of Dorothy Thompson, confirmed the analysis: "Rockefeller, Sr., was of all men the most complete expression of the era of reconstruction . . . He built his industrial empire in the only period in which it could have been built . . . The man was all of a piece; he got in at the right moment and he got out at the right moment." [12]

But what made it the "right moment?" Two New York newspapers expressed clearly what had been implied by most of the press. "Only in America," wrote the *World-Telegram,*

only in the hundred years which his life so nearly spanned, could the phenomenon that was John D. Rockefeller have been possible. In no other country, at no other time, could a poor boy have become a billionaire so quickly . . . because he was born in 1839, and because he was thrifty, and industrious, and — according to standards of our own day — ruthless to the nth degree, he was on the stage and ready to act his part when the curtain rose on the American era that began with the civil war. It was an era of individualism uncurbed, of complete adherence to the Adam Smith philosophy. Rockefeller did not make that era. No more did Fisk and Gould, Hill and Harriman, Carnegie and Frick, Commodore Vanderbilt and Pierpont Morgan. The era made them, in the sense that it gave them opportunity.

With the notion that it had been the "individualism" of the time and place in which Rockefeller had lived that had provided opportunity for him and for others, the New York *Times* agreed: "The life story of the man who started with nothing and accumulated so much and who gave away so much is the outstanding example of the romance of American business, the most dramatic illustration of the opportunity for amassing wealth which was a part of the era of rugged individualism."

A few newspapers applauded the fact that the passing of the era of "dollar philosophy" to that of "social philosophy" made it almost a certainty that there "probably will never be another John D. Rockefeller"; but for the majority of the press, agreement that there would never be another Rockefeller was cause for regret, not approval. "We Shall Not See His Like Again," mourned the *Oregon Statesman:* "Laws, taxes, conditions are unfavorable for a new group [of captains of industry] to rise." The spirit of the age that had made America great — the belief that "'laws of nature' are paramount; that 'natural law' and 'economic law' are identical; that 'economic law' calls for complete freedom of the individual to acquire what he can and do with it what he likes; that this complete economic individualism will automatically work out to the greatest good for all, and that the one rule for governments was the rule of 'laissez-faire,' of 'no interference'" — has vanished, and "we shall probably never again produce . . . another 'John D.'" In the day of "the rugged individual . . . tax laws and similar limitations" had not restricted the activities of entrepreneurs. But the "present civilization will create no more Rockefellers" and millionaires, instead of indulging in "splendid benefactions as Mr. Rockefeller did . . . will be busy saving for the tax day." How then, inquired Walter Lippmann, "when no man will be permitted to acquire such wealth," will "higher learning and research . . . be supported?" [13]

If conditions had changed so drastically that enterprise was placed in jeopardy, then the nation itself was the loser, for the real beneficiaries of business were not its owners but the public which it existed to serve. CIO President John L. Lewis might testify that he was unable to find anything "to say regarding Mr. Rockefeller's contributions to the social and economic progress of this nation" and Ida Tarbell might have "no comment whatsoever," but the vast majority of persons whom the press asked to comment concerning Rockefeller had no hesitation in asserting that his career had been of positive benefit to the American people. Omaha clerk Robert C. Richelieu, spokesman for the man-in-the-street, and

Morgan partner Thomas W. Lamont, spokesman for the financial community, alike were convinced that his magnificent gifts to charity and his pioneering in "large scale elimination of needless waste, in mass production, in scientific management" gave him "as much chance as anybody" to "enter heaven." The statement issued by Henry Ford was typical of the judgment of oil company presidents, meat packers, financiers, political leaders, clergymen, and college presidents: "Mr. Rockefeller filled a long lifetime with useful work which left a notable mark on his times . . . Like all creative workers, the benefits of what he did were shared by humanity everywhere." [14]

Had he not provided employment? "The Rockefeller wealth," the Sacramento *Union* stated, "flowed perpetually into all the channels of trade, making possible the industries which employed millions of men."

"In this day," the Houston *Post* observed, "when unemployment is still widespread, and we are in a position to appreciate more fully what it means to have an opportunity to work, it is easier to realize what a service Mr. Rockefeller rendered to his generation by providing employment."

Had he not helped raise the American standard of living? The courts may have determined that he had formed a monopoly in the oil industry, the Los Angeles *Times* commented, "but an objective view establishes the high probability that petroleum products are both much better and cheaper than they would have been had he never entered the field." The Indianapolis *News* and the *Idaho Daily Statesman* lauded the standardization of oil products, "the efficiency and sound business sense . . . for which Mr. Rockefeller was responsible," for these "resulted in prices for petroleum products far lower than might have prevailed had the producing and selling been done by a host of little independents." Service to mankind was a function of enterprise itself, not merely of philanthropy. As one newspaper expressed it, "formation of the 'oil trust' was the first large-scale 'planning' in industry which has reduced prices and raised the standard of living." For what would "the name of Rockefeller . . . be revered?" For the fact that "Standard Oil and allied enterprises . . . were forerunners of America's greatness and the high standards of living enjoyed by our people . . . And John D. Rockefeller played a major role in building the financial system which prevails today." [15]

Philanthropy, important though it was, was a by-product of enterprise; the achievement of high levels of employment and high standards of living was the very heart of enterprise itself. That Rockefeller's business activities had been of benefit to society, therefore, was not to be attributed to any special generosity on his part, though generous he had been; it was of the very essence of business enterprise that it should be of service to society. "Whatever may be said of the evils of large fortunes, one fact about them is clear. They invariably return to the public use in one form or another. All that their owners get of them is what they spend on their own needs and pleasures; the rest must go back where it came from for there is nowhere else for it to go." If all members of society benefited from successful business enterprise and from intelligent philanthropy, then surely it was fitting that all members of society should mourn the death of the man who was the exemplar of both. "The world should be thankful that it once held a man as great as John D. Rockefeller" — and the world was thankful. Not even labor "assailed him," and all "bowed in grief at his bier." [16]

This was no heartless, soulless corporate symbol whom the people mourned, but a man as much occupied in the performance of nonbusiness as business duties, so much like other men in interests and habits that distinction based on differences in economic roles was obliterated by identity based on similarities in noneconomic roles. "Charitable . . . church-going, insistent on the domestic virtues, an admirable husband and father," Rockefeller in his domestic life differed little from other men. Despite his complex business activities, he

took his job as a father seriously. No one ever heard of his son making whoopee and getting into trouble. He was the richest man of his time but his son escaped the troubles which the progeny of rich men are so often heir to. John D. Rockefeller, Jr., was hand reared. His grandsons, too, have been singularly free from the "high society" mania which has ruined so many fine young men . . . He made a huge fortune but did not neglect his family while he did so. The fact is almost a miracle.

He was not a man for "yachts, polo ponies, and wild parties." His "love of family was deeply rooted," "he raised a good and simple family," and "some of the happiest moments of his life" were spent in its midst.[17]

Like other men he worked, played, chatted with his neighbors, relaxed in the presence of his grandchildren and great-grandchildren, prayed, conversed with his friends — sometimes seriously, sometimes jocularly — about problems great and small. "The American people saw John D. Rockefeller, Sr., in the role of worker, Christian enthusiast, master financier, golfer and finally as a philosopher." Those who knew him not might regard his fortune as his distinction, but he "was famous to his friends not for his wealth but for his sense of humor." A "kindly old man," "singularly humane . . . sympathetic, democratic, even humble . . . a particular favorite among the children," he was not regarded as "a person to be avoided, as one contaminated by great wealth," but "as a neighborly neighbor," held not in "awe but just a simple affection." [18] "If the capitalistic system is to remain in this land of ours," said the Augusta *Chronicle*, "it would be well for our men of vast wealth to take a leaf from the book of John D. Rockefeller." [19]

The pictures with which the newspapers liberally sprinkled their pages portrayed vividly the entrepreneur in his multiple roles and underscored those aspects of the editorial discussion which emphasized both his business success and his humane qualities. Rockefeller at various stages of his career, Rockefeller playing golf with humorist Will Rogers, Rockefeller dandling his great-grandchildren on his knees, Rockefeller passing out dimes to little children, entering church with prayer book under his arm, standing side by side with his wife, smiling shyly at his neighbors — if this was the pictorial representation of a "Success Story Covering 97 Years," of the man "Who Rose from Farm Youth to Builder of World's Largest Private Fortune" — as the captions put it — it was also the story of "The Kindly Old Man Who Made a Billion Dollars, Gave Away a Billion Dollars," whose life was one of "Completeness in Small Things."

Clearly it was not presumption for a man so much like his fellows to draw upon his wealth of experience and achievement so that he might benefit others by educating them in the attitudes which he had found successful in coping with the problems that all alike must face.

Work! Persevere! Be Honest! Save!

One of the most important of the elements which go to make up civilization is the progress of morality and religion.

I believe in man and the blood of man and am confident that everything will come out for the good of all in the end.

Do all the good you can.

Be earnest.

Live within your means.

A clear conscience is worth more and is a greater comfort than is a great fortune gathered by dishonorable methods.

The religion of a man is his most important possession. There is nothing in the world that can compare with Christian fellowship; nothing that can satisfy but Christ.

You won't have a happy life if you don't work.[20]

Whether or not these aphorisms were distillations of Rockefeller's experience, they were, like proverbs, admonitions for the adoption of those attitudes and strategies for dealing with recurrent problems which Rockefeller himself — and the press, too, it must be presumed — deemed desirable.[21] The words uttered by Rockefeller years before his death when he came across a group of French peasant women washing clothes in a stream — "Hark! They are singing. Ah, after all, the secret of happiness in life is to make the best of one's lot" — were of continuing relevance, for the phenomenon which those words were calculated to deal with was, *mutatis mutandis,* a recurring characteristic of American life. Admonitions for action necessary to achieve success and happiness were offered by Rockefeller, and so, too, were words of hope for those less fortunately situated: "Sons of wealthy parents have not the ghost of a chance compared with boys who come from the country with the determination to do something in this world." [22]

In speaking thus to the American people, Rockefeller was speaking with the authority born of personal knowledge and experience, for was his not "the greatest Horatio Alger story of all time — the story of a farm boy who started with nothing but a shrewd head and a capacity for hard work, and created a fortune . . ."? Was he not the "epitome, the acme of the success stories . . . in American history"? "As a young man he had no advantage over any in birth, education or circumstance; he was but one of the many thousands." He had not been "born with a silver spoon in his mouth," and his "boyhood was spent in comparative poverty"; yet by "hard work, painstaking attention, frugality in personal expenditures, and . . . faith," starting "as close to the bottom as a $4.50 per week salary," he had "made his name a symbol for wealth." His career "might well have formed the basis of one of Horatio Alger's books illustrating how success may be attained from most humble beginnings," wrote the Savannah *Morning News.* His life "proves that ambition when combined with hard work can lead from the most humble beginning to amazing success"; it offered a "picture and an inspiration to the boy who starts humbly but who has business acumen and thrift and patience." That all who conducted themselves in accordance with his maxims and modeled their behavior after his might succeed as he had succeeded was the "lesson of a very permanent value and applicability . . . taught by the life" of Rockefeller.[23]

There was, in one sense, little that was new in this aspect of journalistic discussion of Rockefeller's career. Other entrepreneurs before him had been held up as models of aspiration. But in the case of earlier entrepreneurs — of Girard and Astor — those who held aloft the figure of the entrepreneur to be emulated could guarantee success to the aspirants only if their qualities of mind, body, and spirit were identical with those of the entrepreneur. In the case of Rockefeller, however, there was an additional assurance. Rockefeller symbolized America because the American spirit and society which had produced him, nurtured him, and blessed him with success would do the same for any man. Surely, then, that spirit and that society, which offered so much, should be preserved, not altered, defended, not assailed. "Only America could have produced in one person such a colossal builder of wealth," said Colby M. Chester, chairman of the National Association of Manufacturers, and the press agreed. The qualities which led him to the highest peak of success were not his alone but those of all his countrymen. He "typified the American habit of major acquisition, coupled with the even more distinctively American habit of major distribution of wealth." He had become the "richest man in the world by the exercise of those American pioneering traits that have built up the country — Tenacity, Self-Reliance and a Will of Steel." Always would he remain "a symbol of the industrial evolution of America, of its business genius and of the indomitable will of its people," for he had never faltered in "his faith in America," never "overlooked an opportunity to reaffirm his belief in the fundamental principles upon which this country was founded — liberty, unselfish devotion to the common good and belief in God." [24]

If, then, the life of Rockefeller had been "one of those fairy stories of commercial success which are so common in the United States and in which the citizenry has taken so much pride in the past," it was in large measure because the United States itself was "a land of opportunity," a "land of equal opportunity for all men." [25] "The career of Rockefeller," said the Sioux Falls *Daily Argus-Leader,* "serves again to emphasize the fact that this is the land of opportunity . . . Through native ability and energy, he was able to open the doors that faced him along the way. Such an opportunity is typically American. Here it is possible for a man to achieve the rewards his talents and his efforts merit. In many other countries, a situation of this nature does not exist."

Not only did opportunity exist in America, so that the meritorious could be rewarded, but the reward of one was to the benefit of all. Rockefeller's career, said the Galveston *Daily News,* "personified the boundless range of individual opportunity in America and the equally unlimited capacity of private concentrations of wealth to advance human welfare." This was the "association characteristic of American capitalism."

Conversely, of course, consciousness that Rockefeller had performed his services in a favorably regarded political and economic setting implied opposition and antagonism to alternative settings. The "vicious little feists, — demagogues, politicians, anarchists, and a certain class of social reformers" — what had they to offer? Mockery at "self-reliance?" Expectation that "the government . . . would support them, without their having to work or save?" Suppose, as some had suggested, that the profits of industry had been "divided . . . with the public?" What would have been the result in the case of the Standard Oil Company? "The share of the consumers would have been so small as to be almost imperceptible. It would have added but little to the purchasing power of the individual. It would have been dissipated and there would have been no more reserve to be drawn upon for the creation of the great fund set up by John D. Rockefeller . . . which has . . . so benefitted the whole world." This was the "question for which those who seek to destroy the capitalist system must find an answer." [26] "Mr. Rockefeller," said the Charlotte *Observer,*

is not only a stellar example of what the practice of the simple virtues of thrift and industry and frugality and saving will accomplish, but he stands also as a symbol of the unlimited possibilities offered every individual under the friendly climate of a free democracy. As long as he remained within the bounds of law and morals, his government laid no oppressive nor restricting nor impeding hand upon his wealth-making progress and adventures. Such has always been the glory of the American system of free competitive enterprise. It has offered young men, even in poverty of riches, but in plenitude of aspiration — it has offered such as these an open door and fair weather and a hearty wish-you-well! A tragedy for America if this system and this spirit and this encouragement offered by democracy should perish from the face of the earth!

"Thrift and industry and frugality and saving" — dim echoes from the past. "The American system of free competitive enterprise" — the discovery of the new. Paradoxically, perhaps, it was in the gradual fading of emphasis upon the qualities of the entrepreneur himself and in substitution for it of awareness of "system and spirit" that entrepreneurs in the 1930's seemed to find their greatest security.

Like the newspapers, those magazines which looked upon Rockefeller favorably emphasized his life of service and his generous philanthropies, described his rise from poor country boy to richest man in the world, attributed the undesirable practices with which he had been charged to the nature of the times in which he had lived, and concluded finally in placing him solidly in the context of American life and the American temper.

"His fame is not due alone to the size of the fortune which he amassed," wrote *Opportunity,* "nor to the power and influence which he wielded as one of the world's greatest, perhaps its greatest, industrialist. Rather his fame rests on the more enduring foundation of service to Humanity, which he envisioned as the proper function of great wealth."

"His methods of quashing competition" had made him "one of the most hated men in America"; but "through the years his benefactions gradually obscured bitter memories of his business career. On his death many people thought of him as an old man who gave away immense checks and shiny dimes," a "gentle oldster who gave away more money than any man who ever lived." [27]

He "was the perfect 'rags to riches' hero," "America's favorite symbol of great wealth. The story of his life reads like a fairy tale." Farm boy in upstate New York, wholesale grocery clerk in Cleveland, then to the very apex of American industry, his career of upward progress was the product of both parental training and environmental conditions. "John D. got something more than long life from his father. Big Bill . . . had the knack of making money, though he didn't save it. He gave his three sons a thorough training in worldly bargaining. 'I cheat my boys every chance I get,' he said . . . 'I want to make 'em sharp.'" This, however, was but one aspect of his training. "His parents taught him to keep strict account of all money which passed through his hands, and to make regular donations to the church and the poor from his meagre boyhood earnings." It was the combination of habits and attitudes instilled by early training with the "opportunity" afforded by "the old system" when "it was possible for an individual to accumulate such wealth" which led to his success.[28]

If his were "the ruthless tactics of a predatory monopoly," they were the expression of the "social philosophy . . . typical of his age" and a reflection of the fact "that he lived on the frontier, and the methods of the frontier were highly individualistic." Judged "in the light of the times" he was no worse than his contemporaries; if he was ruthless it was because he was "exploiting an historical imperative" and out of that very ruthlessness emerged "modern large-scale industrial enterprise."

"What are one's conclusions to be" concerning Rockefeller? That he had lived "through three periods, all of which were strictly American in scope and environment. There was the first — the struggling poor boy whose object was self-betterment and success. Then the great oil operator buying up the competitors and amassing an economic kingdom . . . Then the philanthropic period." [29]

Only one element which had been of major concern to the newspapers was absent from the magazines. For the newspapers, accurate appraisal of Rockefeller's life proved the superiority of America's economic system. Editors of the magazines, however, felt no need to make that demonstration, perhaps because they thought their readers, unlike those of the daily press, needed no convincing.

Nor, for that matter, was concern for demonstrating the superiority of the economic system a fundamental consideration of those journals which were explicitly designed to present the point of view of the business community to those persons who might be reasonably expected already to be in substantial agreement with it. For such journals, though philanthropy was by no means ignored and Rockefeller was given credit for having "done much to build higher the structure of our civilization and to beautify it," as *Commerce and Finance* put it, the major focus of attention was his business career. That business activity itself, not philanthropy, should be the criterion for evaluating Rockefeller's career was the judgment of the entrepreneur's own colleagues: "But widespread as were his benefactions and far-reaching as they are upon the welfare of nations," read the resolution adopted by the board of directors of the Standard Oil Company of New Jersey,

his achievements in recreating business and industrial processes will, in the end, we think, be regarded as his greatest gift to humanity . . . No man ever revealed a greater genius for industrial organization, and the methods of low cost production and distribution which he introduced into his own business have since spread to practically all basic industries. It was indeed providential for the United States that when one of its great industries, the oil business, was in a condition of reckless exploitation and chaos, a man of his foresight should have occupied himself in its development. Almost from the outset the wage earning classes instinctively regarded Mr. Rockefeller as a friend. Among those with any real claim to knowledge of the facts, his name was always a synonym for fair dealing, and that reputation was the heritage he left to his successors.[30]

The journals of industry agreed. "Primarily" Rockefeller was "a business man . . . He found the oil business a gamble. He left it one of the most efficient business organizations the world has seen. He taught it not only by example but by force of superior competition based on sheer efficiency. He was the supreme organizer whose methods have made American efficiency the model for the world." In his earlier days he "appeared to typify everything that was predatory and unsocial"; but that was a time "of severe commercial competition," when he was "the most rugged . . . in the era of emphasized rugged individualism." And, besides, the passage of time made it possible for his "extraordinary accomplishments" to be "appraised at something like their true value." [31] Rockefeller himself testified that he felt his greatest service of all to be business enterprise itself, not philanthropy. "When I asked him, late in life," wrote the editor of *Forbes*, "what had yielded him the greatest satisfaction of all, instead of referring to the colossal benefits his philanthropies had wrought for mankind, he replied emphatically: 'Having been instrumental in enabling many thousands of bread-winners to earn a decent living.' In other words, he was proudest of all of having been a constructive, large-scale employer." Indeed, business enterprise could not help but contribute to the well-being of mankind. "Would the scattering of wealth into numerous and many incompetent hands be of greater public benefit than its concentration into the hands of one person who could use it in the most practicable way it could be employed, and that is in the production of more wealth?" asked the *Bankers Magazine*.

Missing from the journals which businessmen read were description of Rockefeller's career in terms of the American success story, revelation of his human qualities, emphasis upon those thousand-and-one little things which proved he was a man as well as a businessman. But in the journals which businessmen prepared for others to read, emphasis was altered.

For the editors of *The Sohioan,* employee house organ of the Standard Oil Company of Ohio, the story of the Rockefeller enterprises was the story of the "greatest industrial empire the world has ever seen . . . built in thirty years from the meagerest possible beginnings"; and the story of Rockefeller himself was not that of the man who had been the great organizer of industry but that of the man who had written

> I was early taught to work as well as play;
> My life has been one long, happy holiday.

And when the president of Standard Oil of Ohio addressed his employees it was not to speak of Rockefeller as "economic genius, empire builder, wise and far-seeing philanthropist — so Olympian . . . as to make him seem to many people almost an abstraction rather than a man. But what of the man?" asked W. T. Holliday:

Simplicity, gentleness, patience, kindness, sweetness of temper, interest in others, all nourished by his inherent religious attitude toward life, were the qualities of his personality . . . He kept himself interested in other people . . . When he was present with his guests they had his undivided attention . . . It was all so simple and informal. Sometimes, if music was referred to, he would even sing a song at the table, and he carried the tune perfectly and his voice was clear and unwavering . . . He never indulged in harsh or unkind statements. It seemed as though he were incapable of bitterness . . . Whenever he appeared in public people gathered around him . . . Mr. Rockefeller achieved wealth, power, honor, and fame, but he did not seem to consider those things important as compared with the fundamental qualities of a man's character and personality . . . He had a great intellect and great vision and courage, but he was a great man because in addition to these qualities he had depth of character, serenity, patience, simplicity and kindness.

It was the adulation of such articles that caused Heywood Broun to remark cynically that "every indication points to the fact that life will go on about as usual even though John D. Rockefeller is no more. Life is less easily stampeded than the headline writers." It was not Broun, but the dean of American newspaper editors, however, who caught up in one short paragraph the essence of American journalists' evaluation of the great oil entrepreneur. "Farewell John D.," wrote William Allen White in the Emporia *Gazette:*

You have lived to be a symbol of our age, Mr. Rockefeller. The good you have done has outlived the evil of your day when your shortcomings were those of an age and time . . . Whether you tried consciously or not to choose, the last thirty years of your life have undone the wrong that you and your generation justified in the beginning of your life. You have expiated here on this planet for the sins of your generation. They were not uniquely yours. They were ours. Incidentally, you, the real John D., who has also survived the ravages of time, are also ours. You and your major vices, you and your benevolences, you as a whole are as distinctly American in one character as you are in the other, the great ruthless unmoral organizer, the wise and splendid giver. No other country ever has created giants exactly like ours . . . John D. stands, wherever the English language is spoken, for the high qualities of American achievements, the genius of organization, the joy of intelligent giving. And so John D. you leave the world much better than you found it . . .

May you rest in peace!

During the course of his long editorship of the Emporia *Gazette*, William Allen White had occasion to write many obituaries. On December 23, 1925, commenting on the recent death of a noted newspaper publisher, White wrote:

Frank Munsey, the great publisher, is dead. Frank Munsey contributed to the journalism of his day the great talent of a meat packer, the morals of a money changer and the meanness of an undertaker. He and his kind have about succeeded in transforming a once noble profession into an eight per-cent security. May he rest in trust.[32]

But only a few years later, though he still indicated interest in the problem posed by the career of Munsey — the decline of editorial independence — White's acerbity had mellowed into resignation. "There is arising everywhere something in this country approaching a class struggle," he told the American Society of Newspaper Editors:

Now this class struggle, which I regret, which we all must regret, which is certainly not in the American tradition, has placed us as editors on one side, because we represent property. In the nature of things we have to represent property, because it takes considerable capital to operate a newspaper. So we are placed by our position on the other side of those who are struggling for a fair adjustment of the matter of income for labor . . . We are businessmen merchandising the news.[33]

"The publisher associates on terms of equality with the bankers, the merchant princes, the manufacturers, and the investing brokers," he explained further. "His friends unconsciously color his opinions. If he lives with them on any kind of social terms in the City club or the Country club or the Yacht club or the Racquet club, he must more or less merge his views into the common views of the other capitalists . . . he takes the color of his social environment." [34]

What William Allen White came finally to accept with resignation, others regarded with anger and suspicion;[35] but common to all such critics was recognition of the fact that

Since the mass media are supported by great business concerns geared into the current social and economic system, the media contribute to the maintenance of that system. This contribution is not found merely in the effective advertisement of the sponsor's product. It arises, rather, from the typical presence in magazine stories, radio programs and newspaper columns of some element of confirmation, some element of approval of the present structure of society. And this continuing reaffirmation underscores the duty to accept.[36]

Increasing monopolization of the press and its tendency toward affirmation rather than alteration of existing attitudes are not only "the very conditions which make for the maximum effectiveness of the mass media of communications" but those which "operate toward the maintenance of the going social and cultural structure rather than toward its change." [37] To decide which are the legitimate subjects of public discussion, to enhance the authority of and bestow prestige on those persons, organizations, and social movements deemed desirable by its editors, to reaffirm existing social norms and to expose deviance — these are among the prime social functions of the press.[38]

Certainly the business community has been aware of these functions of the press and has, at least by virtue of its own participation in journalistic activities, shared in the defining of issues, designation of persons, and reinforcement of social norms calculated to strengthen the environment of enterprise. Harknesses and Harrimans, Du Ponts and McCormicks, Reeds and Hannas have utilized the opportunities afforded by investment in journalism. So, for that matter, did John D. Rockefeller himself, whose interests in the Oil City *Derrick,* Buffalo *People's Journal,* Jennings Publishing Company, *Fra, Manufacturers Record, Southern Farm Magazine, The Outlook,* Trinidad (Colorado) *Chronicle-News* and *Advertiser,* Pueblo *Chieftain, Leslie's Weekly, Gunton's Magazine,* and Denver *Post* testified to his belief in the importance to be attached to the press.[39] James P. Selvage, public relations director of the National Association of Manufacturers, indicated not only awareness by the business community of the function performed by the press but also understanding of some of the means to be employed in the formation of attitudes when he wrote in his "Memorandum on Community Public Information Programs to Combat Radical Tendencies and Present the Constructive Story of Industry":

V. Possible Activities. A. Newspapers . . . 2. Get another paper to carry a series of stories and pictures of industrial and business men, with the accent on those who have either started at the bottom and become executives of big companies, or who started their own companies on a shoestring and become big.[40]

Business leaders had every reason to mobilize their efforts to create an environment of security for enterprise, for indications were not lacking that cynicism and disapproval were undermining the structure they had erected. So far as Rockefeller himself was concerned, opposition dated, of course, at least from the time of Henry Demarest Lloyd and in 1905 he was the thinly disguised villain of one of Broadway's smash dramatic hits;[41] but the menacing fact was that no matter how vehement Rockefeller's denials, how firm his statements, opposition would not wholly be downed even after the death of an old generation and the birth of a new.

The sixty thousand men who are at work constantly in the service of the company are kept busy year in and year out . . . It pays its workmen well, it cares for them when sick, and pensions them when old. It has never had any important strikes, and if there is any better function of business management than giving profitable work to employes year after year, in good times and bad, I don't know what it is.

So wrote John D. Rockefeller about his Standard Oil Company.[42]

But his contemporary and great antagonist remembered another Rockefeller company:

A frantic mother clutched me. "Mother Jones," she screamed, "Mother Jones, my little boy's all swollen up with the kicking and the beating he got from a soldier because he said, 'Howdy, John D. feller!' 'Twas just a kid teasing, and now he's lying like dead . . ." I nursed men back to sanity who were driven to despair. I solicited clothes for the ragged children, for the desperate mothers. I laid out the dead . . . The smoke of armed battle rose from the arroyos and ravines of the Rocky mountains. No one listened. No one cared. The tickers in the offices of 26 Broadway sounded louder than the sobs of women and children . . . Then came Ludlow and the nation heard. Little children roasted alive make a front page story. Dying by inches of starvation and exposure does not.[43]

That the majority of Americans believed John D. Rockefeller to have been essentially as he had been presented by the press seems probable. But during his lifetime how many, like Theodore Dreiser, could "not help thinking what an excellent type of Keeper of the Exchequer, Vizier or High Priest our own John D. Rockefeller would have made. The robes! The sanctity!" [44] And at his death how many agreed with Pete Casey, Omaha WPA laborer, who didn't know whether Rockefeller would go to heaven: "I noticed in the paper this morning that picture of him handing out dimes to a little girl. But take me, for instance, if somebody hit me, I'd always give 'em a quarter, if I had anything at all"; with Frank Wilson the rancher who felt "after all the people he's robbed he doesn't have much chance, even if he did try to cover it up by giving some of it away"; or with the anonymous person ("The oil people would get me") who denied Rockefeller had "a chance" to get to heaven: "He was avaricious when he started out. He didn't have any right to make so much money. He has a lot to account for." [45]

But more serious than antagonism directed against an individual entrepreneur was loss of faith in business enterprise itself and in the social system which guarded it. It was a gross exaggeration to say that every broken strike "broke the ideal in the hearts of thousands . . . that America was a government for the people — the poor, the oppressed"; that "little boys" in the mines and mills of the nation "would sell their chance" of rising in the world "any day for good square meals and a chance to play." [46] But exaggeration or not, business leaders, even in the golden twenties, acted to prevent the further contamination of a populace whose precise degree of disaffection was less a matter of dispute than of concern:

. . . businessmen . . . were seeking in every possible way to direct American thinking in lines more favorable to general business purposes . . . And on the whole, of course, they succeeded . . . The booming prosperity of the twenties gave a magnificent gloss to the quality of their leadership, and their control of important avenues of communication permitted no strong heretical gospel to gain a foothold in the United States . . . The first object of business leaders in America in the twenties, just as it was the first object of leaders of all earlier societies, was to eliminate every shade of "radicalism." The threat of world revolution contained in Bolshevik propaganda made American businessmen extremely sensitive to attacks upon the "American way of life." [47]

Discerning leaders of the business community might have noted in the constant decrease in numbers in the popular magazines of articles presenting businessmen as heroic figures evidence of a loss of prestige; and though sophisticated irony had supplanted strident exposure, evidence of continued hostility among the writers of fiction.[48] But even the least perceptive could have seen in the events of the 1930's evidence that business enterprise was under fire and that its environment was being altered after the fashion designed by its critics. The Monday afternoon newspapers which carried articles describing the career of Rockefeller as an epic of individualism carried the news, too, that the Supreme Court had that morning upheld the Social Security Act. And the delegates to the Northern Baptist Convention, who "Voiced Sorrow At Rockefeller Death" on one day, on the very next day adopted a resolution expressing their conviction that "the building of the Kingdom of God on earth lays upon . . . individual Christians the compulsion to work for a living minimum wage for every worker and a maximum income, set by law, so as to make possible the minimum wage." [49] So much had America changed from the days of Rockefeller's youth.

Insecurity wrought by widespread evidence of animosity and change in the climate of business enterprise led the defenders of enterprise not to abandon that which was under attack but, on the contrary, to resist the political and economic ideas which seemed to threaten them and, conversely, to reassert the fundamental, traditional values on which they sought to rest their case.[50] To create a new consensus by converting disagreement into harmony, removing certain problems from the area of controversy and highlighting certain facets of enterprise which hitherto had been obscure — this was an essential prerequisite for achieving that social discipline which results in the active coöperation of all members of society in the performance of the tasks and duties expected of them.[51] That such was indeed a major task of business enterprise was not unperceived:

> The realization is now dawning that there can be only one end to this steady attrition and whittling away of freedom for enterprise; to the constant encroachment of government . . . ; to the persistent poisoning of the public mind with regard to the motives and integrity of industrial leaders. That end is the undermining, and possible eventual overturn, of the American enterprise system. The recognition of this fact has led to searching diagnosis and critical self-examination . . . The conclusion becomes almost self-evident that the first task before industry is revision and restatement for present capitalistic philosophy. The old economic phraseology, largely inherited from the days of Adam Smith, must be discarded. It is no longer adequate. It neither meets the needs of the times nor commands the public's respect. Its ideology must be completely modernized . . . The emphasis formerly placed upon individualism, under which capitalism grew, can be broadened into new concepts without any surrender of private ownership rights.[52]

To achieve these results, business leaders made use to an unparalleled degree of a series of identifications which removed from enterprise certain of the stigmas its opponents had attached to it and which associated it with those values for which people reserved their deepest loyalty and affection.

What was the relation of business enterprise to the American past?

Capitalism was underwritten by the Declaration of Independence, Representative Charles A. Eaton told the Congress of American Industry:

> We enjoy the highest level of comfort and the widest distribution of wealth ever known in any society since time began. Consciously or unconsciously we have decided to retain the capitalistic system, the oldest system known to man. We propose to solve and to eliminate the evils of the capitalistic system by the simple process of making more capitalists and, in this effort, we have found a solution for many of our most important economic and social problems . . . We are a nation of capitalists.[53]

What was the relation of business enterprise to present-day America?

> Our American system of free enterprise is far more than just a way of doing business. At its best it comprehends good sportsmanship; gives free play to the laws of supply, demand, and competition; develops discipline,

character, and initiative; raises the standard of living, and improves the morale of the people . . . The institutions of political democracy and economic freedom have grown side by side. They have grown together and lived together; their epoch has been marked by the emancipation of the common man and by humanity's most impressive advances in the arts and sciences . . . Everyone must have his chance; and under our American system of free enterprise and equal opportunity everyone gets just that chance.[54]

What was the relation of business enterprise to Christianity?

One spokesman, who had attended a meeting of executives which had opened with "one of the most basic prayers" he had ever heard, asked if it were standard procedure in that company to begin its deliberations with prayer. " 'Why, yes,' " the head of the company replied: "and more than that, we never even have a directors' meeting but what there stands at one end of the table a vacant chair, and never do any of us make a decision or cast a vote but what we first think of the Man of long ago were He sitting there, and say to ourselves, 'What would He have done?' I don't know . . . just what such things have meant to us. We are not religious, but somehow or other we always seem to be going ahead."

If the head of the company did not "know . . . just what such things have meant" his interviewer did: "So far as I know that firm has never had a strike, labor trouble, financial trouble, or any of those business disturbing things." [55]

Identification of business enterprise with the public interest by emphasis on the responsibility it assumed for the welfare of society, on its accomplishments in raising living standards, on the complete congruity between its ideals and those of nation and religion was the image projected by the leaders of business themselves. Business community and nation were functioning parts — at times even interchangeable parts — of a general unity. American society, in the imagery of business leaders, was one in which harmony prevailed and should prevail because business enterprise was essentially social service.[56]

By presenting their point of view in such fashion in the organs over which they had full control, entrepreneurs expected to achieve concrete results. "Education for employes is the only possible escape from the crisis of the railroads," wrote the assistant to the editor of *Railway Age*. "The railway employe can save the day for the privately operated railroads if he is given the tools of knowledge with which to do the job." Originally, "all the employes were expected to do was to provide transportation — to animate the railway plant." But given the proper education they might be counted on "to speak for the railroads — to keep the public friendly — to go to the front for the railroads in national and state legislation — to soften up railway regulation — to oppose the establishment of competition menacing railroads — to see that proper regulation is set up for such competition — to see that regulation so set up is enforced — to organize in ways that will best demonstrate to the public the strength of railway morale — to solicit traffic — to increase the safety of both employes and patrons — to reduce loss and damage and to conserve materials — to oppose excessive railway taxation — to welcome the public to demonstrations of railway safety, efficiency, and progress — and to spread good-will and publicize the railroads in other ways." If the railroad employee "is not given these tools and hence does not do this job, then . . . we are headed for an era of 100 per cent state socialism in transportation." [57]

The daily newspaper was, of course, not identical with the corporation house organ, nor was the audience of the one coextensive with that of the other. But no less than the house organ, though in somewhat different ways, did the daily newspaper attempt to integrate its readers into a coöperating society in which, if there was rivalry, that rivalry was motivated by a desire to attain those goals which sanctioned business enterprise.[58] As the editorial written by one great newspaper publisher put it:

The Hearst papers are American papers published for the American people.
They support the American system of government, the American Constitution, American institutions and American ideals.
They labor to maintain the American standard of living . . .
They are in favor of American independence, American rights and liberties, free speech, free assembly, freedom of thought and action, and freedom of the press.
They are advocates of rugged individualism, and of the industrial independence and enterprise which have made our country the richest and greatest in the world.
They are opposed to paternalism in government . . .
They believe in opportunity for all and equality before the law.
They believe in the capitalistic system, so-called, which is the only practical economic system of proven worth and with adequate reward for merit.[59]

On this issue, though not on others, the major difference between William Randolph Hearst and his publishing colleagues was in his greater degree of explicitness.

Recognition that the very social system which supported business enterprise was itself under attack required newspaper editors, in their analysis of the reasons for the success of such a great entrepreneur as Rockefeller, to incorporate the social system as a fundamental element into the explanations they offered. The aspect of the social system which received greatest emphasis was that of social mobility. In one sense, emphasis on social mobility had been characteristic of discussion of successful entrepreneurs at least as far back as the time of Stephen Girard, and as early as the 1840's it had received explicit recognition. In the catechism which the noted educator Henry Barnard prepared to help teachers give the correct answers to questions raised by workmen's children there appeared the following dialogue:

Q. Suppose a capitalist in employing his capital makes large profits, would that harm the working man?

A. No. There would be more capital to raise wages . . .

Q. Are you sorry, then, that capitalists should have great profits?

A. Glad . . .

Q. If there are two boys starting in life, one the son of a man who has accumulated capital, the other of a man who has not, shall I be right in saying that the boy without this advantage can never be a capitalist?

A. No.

Q. But what is to make him a capitalist?

A. Saving.[60]

This was, indeed, recognition of social mobility; but in this form, and in the form in which the careers of early entrepreneurs had been discussed, evidence of the existence of mobility was expressed as a tribute to the man who had the qualities necessary to overcome obstacles.

In the discussion of Rockefeller, however, the emphasis shifted. "Such has always been the glory of the American system of free competitive enterprise," wrote the Charlotte *Observer*, that "It has offered young men, even in poverty of riches, but in plenitude of aspiration — it has offered such as these an open door and fair weather and a hearty wish-you-well." [61]

This, too, was recognition of social mobility; but in this form evidence of the existence of mobility was expressed as a tribute to a society which interposed no obstacles to a man's upward progress. The successful entrepreneur had once been offered as a testimonial to the value of good character; now the successful entrepreneur was being offered as a testimonial to the worth of the social system.[62]

Stressing the social system in the explanation offered for the success of the entrepreneur would include that system itself within a new consensus. So, too, would the new emphasis on the nonbusiness activities of the entrepreneur serve to include him in that consensus. Just as with the problem of social mobility, newspapers had always discussed the personal qualities of entrepreneurs; but not always had they discussed — as they did to an overwhelming degree in the case of Rockefeller — those nonbusiness activities which the business leader had in common with even the lowliest of men. The entrepreneur at work and at play, worshiping in church and relaxing in the bosom of his family, pronouncing simple judgments on all the problems that confront ordinary people, like his countrymen in every respect save that of his wealth, and even then deferring to

them in his conviction that money was the least important of all possessions — on such a large number of shared activities, purposes, and
dreams in commonplace daily acts and thoughts could identification be
built and the entrepreneur be presented as instructor and guide. What
had once been considered in the sphere of private life had been endowed
by the press with a public function; and dissent that might arise from the
real public functions of entrepreneurs — their business activities — could
be weakened by the unanimity of approval that flowed from appreciation
and understanding of "the pathos of their position as individuals." [63] To
portray Rockefeller as a symbol had been the achievement of the press,
and, as with all symbols, the ideas associated by the world with the name
of Rockefeller had no necessary correspondence with the reality behind
the name. Rockefeller might protest to B. C. Forbes that, while people
persisted "in thinking I was a tremendous worker, always at it early and
late, summer and winter," the "real truth" was that "I was what would
now be called a slacker after I reached my middle thirties . . . I never,
from the time I first entered any office, let business engross all my time
and attention." [64] But for the press such protestations, even when they
came from the man being canonized, were of little significance; for like
all makers of symbols the press was less interested in the question, What
are you? than, What can you make of others? [65]

One of Rockefeller's adversaries, in writing his obituary, commented:
"So old Skull and Bones is dead . . . I don't envy Harry Emerson
Fosdick the job of thinking up a snappy funeral oration." But his ironical
shaft, shot as it was in expectation that Rockefeller's business activities
would be discussed, was far wide of the mark. Rockefeller had been a
man, preached Dr. Fosdick, of "creative foresight, persevering courage,
high standards of character, consciousness of stewardship . . . world-
wide philanthropies, inner serenity, love of his family, loyalty to friends,
faith and hope." [66]

VI

Henry Ford

In 1923, Arthur H. Vandenberg, editor and publisher of the Grand Rapids *Herald*, sharpened his pen to prick the rapidly swelling "Henry Ford for President" bubble. "Ford has to his debit," the editor wrote, "more erratic interviews on public questions, more dubious quotations, more blandly boasted ignorance of American history and American experience, more political nonsense, more dangerous propaganda, than any other dependable citizen that we have ever known."[1]

On April 9, 1947, the same Arthur H. Vandenberg, now senior United States Senator from Michigan, rose on the floor of the Senate to appraise the automobile manufacturer once again. "Mr. Ford's death," the senator said,

ends one of the most thrilling and greatest careers in the life of this country. It is the vivid epitome of what one man can do for himself and for his fellow men under our system of American freedoms. Through his own irresistible genius and courage he not only rose from humble obscurity to fame and fortune, but he also founded a new national economy of mass production which blessed his hundreds of thousands of employees with his wages and his millions of customers with low prices. He has probably had as great an impact on his times as if he had been a President of the United States. With it all, he continued always to be a modest, kindly, gentle friend with a constant interest in the welfare of his country and of his fellow men.[2]

The passage of time and the emergence of new issues led others besides Senator Vandenberg to reconsider earlier judgments and to focus upon criteria which, however unimportant they appeared in an earlier day, seemed now to be those upon which appraisals should be based. Shortly after Henry Ford had taken the witness stand in 1919 during his lawsuit against the Chicago *Tribune*, the New York *Times* commented tersely: "Mr. Ford has been submitted to a severe examination of his intellectual qualities. He has not received a pass degree." [3]

But in 1947 it was not Ford's "intellectual qualities" which concerned the *Times*. That he incarnated the opportunities in which American society abounded, that his had been a life of service, that he embodied the simple virtues — these were the bases on which the new evaluation was erected:

> To a peculiar degree he was the embodiment of America in the era of industrial revolution . . . It was the American success story . . . His was a single-minded devotion to the fundamentals as he saw them: hard work, the simple virtues, self-reliance, the good earth. He profited by providing what was new, but also he treasured that which was bygone . . . He built "for the great multitude," and they were, both directly and by accident, the great beneficiaries of Henry Ford, master mechanic.

For all the doubts which Senator Vandenberg and the New York *Times* had expressed concerning various facets of Henry Ford's career, neither, of course, had been antagonistic to his business activities, and it required no great sleight-of-hand on the occasion of his death to convert early doubt into present praise. But in 1947 not only former skeptics but former enemies found common ground on which to stand in sanctioning what had once been a target of attack. Ten years earlier, on May 26, 1937, several members of the United Automobile Workers of America, the CIO union attempting to organize the employees of the Ford Motor Company, were attacked by the Ford Service Department while distributing leaflets at the gates of the River Rouge plant in Dearborn, Michigan. But in April, 1947, Walter P. Reuther, now president of the UAW-CIO and one of those who had been most severely mauled in the earlier attempt at organization, issued on behalf of his fellow union officers a laudatory statement concerning the automobile manufacturer. And for the president of UAW-CIO Local 600, the union which bargains for the employees of the River Rouge plant, there was no place for enmity based on memories of an earlier day. Writing in *Ford Facts,* he said:

> The greatest tribute that could be paid to Mr. Ford is that his roots were firmly imbedded in the soil of his birth — the banks of the River Rouge. From humble beginnings on a farm . . . he welded together a vast industrial empire . . . without leaving the banks of the River Rouge. His friends and his neighbors were important to him. No absentee ownership on the banks of the River Rouge for him! Part of his greatness arose from his willingness to pioneer. Like his rugged forbears, he was never afraid to venture forth into uncharted

seas. He recognized that increased purchasing power in the hands of the workers meant more contented workers and a greater potential market — a greater America . . . His mistakes were never mistakes of the heart.

What, then, were the criteria the application of which resulted in an evaluation of the automobile entrepreneur in which the area of approval was wide enough to encompass even the leaders of groups which hitherto had remained outside the consensus of acquiescence?

Henry Ford "was a benefactor of mankind. Simplicity was the keystone of his life," Republican Congressman George Dondero of Michigan said in the first of six speeches delivered by members of the United States Congress on the occasion of Ford's death:

> Born of humble parents, and with meagre education, he rose from obscurity to build the greatest industrial empire of his time . . . The poor man should never forget him. He provided transportation for him at a cost within his reach. The laboring man should never forget him. He doubled his wages voluntarily. Henry Ford and his family have been manufacturing cars, not because they needed bread but to provide employment for those who needed it.[5]

For Democrat as well as for Republican, service had been the major characteristic of Ford's life. "Henry Ford was a practical idealist who believed in helping his fellow man to help himself," Representative John Dingell asserted. "How well he succeeded can be judged by the prosperity of hundreds of thousands of his workers, associates and coordinated industries . . . As Henry Ford grew and prospered so did everyone who worked and associated with him." [6]

Other congressmen embellished the portrait. Republican Edith Nourse Rogers of Massachusetts was not concerned with Ford's business career. "He bought the historic Wayside Inn at Sudbury," she told her colleagues. "He was tremendously interested in all the old traditions of the country. He was interested in art in all its forms. The Ford Sunday symphony orchestra is heard by millions . . . He had some of the finest cattle in the United States. He made splendid contributions to agriculture." [7] Conservative Democrat John Rankin of Mississippi asked different questions of Ford's career but nevertheless came to a similar conclusion: "If it had not been for Henry Ford," he prophesied retroactively, "the average American would not be able to ride in an automobile today. There is one thing characteristically American about Henry Ford's life . . . simplicity . . ." [8]

Henry Ford as a man for whom principle prevailed over profit, for whom service to humanity was the fundamental law of conduct, rooted in the traditions of his country, exemplifying its opportunities, and governed by sentiments of warmth and friendship for his fellow man — this was the portrait of Ford presented by those congressmen who chose to discuss the matter. Whether or not the portrait corresponded in every detail to reality, it was one which both reflected and yet reconciled important conflicts in the society in which Ford had lived. The veneration of goodness and the rewarding of success, while always approved in the abstract, nevertheless created serious problems when applied to concrete cases; for always there had been those who insisted that the good were not always rewarded and that the successful were not always good. But in the case of Ford there could be no such problem. He had helped himself because he had helped others — not because he needed bread but because he wanted to provide bread for others had he manufactured automobiles, the congressman had said — and so, for the idealists, the problem was solved because there was no problem. For those less concerned with resolving apparent paradoxes but inclined rather to accept situations as they found them, the answer was no less satisfactory. Henry Ford had proved it was possible neither to be so self-seeking as to be branded inhuman nor so good as to be condemned to poverty.

Once the portrait of the entrepreneur had been drawn, it remained only to sketch in the background in such a way as to suggest that, without the appropriate setting, the painting would be meaningless. Republican Senator Albert W. Hawkes of New Jersey and radio commentator Samuel B. Pettengill jointly undertook that responsibility. "Henry Ford's life," Senator Hawkes asserted, ". . . sounds almost like a review of the opportunities open to all people under the American system of free men. Mr. Ford benefited humanity by giving them an opportunity to benefit themselves through honest effort, work, and thrift."

For the instruction of his colleagues, Senator Hawkes read the radio address which Samuel Pettengill had delivered on April 20, 1947:

Abraham Lincoln and Ford mean America throughout the world — log cabin to White House — machine shop to industrial empire. Henry Ford and the other automobile manufacturers who, like him, have developed and applied mass production methods represent the American system at its best. They show what competitive individual enterprise can do — and I stress the word competitive . . .

Has big Government, and the cost and the waste of Government, made it impossible for America to ever have another Henry Ford? . . . Contrary to the teaching of Communist professors that "one man's gain is the other man's loss," he demonstrated on a world scale that it is possible to make more money, pay higher wages, and reduce costs all at once and at the same time — investor, worker, and consumer all gaining and no one losing by the process. The secret of this miracle of economics is high production per man-hour, which brings costs down . . . The best manager of a machine is the man who owns it; if he takes pride in his job. This is the miracle of America. It is hard to see any limit to this progress . . . if . . . If we don't lose the magic formula in a struggle between class and class; if investor, and manager and worker all play fair with each other . . . But even the magic formula cannot work except under a government friendly to achievement, a government that protects a man in the fruit of his toil. Great as he was, I firmly believe Henry Ford would be a name scarcely known beyond the county limits of his home, if he had not lived under the protection of the Constitution of the United States . . . Ford's career was possible only in an America with constitutional government and competitive free enterprise unhampered by confiscatory taxation of able men — as it was when he was born.

These, concluded the speaker, were "big facts that tie in with the argument as to whether communism, socialism, or the individual enterprise system is best for America — and the world." [9]

Never before had the identity of business enterprise and the entrepreneur with the symbols of nationalism been so explicit, and in that explicitness of identity lies the clue to the realization of the new and broader consensus. If the entrepreneur, like Abraham Lincoln, "represented the American system at its best," if competitive free enterprise and constitutional government were interchangeable parts of the same mechanism, and if — as the speaker said — these "big facts . . . tie in with the argument as to whether communism, socialism, or the individual enterprise system is best for America," then to deny the identities or to evaluate Ford differently was to court the risk of being considered antagonistic not only to business enterprise but to the nation itself, at a time when its very existence seemed to be challenged and when the conception of loyalty was being increasingly invoked as the acid test of all political and economic pronouncements. The equation of business enterprise and patriotism was not one which was derived for the first time on the occasion of the death of Henry Ford. It appeared at least as early as the time of Commodore Vanderbilt; with the discussion of J. P. Morgan it received a new impetus; and it had been utilized by Ford himself. From 1937 to 1941 he had sought to protect himself against union organization by describing the CIO as "un-American," as a Russian importation; and in November, 1941, when Ford employees in Canada were preparing to elect their bargaining representative, he had asked them to remember that the UAW-CIO was an "American" importation and to vote against that union out of loyalty to the "Canadian way." [10]

The congressmen who lauded Ford's simplicity, emphasized his career of service, and insisted that all he represented was the very essence of that which the country was mobilizing to defend were speaking, of course, to a relatively limited audience. But through the news and editorial columns of the daily press, which deviated hardly at all from the appraisal of the congressmen, the American public was saturated with obituaries which, though they purported to examine Ford's career, subordinated discussion of the man to praise for what he was alleged to symbolize.

"Only America could have produced the kind of man he was," wrote the Grand Rapids *Herald* of Ford:

Only in America could he have revolutionized a civilization and built a powerful empire of such vast extent. For he was both the product and the exponent of the free enterprise system functioning at its best in a democratic atmosphere . . . Mr. Ford's eighty-three years give us a vivid, bright example of the opportunity America offered in his lifetime and still offers to a man with the foresight, the unswerving purpose and the indefatigable energy to grasp it . . . Thus in one man, with his foibles as his wisdom, is summed up the opportunity and the spirit of America.

Other newspapers were equally convinced that the essential clue to an understanding of the entrepreneur's career lay not in his character but in the nature of the time and place in which he had lived. "Henry Ford . . . was distinctly a product of America. In no other land and no other age could just such a career have been enacted and such a personality have flourished," the Atlanta *Journal* stated. "The times were ripe and the country of free enterprise and individual initiative was favorable to talents like his." He was, that newspaper concluded, "one among many in the long tradition of pioneering characters and inventive minds whom America has brought forth and who have made America in turn."

"In some areas of the world Henry Ford would not have been permitted to have carried out his ideas. He would have been refused a permit," one newspaper stated. But in America things were different. "Since this nation's infant days, men have climbed to marvelous heights of success on the ladder of opportunity fashioned by the American system. Like many others, the name of Henry Ford will endure as an eminent example." His was "the story of a Michigan farm boy who went to work at $2.50 a week . . . Henry Ford went on to achievement in after years which gave him world renown and gave to the world more of the benefits which constantly flow from the exercise of courage and genius under the American economic system. Henry Ford's career stands as an illustration of the American way of life at work." Newspaper after newspaper from every corner of the land reiterated the argument of the reciprocal relationship between the man and his environment — the nation had made possible the career, and the career had benefited the nation. "America gave Henry Ford his opportunity . . . Only in a free society can there be a Henry Ford; only in a free society can the productive, imaginative, able person produce for society what his own mind and courage dictate." He was, indeed, "the embodiment and example of the freedom of opportunity and enterprise that is America." [11]

That it was the quality of freedom in the American environment that had produced Henry Ford all newspapers agreed, but the precise nature of that freedom was somewhat obscure. In some analyses it seemed to refer to political institutions; in others, to that particular set of economic relationships which had become known as "free enterprise"; and in still others both concepts of freedom were so merged as to create the impression that they were, indeed, identical. None expressed the mingling of concepts so eloquently nor so clearly revealed its usefulness for the purpose of strengthening the traditional forms of enterprise than did editor William Griffin of the New York *Enquirer*. Ford's

. . . record serves to emphasize, at a crucial period in our country's history, the superiority of the American system of free government and free opportunity, as an instrumentality for the protection of the liberties and rights of the individual and of the masses, and the promotion of their well-being, over every other system known to man in the past or in the present . . . Wealth was not his by inheritance, but genuine Americanism was . . . Because long and toilsome hours did not dismay him, because he was self-reliant and farsighted, and because he was animated by the Americanism which he learned at home and at school, Henry Ford in time conferred upon his countrymen and his country benefits beyond the capacity of human calculation . . . The great American whose death our country now mourns did not receive an expensive education, with the taxpayers footing the bill. He left school when he was 16, not to dodge work and have a good time, but to busy himself as an employe in a Detroit machine shop. Those were the horse-and-buggy days before the philosophy of maximum pay for minimum effort began to wreak such horror in our national life. Henry Ford was a self-reliant individualist. Life in his parental home was American. The education he received was an American education, not the type of instruction so prevalent in our land today, when so many young Americans are the victims of an educational system that destroys patriotism and self-initiative, leads boys and girls to believe that the world owes them a living, and saddles the hard-pressed taxpayers with a burden that is of no benefit to anyone but on the contrary maintains a system which is a national destroyer . . . No country save America could have produced a success story even approaching that of Henry Ford. Ours is the task and the duty of guaranteeing that this land shall not become the victim of the totalitarian philosophies that have enslaved the Old World and are threatening to enslave the New. Henry Ford will live in history as one of America's foremost patriots and one of the greatest benefactors of mankind.

Was it free America which had produced Henry Ford, or was it free enterprise? The newspapers obviated the necessity of making a choice by presenting the two as if they were in fact one. "By utilizing the American system of free enterprise, he started from financial zero and built up during his lifetime the greatest private fortune the world has ever known," The Burlington *Free Press* editorialized. Henry Ford, stated the Charlotte *Observer* in an editorial which equated nation and economic system,

has been the living symbol of everything that we mean by American private enterprise — its initiative, its daring, its urge to achievement, its freedom from hide-bound tradition and taboo, its incomparable rewards in both material and spiritual satisfaction for work well done, and, above all, its opportunity. The superiority of our system over all others was never better exemplified than in the life of this man, who demonstrated that in this land of ours humble birth is no barrier to greatness, that genius can win recognition in a ramshackle garage, that a man's capacity for attainment is limited only by his own short-comings . . . His life was a practical demonstration that the impossible collectivist ideal of equal distribution has been attained least of all in the collectivist countries; the nearest approach to it has been made by American private enterprise.

"With the system of free enterprise we embrace in this country, more" great entrepreneurs "will follow" Ford. But "if ever the time comes when" individual initiative and private enterprise will be lost, then "it will be time for America to close up shop and call it a day." [12]

If that which was responsible for Ford's career was, however expressed, something in the American environment, then surely the career itself, capped as it was with extraordinary success, was American in a special sense.

"Mr. Ford's life story," one paper commented, "tells us that there is no limit in America to what a man can accomplish, and that it is possible to rise to the top and still walk unaffected with one's fellowmen." There could "be no better illustration of the old slogan that 'America is another word for opportunity.'" The success he had achieved was not at all unusual; indeed, "Ford may be rated as a typical American, in that he demonstrated in a monumental way the heights to which American opportunity can lead. In no other land could he have achieved the tremendous results that he did." [13]

Indeed in every aspect of his life, private as well as public, Ford was authentically American. A "man of simple tastes and of peace," he was "quite the antithesis of the Krupps or the Kruegers, his counterparts on the European continent." His qualities of "individualism . . . self-confidence . . . inventiveness, pliability and industry" were not uniquely his own, but those "of America." He was "a great American," and like "great Americans," he had been "simple and human." Americanism permeated his very being. "Like the many-sided Franklin and the versatile Jefferson, Henry Ford was, in accord with one of America's more picturesque traditions, a man of many facets. His active interests ranged from world peace and reforestation to dietary reform and folk dancing."

"There was something very earthy and American about Mr. Ford. His hobbies, expensive though some of them were, were also wholesome and much in the American tradition"; and no one had done as much to keep that tradition alive, for he had been "greatly interested in early American culture and in the perpetuation of the ideals and the virtues that have made America great." His "American saga" had been "many chaptered." His career, of course, was thoroughly in the American tradition. But there was another chapter "for the father — an immigrant out of Ireland"; and above all there was the chapter "for the widow who mourns," whom he had married "59 years ago," and who had been "his helpmate . . . his inspiration. Such long loyalty and constancy — that's American, too!" Surely this was a man who had "built himself into the history" of his country.[14]

On the basis of such evidence, the conclusion reached by the press was logical and appropriate. Henry Ford had been "an inspiration to Americans in this and future generations" and a "symbol of the United States," of "individualistic American drive," of "American productive genius and of America itself." His were "the qualities the nation must more and more appreciate for they" were "the qualities which forged the greatness of this nation, and the qualities which alone will keep it great." [15]

If this was discussion of an entrepreneur, no less was it discussion of the setting in which that entrepreneur had acted and, more precisely, discussion which held setting to be of greater consequence than agent in accounting for the nature of an entrepreneurial career. Never before had interest focused so sharply on entrepreneurial setting rather than entrepreneurial character, and never before had the defenders of business enterprise disclosed such sensitivity to problems relating to the fundamental economic structure of society. Indeed, recognition that they were concerned with such problems and that the real importance of Ford's career lay in the light it shed on the merits of competing economic systems was frankly avowed.

"You political and economic theorists," asked the Portland *Oregonian*, "you proponents of the isms, you critics of the American way of life who believe that democracy is in decay, where are the Fords and the Edisons of your school? Where are your Lincolns? It is more than mere coincidence that the story of Henry Ford, inventor and industrialist, is essentially an American story."

"The rise of Mr. Ford, a one-time obscure farm youth, to the position which he occupied in the industrial world," the Lansing *State Journal* observed, "is one of the most effective lessons the world has ever had in the virtue of the American system of free individual enterprise. At a time when that system is under attack from some quarters it is of the greatest importance that there be reflection upon what an obscure farm youth was able to accomplish with the opportunities which were open to him under a system which made it possible for him to use his individual ideas . . . Had he operated under a system which did not permit freedom of individual enterprise he might have remained in obscurity." If "freedom of individual enterprise" was the basic element of the system which had produced Ford, and if that system was characteristically American, then those who advocated alterations in it were not only guilty of tampering with the material prosperity of the nation but of injecting "alien poisons" into the American environment. Those who called for the "replacement" of this system "by more and more government control, through such alien governmental forms as communism"; the "cheap political demagogues" and the "communist infested CIO local union" which controlled his plant; "the collectivists and the left of center planners"; "the Judas fringe of the left"; the advocates of the "alien economic and political sophisms that, having failed to create, would attempt by force, casuistry and deceit to pervert our democratic processes to their own gain" — only such persons as these could be found among the opponents of Ford, the press argued, because, by definition, only advocates of alien ideologies could oppose him. Ford had succeeded because he was "untouched by the precocity of decadent foreign doctrines" and because he was "the personification of strong Americanism." "If there is a defense for a free economy, nothing speaks louder than the deeds of Henry Ford." In this lay his triumph and significance, that the "whole career of Henry Ford presents a glamorous testimonial for the American system . . . The achievements of the elder Ford will intrigue young Americans so long as our free enterprise system endures." [16]

If Henry Ford's career was a testimonial to the environment which had shaped it, it was, in another sense, a testimonial to business enterprise itself; for, so at least the newspapers argued, service to humanity was the real product of the Ford factories as it was of all industry. Nor, indeed, could it be otherwise; for mass production, with which Ford was so closely identified, was, in the view of the press, to be considered less a technological aspect of the process of manufacture than an instrumentality for the elevation of standards of living. The fundamental result of mass production was to "put the motor car within the reach of the common people," to give "the lesser man not only an instrument for a freer, wider life, but . . . the purchasing power to enjoy the better things of living," to lighten "men's labor, improve their efficiency, their wages and their living standards." Appraised in terms of the results wrought by his work — "increased national wealth, convenience in travel, progress in the making and distribution of useful articles of commerce, rational philanthropy, and patriotism" — there could be no dissent from the double verdict that Ford's "enterprises enriched his country and the world at large in spiritual and cultural as well as in material ways" and that "not mass production alone" but "mass service to all was the sparkplug that made the Ford ideal click." [17]

"He conceived that his own prosperity lay in that of others," wrote the Detroit *News*. "To place in the reach of the greatest number of people a useful product which would lift the whole level of living was, therefore, a purpose to which he committed a boundless originality and inexhaustible energy." That he had succeeded in his purpose was abundantly evident in every aspect of American life. "He released his countrymen and people everywhere from the older restrictions of locality . . . With the new freedom of movement and thinking came a new, more commodious freshness of the spirit." His "initiative and daring raised directly and indirectly the wages of millions and his mass-production methods . . . lifted living standards, comforts and conveniences to a new 'high.'" He increased the strength and prosperity of the nation. His "genius meant the making of jobs in a big industry and the building of a business which directly and indirectly contributed tremendous pay rolls of employment as well as taxes to the American economic system." His automobiles "probably accomplished more than any other agency in the past hundred years in increasing unity between city and country," for they "brought within easy range of rural families markets and recreational and cultural advantages." [18]

"Although Henry Ford showed no sentimentalism in business," the *Arkansas Gazette* concluded approvingly, "his policies were humanitarian in their results, as well as practical." He had raised the "living standard of the common people of America" — his achievement gave him "a sort of immortality," the immortality "that is reserved for those who dream and toil for humanity's sake."

In that conclusion the Negro newspaper, the Chicago *Defender*, concurred. Ford had been "an industrial genius at the service of society." But other Negro newspapers exhibited greater interest in more concrete demonstrations of the automobile manufacturer's humanity. He had befriended the noted Negro scientist, George Washington Carver, and his "high wages and revolutionary assembly line production" acted as a powerful magnet to draw Negro migrants from the "farm-bound South." Above all he had not refused to hire Negroes in his factories. "There would be no need for an FEPC if all employers took a page from the

Ford book. In his passing, we have lost a real friend," mourned the *Afro-American*. This was high praise indeed for Henry Ford, but it was not praise from which enterprise in general could derive much satisfaction; for the Negro press applauded Ford not because he typified standard business practice but because, in their view, he had departed from it.

So far as Ford himself was concerned, however, editorial opinion was virtually unanimous in holding not only that the consequences of his acts were of widespread public benefit, but that consideration of public service was the compelling motive which dictated his acts and decisions. One of the cardinal principles of classical economics was, of course, the compatibility of private striving and public welfare, but the two had been linked in such a way as to make the latter dependent on the former. In the economic theory of the newspaper editors, however, there was no place for explicit avowal of private striving. Service had replaced profit as a basic category of entrepreneurial motivation. "The acquisition of a personal fortune counted for little with Henry Ford," wrote the Galveston *Daily News*. "He was not by nature a money-maker." On the contrary, his "mind was dominated by constructive motives, the desire to invent and to invent in such a way as to lessen human labor." The very ideas which made of Ford "one of the greatest benefactors of his day" stemmed from "his love for his fellows with whose struggles he sympathized and for whose betterment he worked, his own wealth being incidental to his performance." That this was so the Ford Motor Company itself revealed. "The impression has somehow gotten abroad that Henry Ford is in the automobile business," the Company had said. "It isn't true. Mr. Ford shoots about fifteen hundred cars out of the back door of his factory every day just to get rid of them. They are the byproducts of his real business, which is the making of men . . . Mr. Ford's business is the making of men, and he manufactures automobiles on the side to defray the expenses of his main business." [19]

Indeed, the money Ford had made was really a reward both for the risks he undertook and the benefits he conferred. "He and those who lent him money took all the risks of possible, even probable, failure," the New York *Daily Mirror* stated. His "vast personal fortune" was a "reward for the billions upon billions that have been made for those who have been associated with him, either as management or labor, or connected with other concerns that have profited by his production methods; and for his contribution to the happiness of the so-called 'common man.'" But in either case, whether construed as reward for risk or as reward for service, his fortune was only "a by-product," "only incidental," merely "nominal," and considerably less than the value of his "services to . . . country and to mankind." Not "by exploitation of labor and financial finagling" had he made his fortune, but by concerning himself with "the general welfare of his country and of the world." There was, in this example of the relationship of private wealth and public service, a profound lesson in political economy:

It is individuals who have big ideas, not nations . . . It is individuals who have the drive, the patience, the persistence, to put big ideas into effect, not nations . . . If, in the process, the individual acquires a great fortune and great power, that is not necessarily worse than the acquisition of greater resources and power through the domination of government. It can be better, and often is, because government is still left to help keep the individual from getting too far offside, whereas the man who dominates a government is often beyond anyone's reach.[20]

Not even the high eminence which Ford had attained, however, placed him "beyond anyone's reach," and the fact that — as most of the press agreed — he had begun the climb to that eminence from a position no higher than that occupied by most men served less to emphasize his exceptional qualities than to place him squarely amidst the general body of his fellow men. A few newspapers, to be sure, felt that Ford's climb up the ladder of success had begun at a rung somewhere higher than at the bottom. His father, said the Chicago *Journal of Commerce*, had been "well-to-do," and the Detroit *Free Press* was even more favorably impressed with his father's economic status: "At the time of Henry's birth, his father had prospered until he held 240 acres of land. He was a progressive man. He owned and operated the latest and best of farm machinery of that day." But most editors chose not to quibble over the exact elevation at which Ford had begun his climb; the fact of his ascent and the eminence which he ultimately attained were the matters to be emphasized. "The saga of Henry Ford's rise from farm boy to the world's richest man, head of a billion-dollar company," said the New York *Daily News,* reverting to a time-honored theme, "reads like one of the novels of Horatio Alger who was one of Ford's favorite authors." His was a "life story more strange and wonderful than any spinner of tales ever dared put into words. Even the bare details . . . still seem incredible. If they had not happened before our very eyes we could not believe in the farm boy turned mechanic, inventor, racing car driver, motor manufacturer, head of one of the greatest industrial empires in the world. Yet it is all true." He "was the King Midas of all time," compared to whom "Croesus . . . was a piker"; but he had started the trek which led to such wealth "as a $2.50 a week mechanic." In this, as in all else, Ford's career was "traditionally American," for it was the "realization of the American dream" and he had written still another chapter in the history of a "country famed for its astounding episodes of the 'rags to riches' variety." [21]

In all of his undertakings, concluded the editor of the New York *Enquirer,* "Ford was a big business man with a big heart, a big understanding and sympathy with his fellow man, a big regard for the rights and advancement of his employes, a big eagerness to serve the masses, a big contempt for the detractors of the American way of life, a big faith in America and a big confidence in her future." But though he was big in the things that required bigness, the press argued, he was no different from his countrymen in those areas of life in which true qualities of humanity were likely to manifest themselves.

"With all of his vast wealth and his world wide prestige," said the Atlanta *Journal,* "Mr. Ford remained the simplest of men, a good neighbor, a loved companion to those who knew him, with never a tinge of ostentation . . ." "Mr. Ford was a good man and his tastes, regardless of his ability to have anything money could buy, remained modest." He loved automobile and boat racing, skating, and baseball. "Henry Ford's identity with sports was more than sufficient to humanize him," said the Detroit *News.* To the very end of his life he remained "a family man," with "strong family loyalties," and he "often said, in his latter years, that his chief aim in life was to provide happiness for his wife." But his family was not the only recipient of his kindness. "Henry Ford was the kind of man who was so worried about the chance of accident in the 1936 500-mile Speedway race that he insured all drivers and mechanics," the Indianapolis *Star* revealed. This was a demonstration, "in a practical way," of his advocacy of the Golden Rule; "he believed in it, he preached it — and within limits — he practiced it." He was, in short, "a down-to-earth human being," "a humble, God-fearing, eminently respectable and wholesome citizen." [22]

To these qualities of plainness and humanity, James Kilgallen, a columnist of the Hearst newspapers, devoted his attention:

One of the greatest things about Henry Ford was his simplicity. He was a plain, easy-to know man, the kind you'd run into if you suddenly dropped into the village barbershop. True, he was a multi-millionaire but he never talked to you in dollars and cents. In fact, he often traveled around without a dime in his pocket. There was no pretense about him, nothing of the "phony," no consciousness of the fact that he was a man of note whom many regarded with awe.

In Ford's personality, Kilgallen concluded, all facets of the American character were revealed and in him each American could find something of himself. "To me, Henry Ford was like . . . Tom Dewey, Jim Farley, Peggy Hopkins Joyce, Eddie Rickenbacker, 'Peaches' Browning and others who were sure-fire Page 1 copy . . . He was just plain Henry Ford. In a word, he was democratic." Reporter Robert J. Casey captured still another aspect of the man's character. The people of Detroit, he said, "spoke of his affection for children and linked him with legends like that of St. Francis and the birds." In the face of such evidence, could anyone deny that "he was fundamentally a man of the people?" [23]

But the riches which Ford had attained were more than those of the monetary variety. He had accumulated, as well, a great store of experience and wisdom. "It wasn't mechanical ability alone" that characterized him; his "other impelling and powerful" characteristics — "faith" in himself, "his distinguishing quality of intellect," his "hard, common sense," "his disposition to set impossible objectives and then achieve them," his "fierce individualism" — were applied with distinction in non-business as well as in business activities. His was a career, therefore, "that had many facets. He was an ardent pacifist, a prohibitionist, deeply interested in sociology and in the development of agriculture as an adjunct to industry." He was "a humanitarian"; he "developed antiquarian interests" and was "a patron of American folkways"; and, "something of a philosopher," his thought was that of "a shrewd, kindly sage." If "as an individual" he exhibited "all sorts of misjudgments and prejudices," they were simply those which "he shared with the rest of us"; and besides, "if he exposed himself to ridicule by some of the convictions he expressed and the causes he espoused, more often than not his critics came to agree that he had been right." [24] Nowhere was this better illustrated than in the field of science. Once he had told a reporter:

I believe that the smallest particle of matter — call it an atom or an ion or what you like — is intelligent. I don't know much about atoms and the like, but I feel sure that they know what they are doing — and why. They swarm all around us. If a man is working his level best to do what he believes is right, these invisible elements pitch in and help him. If he is doing what he knows is wrong, they will work just as hard against him.

And the critics scoffed. But "today," wrote the Detroit *News*, "scientists are coming close to Henry Ford's concept in their belief that inherent spirituality is a basic function of all matter."

Since Ford remained a man of the people despite the towering heights he had attained, he was, in the view of the press, eminently qualified to impart to his countrymen the wisdom which had served him so successfully. In presenting Ford's views to the public the press was offering more than simply an interior view of the man; it was also, in effect, advising its readers that the policies which the automobile manufacturer had found serviceable in coping with problems were in the public domain and would be of equal utility to all. The practice of presenting Ford's views to the public was hardly new. For years journalists had quoted Ford's opinions on all manner of problems, and as early as 1923 a booklet had been published containing 365 — one for each day of the year — of the auto maker's aphorisms.[25] What was new was the content of the aphorisms which the press chose to print on the occasion of Ford's death. There was available in the public record a body of statements by Ford on almost every conceivable subject:

I cannot conceive how we tolerate hunger and poverty when they grow solely out of bad management.

It is not necessary for people to love one another in order to work together. In a factory the sole object of everybody should be to get the work done and get paid for it.

It is pretty well understood that a man in the Ford plant works.

Wars are manufactured by war campaigns along definite lines. First the people are worked upon, their suspicions are aroused. All you need are a few agents with some cleverness and no conscience working through a press whose interests are bound up with those who benefit by war. Then the "overt act" will soon appear.

The paramount right is the right to work.[26]

It's a good thing the recovery is prolonged. Otherwise the people wouldn't profit by the idleness.[27]

The nations of Europe could come together more easily if it were not for their capitalistic governments.

A certain stream of nasty Orientalism has been observed in this country to be affecting our literature, our amusements, our social conduct and our business standards. It is traceable to one racial source. Whether this impress is to be changed or not is wholly in the hands of the Jews themselves.[28]

The cow must go.[29]

Successful persons often say that opportunities are just as plentiful as they ever were, but they don't tell you what they are, where to find them, or how to use them . . . They deal in glittering generalities that mean nothing.[30]

Maxims such as these were not, however, those which were quoted by the press at the time of Ford's death. Rather did the press select from the general body of available material those aphorisms which conformed more closely to the image of Ford it had chosen to present:

Competition is the great teacher.

It is all one to me if a man comes from Sing Sing or Harvard. We hire a man, not his history.

I am in business not to make money as money, but to do many things which I believe are of public benefit.

I have tried to live as my mother would have wanted me to.

History as sometimes written is mostly bunk. But history that you can see is of great value.

I am not interested in money but in the things of which money is merely a symbol.

The only right use for money is to capitalize industry. One might give it away but giving it away doesn't do any good.

Gold is the most useless of all things.

Profits are a public trust.

Endowment is an opiate to imagination, a drug to initiative . . . One of the greatest curses of the country today is the habit of endowing this and endowing that.[31]

It was to this Henry Ford whom the nation's leaders from every area of activity joined to pay tribute in an unprecedented display of mourning. "He typified the best in American enterprise . . . He contributed directly and by example to our high living standards," said Alfred P. Sloan, chairman of the board of the General Motors Corporation. "A great man and a wonderful example of American civilization and opportunity," proclaimed Mayor Edward Kelly of Chicago. "He was a genius in many respects and an example of what continuous and hard work may do for ambitious Americans." To his friend Harvey S. Firestone, Ford "exemplified the virtues of hard work, vision and service which made this country great, and sought to preserve these virtues through his philanthropy so that the human, simple, pioneering spirit of America might be perpetuated." Ford's former associate William S. Knudsen expressed the verdict and the wish of all: "He will be remembered forever . . . for the things he has done and the beautiful example of his personal life. May God bless him and give him the reward he has so richly earned." [32]

But more than the great and the near-great exhibited their sorrow at Ford's death. It was, the Detroit *Free Press* suggested, entirely appropriate that the funeral of the man to whom "service was the watchword, profits . . . a byproduct," the man who "took the burdens off the backs of men and made the machine the slave of man," should not be a private service but a vast public display of appreciation and affection. The members of the Michigan legislature paused "in commemoration of the passing of a great man"; Governor Kim Sigler ordered all flags on state buildings to fly at half-staff until the funeral; the Detroit common council "directed that a large portrait of Ford, draped in mourning colors, be displayed on the front of the city hall for thirty days, and that mourning posters be displayed on buses"; the mayor of Dearborn proclaimed thirty days of official mourning; all Ford plants were ordered to shut down on the day of the funeral and in all automobile plants in Michigan preparations were made to stop fast-moving assembly lines for one minute of mourning; Ford dealers throughout the nation closed their establishments the afternoon of April 10; and all automobile traffic in the city of Detroit was observed to come to a complete halt as Ford's body was lowered into the grave. George W. Mason, president of the Automobile Manufacturers Association, said that "about seven million workers probably would take part in the demonstration of sympathy." [33]

For two full days before the funeral, countless numbers of persons — thirty thousand, according to the Montgomery *Advertiser;* seventy-five thousand, according to the New York *Times;* one hundred thousand, according to the Louisville *Times* — filed past Ford's bier. What mattered was not the number of those who came to pay him tribute — in any case that was large — but the social groups from which they came. "Factory workers and business men rub shoulders in a silent procession," said a reporter at the scene, because with Ford "both groups had something in common." So, indeed, did all mankind — the corporation executive who saw in Ford the model of successful enterprise, the worker and the farmer who saw in him the model of aspiration and benevolence, even the "bridal couples" who would "miss his smile" and the sad old lady, Miss Mae Tabor, his schoolmate, who "was heard to whisper, 'Good-by, Henry. You were such a good boy.'" It was for all of these that Dean Kirk B. O'Ferrall spoke as he laid Henry Ford's body down to its final rest: "I speak to you of Mr. Ford's simple personal tastes and habits and his humility; his devotion to his home and his belief in everlasting life. I doubt whether any man of great wealth ever gave more away without the knowledge of the world and his fellows generally." [34]

Rarely before had the nation's daily press so nearly approached unanimity in its evaluation of the work and character of an entrepreneur. Occasionally, of course, evidence was presented which did not quite conform to the almost universally presented description of the man. For the editorial writers of the Detroit *Free Press,* Ford "never lost the kindly touch of genuine friendship. He found joy in mixing among his fellows and would spend a day with some mechanic who did not accept him in awe, but respected him as a fellow mechanic." That conclusion stood, although reporters of the *Free Press,* interviewing long-time employees of the Ford Motor Company, found one mechanic with thirty-two years of service who could not "recall ever speaking to Mr. Ford"; and another with thirty-one years of service who "told how Mr. Ford used to walk through the Highland Park plant, watch carefully the work of the men at their machines and then pass on without speaking." The same newspaper revealed that George W. Frazier, patternmaker of the first Ford car, who was buried only two days after Henry Ford, had been deprived of his pass permitting him access to Ford property fifteen years earlier, and never "thought of asking for another, although he often wanted to renew friendship with Mr. Ford. He simply stopped going."

Significantly, even the few organs among the daily press which looked askance at Ford confined their remarks largely to his nonbusiness activities. For columnist Kenesaw Mountain Landis II of the Chicago *Sun,* "Ford democratized the automobile, distributed undreamed wealth to the nation and built the greatest private empire in the world"; and for that he deserved credit and appreciation. It was "his opinions . . . in matters of philosophy, history, sociology and morals" that earned him ridicule. Max Lerner, writing in the newspaper *PM,* drew a sharp distinction between "Ford's racist and reactionary views" and "his achievements as a technician and an industrialist." As to the latter, "mass-production, standardization, high-speed belt-line, high wages, large volume" were his accomplishments. As to the former, "his mind" was "a jungle of fear and ignorance and prejudice in social affairs." "Henry Ford is dead but the stew of hate churned by his long-defunct newspaper the Dearborn *Independent* still fouls up the atmosphere," that newspaper commented. "Only last week, the Council Against Intolerance in America received a letter from a Ford Motor Co. official, regretting that the *International Jew* was in circulation again, under the sponsorship of Gerald L. K. Smith." The conclusion of the *New Republic* was cut from the same pattern: "The mechanical genius which could conceive the Ford assembly line could never quite figure out that a man's dignity is not measured with calipers." The *Christian Century* felt that what had made Ford "one of the most appealing figures in the America of his time" was "the simplicity of his public character and way of life . . . his venturesome adoption of the principles of high wages and low prices, his interest in the social rehabilitation of men who served prison terms . . . his encouragement of technical education for boys." But "he did not understand . . . much of the world," became "involved in blunders and senseless tyrannies and even outright injustices," and because of "the power which his enormous wealth gave him" became surrounded by "men with warped or reactionary purposes who studied how to use him for their own ends."

With the commercial press approximating virtual unanimity in its reaction to Ford, ideas that differed sharply from the portrait it presented — including opposition to his business activities, dissent from the laudatory accounts of his personal character and nonbusiness activities, and denial that all Americans felt a sense of loss at Ford's death — became restricted largely to those newspapers representing political groups which openly expressed their hostility to capitalism and to that decreasing number of trade union papers which still remained under the influence of anticapitalist thought.

Missing from the columns of the Communist *Daily People's World* were the usual pictures of Ford giving slices of his birthday cake to children in Dearborn, or relaxing around a campfire with his friends Thomas A. Edison and Harvey Firestone, or standing at the side of his wife and smiling shyly at the first Ford car. Instead, that newspaper decorated its obituary of "The Paragon of Free Enterprise" with a picture of Ford receiving the Grand Cross of the German Eagle from German consuls Earl Kapp and Fritz Heiler at Detroit in 1938 on his seventy-fifth birthday. "Ford was a philosopher all right," said the *People's World.* "But his philosophy was hardly original. It was written down in Hitler's Mein Kampf. Ford was a bigoted and active anti-Semite. He was an early admirer of Nazism. He financed almost every fascist movement in America." As to the vaunted efficiency of his assembly line, "thousands of workers were consumed by its relentless speed-up, used up in their youth and dumped on the scrapheap of humanity." This was no servant of mankind; "to the people of Detroit, Dearborn, and Highland Park, who built his empire, the Ford name meant police terror, anti-labor activity, anti-Semitism, discrimination against Negroes, and reaction in politics." Nor, indeed, could it have meant anything else, for Ford in reality was but "a symbol . . . of the American economic royalist who makes the vaunted 'free enterprise' system an instrument of social and political domination." Writers of the *New Masses,* applying similar criteria of evaluation, stressed aspects of Ford's career which were held to be inevitable consequences of the system which produced him. For them, the memorable events — and the ones on which ultimate appraisals should be based — were those associated with the shooting of four demonstrators at the "Ford Hunger March" of 1932; the beating of union organizers in Dearborn in 1937; the conclusion of National Labor Relations Board Trial Examiner Robert N. Denham that members of the Ford Service Department were "most brutal, vicious and conscienceless thugs"; the hectic pace of the assembly line, geared "to get the maximum work and profit out of each individual"; the "good money" Ford made "out of both world wars . . . despite his professed pacifism"; "Ford's anti-Jewish prejudice"; and "the Hitler medal" he had been awarded. Had such a man won for himself a place in the hearts of his countrymen? "Henry Ford could never buy from his workers and the people the affection and loyalty the union commands."

"The newspapers and his paid sycophants are singing weird tales about this two billion dollar tycoon and his spendings on 'charity,'" the Chicago *Fighting Worker* asserted. "Everything is done to gloss over the fact that Henry Ford was merely another capitalist brigand, who made his fortune out of the sweat of Ford workers' brows." Why had not the daily press discussed his "anti-labor gangsters, private detectives and . . . involved system of spying on labor"; his "notorious anti-Semitism" and "support of Fascism"; his "brutal speed-up"? "Judge Capitalism by Its No. 1 Hero!" adjured the *Weekly People*. Such activities were manifestations of a disease rooted in the structure of society, not in the individual, and the remedy must be equally comprehensive. "The working class . . . will remember Henry Ford and vow to end the system that can give rise to such people," provided only that they "awaken and organize their economic powers."

Expressing their ideas in language less acid than that of the radical political parties, a few trade union newspapers — some still influenced by radical thought, others simply reflecting opinion in the plant — evaluated Ford in such a way as to indicate that less than universal approbation existed at the lower levels of the social structure. "Under the veil of decent regard for the dead," said the Federated Press news service, "there was little mourning for the individualistic anti-union auto maker in the Detroit area. At UAW-CIO headquarters the privately expressed sentiment harked back to the long years when Ford stamped out or tried to stamp out unionism with thugs and goons under his crony Harry Bennett. In barbershops envy and resentment overtopped expressions of esteem." Had Detroit automobile traffic really stopped — as the daily press had said — at 2:30 P.M. on the day of the funeral? "No motorists in Detroit's central district were observed to do so, except out of respect for red lights." And did the shutting down of automobile assembly lines throughout Michigan really prove the existence of warm sympathy and respect for Ford? Writing in the *Dodge Main News,* official organ of Dodge Local 3, UAW-CIO, shopworker Frank Stawski, correspondent of the Body Unit section, observed: "I was asked to put this item in the unit column. There was a pause for Henry Ford, yet on Good Friday we did not pause. God commandeth his love toward us, in that, while we were yet sinners, Christ died for us." For the daily press, consideration of Henry Ford's career had led to the conclusion that free enterprise must be maintained; but Frank Stawski, reflecting on Ford's career and focusing his attention upon speed-up and layoffs, concluded: "That is one of the main reasons why we must have a union, to protect our jobs." The "Shop News and Views" editor of the UAW-CIO *Local 599 Headlight,* newspaper of the Buick shopworkers in Flint, Michigan, cast doubt, indeed, on the degree to which even automobile industry management felt sorrow at the death of Ford.

The tribute paid to Old Henry, the King of all auto tycoons, was meant to be a publicity gag . . . The public probably thinks that dear old G.M.

[rivals for market] are not deadly enemies when it comes to respect for each other. Thursday, after we went to work, they placed the notice [to stop work for one minute at 2:30 P.M.] on the bulletin boards not at 6:00 A.M., on the time clocks. Nor at any time did our Bosses ask us to pause at 2:30 P.M. Also no whistle was blown. I point this incident out to you, not that Henry was kind to labor, but to the fact that this man did more to promote mass production which G.M. copied. Their tribute was a farce. Just a publicity gag of the lowest type . . . More than likely if we had paused, we would have been slapped around with a reprimand . . . I would be ashamed to print what some of our supervision said when asked why we did not pause . . . Just a lot of hot wind looking for a place to cool its heels.

And was the closing down of Ford plants throughout the country on the day of the funeral to be considered as a day of mourning — as the daily press termed it — or as a "compulsory workless day"?

"We urge you to correct this gross blunder," said the Reverend Donald Harrington, minister of New York's Community Church and national chairman of the Workers Defense League, in a telegram to Henry Ford II. "Depriving your employes of pay for the day's mourning for your grandfather does not constitute a memorial to him which you would want your workers to remember." [35]

Exactly what Ford workers would remember about their employer no one could state with certainty, but that in all probability it would not be identical with that which the daily press felt to be memorable was made clear by the editorial which appeared in the Ford workers' own newspaper, *Ford Facts:*

Henry Ford placed his reliance primarily on individuals like himself rather than on government or social action. As the foremost exponent of assembly line mass production, he revolutionized industry and with it society. Thus he did as much as any man to bring into being a world in which his own intense individualism no longer provided an adequate answer to the burning problems of either society or the individual . . . Ford's individualism brought into being its opposite — the need of collective action and thinking, of cooperation on a far-reaching scale . . . The world which he leaves behind calls for new qualities and new values.

Like the daily press, the newspaper of Ford's employees gave credit to the man for his industrial innovations. But from the conclusion that those accomplishments testified to the need for maintaining what the press called "individualism" it sharply dissented; and in that dissent lay the hint of an alternative morality and economy.

But not all, even of the labor newspapers, discussed Ford's accomplishments in the light of alternative economic systems. For the most part they applied to the appraisal of Ford criteria similar to those used by the daily press, and from similar criteria emerged similar conclusions.

"Neither the saga of American industrial progress nor our rise to hitherto unknown standards of living and comfort can be understood without Henry Ford. In his own, admittedly individualistic way he did more to promote the workers' welfare than a great many men who pride themselves on their sympathies for labor," the *International Molders' Journal* said. Speed-up, opposition to unions, anti-Semitism — discussion of such issues was no more prominent in this sector of the labor press than it was in the daily press. Weighed against "the great benefits that have accrued . . . through his genius and energy," his "personal eccentricities" were as nothing. That his method of "assembly line production . . . revolutionized the nation"; that he had "held each worker is entitled to a living wage"; that his triumph was a demonstration that "democracy, being the right way of life, can recruit its leaders at the grass roots" — these were the important conclusions to be derived from a study of Ford's life.[36]

In praise of Ford both labor leaders and antilabor spokesmen united, and the common ground of their admiration for him was broad enough to support mutually exclusive reasons for approbation. The officers of the Michigan State CIO Council, for example, applauded Ford for the fact that he "was one of the first industrialists to recognize the CIO as an organization here to stay by accepting collective bargaining." [37] But one southern newspaper, the Augusta *Chronicle,* praised him because, the "essence of rugged individualism, he remained to the last an economic and political conservative and never became reconciled to trade unions even after recognizing them . . . If there is a defense for a free economy, nothing speaks louder than the deeds of Henry Ford." Both, no doubt, would have agreed with the statement of the Buffalo *Catholic Labor Observer* that "the death of Henry Ford focuses the attention of world industry and world labor on America's success in the field of mass production. Nowhere else are so many useful products of the teamwork of labor and management so available to so large a number of well-paid men and women" — for in that statement was recognition and approval of a mutuality of interest between "labor and management." To the degree that that mutuality of interest was affirmed by leaders of the labor movement — and certainly such statements were elicited to a greater extent by discussion of Henry Ford than of any other American entrepreneur — the leaders of business enterprise were assured that they would continue to function in a climate of security.

The journals of industry, of course, spared few adjectives in their portrayal of Ford as a "Courageous, far-seeing pioneer — Giant of Industry — Genius of Production — Master Craftsman in many fields — Humanitarian — A man whose life story is written in the minds of all people, whose life work benefited all mankind." To be sure, such journals felt, to a greater degree than was the case with the daily press, that while Ford "had an uncanny knack for doing the right thing and saying the right thing when it came to building motor cars," he had "a similar uncanny knack for doing just the opposite when it came to public utterances and activities in world affairs." Even that, however, had its advantages: "In the long run his own embarrassment probably was counterbalanced by the valuable publicity accruing to the company." But regarding his accomplishments in industry, his influence on society, and his contributions to human welfare, there could be no doubt. Certainly his services "cannot and should not be forgotten until time has erased the last remnants of western civilization."

"Thorough and untiring in his methods," vividly imaginative in the generation of ideas and forceful in their application, he succeeded in manufacturing a product "within the reach of everyone"; if that was "good business policy" which resulted in "a tremendous fortune" for him, it was also "a very unselfish attitude" which "promoted the welfare of mankind." No wonder then, that "workmen in overalls and fashionably dressed business executives" alike respected and loved him. They loved him because he had served them and because his life was an exemplification not only of "the creativeness of mind and the energy of our nation," but of "those enduring qualities and the high purpose . . . the simplicity and vigor" which represent "America in its finest tradition." He was, in this sense, a product of his country, but he had been one of its creators as well: "Henry Ford's favorite philosopher, Ralph Waldo Emerson, has said that great institutions are but the elongated shadow of a man. If this is true in any case it was true in the case of Ford." [38]

The magazines of public opinion agreed with the organs of industry. Through watching Ford, claimed *Time*, "two generations" of persons the world over "caught a glimpse — however distorted — of U.S. capitalism's great adventure." And great indeed had that adventure been. "The real Industrial Revolution of our day — the one which Henry Ford led and symbolized — was not a technological one, was not based on this or that machine, this or that technique, but on the hierarchical co-ordination of human efforts which mass production realizes in its purest form." Economist Peter Drucker gave Ford full credit for unsurpassed "success in technology and economics," but felt that he had failed "to solve the problems of the new industrial system." If the relatively few readers of *Harper's Magazine* were given the impression that in that sense at least Ford's life had been a failure, the millions of readers of *Life* were given no reason to qualify their approval. "The philosopher's case against Ford," that magazine asserted testily, "is that he . . . cast up economic and social problems for which he could discover no acceptable solution. But why expect him to? His apologia, if one is required, is the American standard of living, the power of machines that made it possible for this nation in two world wars to escape the frightful human toll of the war of hordes. The rest is up to the philosophers."

Other magazines, less modest, donned the philosopher's garb which *Life* had forsworn and inquired into the real meaning of Ford's life.

"Henry Ford was as American as Pike's Peak," wrote Ira E. Bennett in the *National Republic:*

It was only in a giant land of free men that he could have developed himself and his work . . . The USA offered opportunity to a free man to develop the gifts which God bestowed upon him. The result was an astounding phenomenon of production on a continental scale, and that application of revolutionary processes that have spread benefits to all mankind, including the enemies who would destroy such free enterprise . . . Any Russian, Communist or otherwise, who should try to follow the path blazed by Henry Ford would be slaughtered as soon as the NKVD could amass the damning evidence of his individualism . . . When the New Deal was in its poisonous heyday Henry Ford refused to comply with its impudent demands. He detected the inherent baseness and un-Americanism of the NRA and its defeatist "blue eagle" of industrial servitude to bureaucracy . . . He could have been a billionaire thrice over if he had been eager to make money. But he did not crave wealth. He used money as a tool or necessary adjunct of operations . . . A free country enabled him to acquire this money-tool . . . No greedy state-tyranny snatched away in taxes the money that freely flowed toward Henry Ford in payment for his enterprise . . . He saw the dangers of communism in 1917 . . . Until his last breath he resisted the encroachments of communism in whatever guise it assumed . . . Is it true that the US is now committed to a tax policy that will forever destroy the possibility of developing private enterprise on a scale like Henry Ford's achievement? Is it possible that a new theory of government is killing individual enterprise by preventing it from accumulating and using capital as a tool of industry? Some observers think so . . . The conflict between Americanism and communism sharpens the point of the argument in favor of individual freedom, including freedom to use money for industrial development. Let the showdown come — the sooner the better.[39]

In identifying Henry Ford with the "free enterprise system," in identifying "free enterprise" with Americanism, and in regarding Ford's career as proof of the superiority of that system over all others, the *National Republic* was simply stating what the vast majority of the written media of public opinion had already in large measure affirmed. Not only Ford himself, but the economic system of which he was held to be the proudest product, was granted the high sanction of patriotism. More powerful support the press could hardly have offered; and it was as if in recognition of this that *Ford Times* — official house organ of the Ford Motor Company — felt no apparent need to make an original contribution to the discussion, as the Standard Oil Company had done when Rockefeller had died, but instead contented itself with quoting what others — political figures, industrialists, labor leaders, and the press — had said. The image that the Company wished the American people to have of Ford was embodied in the poem declaimed by Edgar A. Guest on the Columbia Broadcasting System during the Ford Hour:

> Not many came to earth so wise,
>> So tender and so true
> To show what faith and enterprise
>> And willing hands could do.
> Who proved how great a man can be,
>> And gave so much to us,
> Now Lord, we give him back to Thee
>> A soul victorious.

Not always had such pleasant verse been composed about Henry Ford. An amateur poet writing in the *United Auto Worker* had once expressed his feelings regarding Ford and the Ford Sunday Evening Hour in phrases considerably more pungent, if no more complex, than those of Edgar Guest:

> Now the music dies out in the distance,
> They announce a lovely old hymn,
> Giving all glory to God
> And singing their praises to him.
>
> But I wonder if those up in heaven
> Ever look down from above
> And see guns, tear-gas and night-sticks,
> A symbol of Ford's brand of love.
>
> Do you think, Henry Ford, you exploiter,
> You can buy with this kind of stuff
> The thanks and goodwill of thousands
> Who haven't nearly enough?
>
> So you might as well keep your music
> And shut old Cameron's yap,
> For while we enjoy your music
> We haven't time for your crap.
>
> So we'll stick to the union forever,
> Yes, forever and a day,
> Till the power of Ford has vanished
> And the workers have gained a new day.[40]

Clearly such an estimate rested upon quite different criteria — both of Ford and of business enterprise — than those used by Edgar Guest.

Only a decade and a half before Ford's death, the author of one of the country's most highly acclaimed novels — applying criteria which he considered relevant to the circumstances of the times — concluded:

> Henry Ford as an old man
> is a passionate antiquarian,
>   (lives besieged on his father's farm embedded in an estate of thousands of millionaire acres, protected by an army of servicemen, secretaries, secret agents, dicks under orders of an English exprizefighter,
>   always afraid of the feet in broken shoes on the roads, afraid the gangs will kidnap his grandchildren,
> that a crank will shoot him,
> that Change and the idle hands out of work will break through the gates and the high fences;
> protected by a private army against
> the new America of starved children and hollow bellies and cracked shoes stamping on souplines,
> that has swallowed up the old thrifty farmlands
> of Wayne County, Michigan,
> as if they had never been).[41]

But the passing of even so short a span as fifteen years gave rise to new problems, softened former appraisals, and — with both — created the possibility of rephrasing the discussion of the entrepreneur in terms which had greater relevance to the needs of the period. Certainly the American press was virtually unanimous in presenting Ford in such a way as to elicit the widest possible approval both for himself and for the economic system which he was held to represent. The methods by which this was accomplished consisted largely of a series of statements which tended to identify both Ford and that economic system with service to the needs of the people and with those cultural values which were the objects of deepest loyalty and affection and which were held to be in gravest danger.

So far as Ford himself was concerned, discussion of his role as a businessman was hardly more important than discussion of the nonbusiness phases of his life. That he had had an amazingly successful business career, that this success had been based on the combination of personal abilities and a society which rewarded possession of such abilities, and that his business activities — while profitable to himself — were important primarily because of the effect they had in raising the standard of living — all of this was, of course, emphatically affirmed. But no less emphasized was the fact that Ford was more than a businessman. He had been patriot, sportsman, philanthropist, scientist, philosopher, sociologist, reformer, economist, teacher, historian, and, above all, a simple homebody. That a few, reading the accounts of Ford's career at the time of his death, might have discerned contradictions in the roles imputed to him was doubtless of less significance than the fact that a great many could find in those accounts such a range of gratifications as to make possible the eliciting of a favorable response.

And gratifications enough there were.

For the multitudes who already felt that a career such as Ford's was one of social utility and whose system of values sanctioned such activities, the portrayal of Ford by the press was gilt for the lily. Not all, however, felt so firmly that such careers were socially useful, that the success attained by Ford or other great entrepreneurs was to be attributed solely to their ability, that opportunities for advancement were distributed equally throughout the social structure, that they owed "honor and service" to the economic organization of which Ford was a part, or even, indeed, that it was desirable to show devotion to a society in which upward progress — even if based on superior abilities — was measured in terms of added income received at each rung of the ladder. When the victory is always to the swift, the slow grow weary of perpetual defeat and may begin to argue either that no one ought to race for bread and butter or that the rules of the contest are unfair and in need of change.[42] The majority of large businessmen may believe that ability — without qualification — is at the root of economic success and give no place to "pull" or "luck," but only a minority of unskilled workers believes so. Every successive penetration downward into the social structure reveals an increasing number of persons who deny that success is a function of ability and that opportunity is distributed equally.[43]

In this gap between economic reality and acceptance by all of that reality lurked the danger to business enterprise and to the sense of common purpose vital to the functioning of society.[44] To bridge this gap by informing the American people of the new significance of the entrepreneur in the changing conditions of American life was the achievement of the press. From the praise which the press bestowed upon Ford those who had attained even a moderate degree of economic success could take comfort, for they had a convincing demonstration that their activities were appreciated and that the system which maintained and encouraged those activities was being staunchly defended. But satisfactions could be derived by others as well. Henry Ford had indeed been a hero, but a special kind of hero. He had been, the press insisted, a hero in spite of himself, a man who would have liked nothing better than to be simply father and husband in his own house.

How was it possible to resent his superior position? Had he not remained unspoiled despite his success; had he not abundantly demonstrated that he was made of the same clay as others; had he not shown solicitude for the welfare of those who had not even the slightest claim on him? And had he not, moreover, constantly emphasized that success was not a proper goal for mankind; that he personally had not followed its siren song; and that the only true goal was that of service to one's fellows? From this even the unsuccessful could draw assurance, for they had it from the mouth of Ford himself that not wealth, but virtue, counted. By this standard, so the unsuccessful might infer, who could say that the successful were really worthy and the unsuccessful unworthy? And so far as Ford himself was concerned, if it was position in the hierarchy of virtue, not in that of economic status, which really counted, and if Ford's position in the former was at the apex, then who could deny that he deserved the tributes he received? Judge not the man of business by his balance sheets, the press admonished its readers, for by that standard what would be the verdict as to you? Judge him as ye would wish to be judged — by a higher standard of accounting, the standard of morality.[45] This was, to be sure, emphasis upon the personal qualities of the entrepreneur, but it was not emphasis upon those qualities which had characterized discussion of early nineteenth-century entrepreneurs. Then the press had been concerned with stressing those aspects of character and personality which made of the entrepreneur a unique individual, which set him apart from his fellows. Now the press stressed less those qualities which helped account for his success than those which he had in common with all others, those which drew him into and made him part of the great mass of mankind.

Nor was this the only difference between early and late newspaper discussion of great entrepreneurs. Gone was the early implication that the entrepreneur was a free-swinging individual, unaffected by considerations of time and place and circumstance and restricted only by the potentialities of his own character. The unique qualities of American social and economic organization were given full, even lavish, credit as conditions without which entrepreneurial success was an impossibility. Only in America did opportunity exist and only in America was entrepreneurial talent recognized and nourished. But the argument did not work in reverse. Society could be expected to do no more than to interpose no obstacles in the path of success; it could not guarantee success. Failure remained a function of the individual for which society was not accountable. No less an authority than John D. Rockefeller had stated one side of the case:

. . . the failures which a man makes in his life are due almost always to some defect in his personality, some weakness of body, or mind, or character, will, or temperament. The only way to overcome these failings is to build up his personality from within, so that he, by virtue of what is within him, may overcome the weakness which was the cause of his failure. It is only those efforts the man himself puts forth that can really help him . . . It is my belief that the principal cause for the economic differences between people is their difference in personality, and that it is only as we can assist in the wider distribution of those qualities which go to make up a strong personality that we can assist in the wider distribution of wealth.[46]

Nowhere, at the time of Ford's death, was the special relationship between entrepreneur and system, success and failure better expressed than in the Grand Forks *Herald:* "'American System' Made Ford's Rise Possible" — this was the title of the editorial. But — and this was the concluding sentence of the same editorial — "Not everyone can hope to become a Ford, for his was a rare combination of vision, mechanical ability, and perseverance."

The effect of such an explanation, of course, was to allow the economic system to be included in a consensus of approval, by making it responsible for permitting success, and yet at the same time to exclude it from the arena of potential controversy, by making the individual responsible for failure.[47]

But in still another way did the press clothe business enterprise in a coat of armor that had the magical property of warding off blows even before they were struck. By identifying enterprise with the nation itself, the press was able to invest the one with the qualities of the other, to enlist in the cause of an economic system the patriotic sentiments of love and loyalty usually associated with defense of the nation.[48]

In one sense, this was an effort to influence the thought of individual men — and therefore their action — by the use of a symbol which embodied widely held concepts of morality, tradition, religion, and patriotism, with the ultimate end of attaining a social order in which, in part through the acceptance of that symbol, all groups would participate harmoniously and act in the manner that had come to be expected of them.[49] "When you affect the economic thought of the people, you automatically affect their political thought," [50] said one spokesman of the business community, and the press had at its disposal powerful weapons for the affecting of both. Not the least powerful of those weapons was the virtual monopoly of the daily press in the purveying of ideas. Who beside a scattered handful of radical and trade union papers expressed a dissenting opinion? [51]

As to the majority opinion, it performed two basic functions. In the first place, the nature of the newspaper discussion of Ford was such as to encourage emulation and win acceptance because, in Walter Lippmann's phrase, the drama of his career was presented as having originated in a setting realistic enough to make identification possible and as having terminated in a setting romantic enough to be desirable, but not so romantic as to be inconceivable.[52] In the second place, the nature of the relationship that was alleged to exist between career and system

was such as to permit the system to become the object of approval
while insulating it from criticism. The system was responsible for the
success of the successful; it was not responsible for the failure of the
failures.

The judgment of the trade union editor — "Great riches may or may
not have turned Henry Ford's head. But they surely reached the heads
of the editorial writers" [53] — was too harsh. Modern journalism "tended
to speak the language of corporate business instead of that of the little
fellow . . . not because it is corrupt and venal but because it is itself
a big business, a powerful institution with its interest vested in conservative economics." [54]

That journalism did, indeed, "speak the language of corporate business" is quite clear.

For years those who sought to interpret business enterprise to the
public had shown increasing sensitivity not only to attacks on individual
entrepreneurs but on the system of enterprise itself. Reviewing the
history of corporate public relations in the thirtieth anniversary issue
of his magazine, B. C. Forbes recalled that in the very first month of its
publication he had asked: "Is it to be Democracy or Socialism?" and
that in almost every succeeding issue he had hammered at the theme
that unless it could be "so consistently and convincingly demonstrated
to the people of humble social status that their attitude toward business
and toward business men" should "be one of respect and esteem . . .
the present economic order, cannot, to my mind, last." The cure for
"economic illiteracy" — then as now — lay in proof to the public that
the "basis of modern business is Service," and demonstration of that
proof called for "the most energetic efforts of every agency in the land
capable of reaching the public: daily and weekly newspapers and other
periodicals, owners of radio stations, educational institutions from primary schools to universities, commercial banks and savings banks, as
well as all other financial organizations, insurance companies, stock
exchanges and all their members, manufacturers, distributors, retailers,
chambers of commerce, trade associations, every enlightened, responsible citizen." [55] Businessmen were alarmed that "the US working class"
might be "entirely losing faith in capitalism's ability to maintain employment, let alone guarantee prosperity and avoid wars"; that increasing leisure for "the worker" gave him "more time to think up grievances,
more inclination to listen to agitators"; and in that frame of mind even
the use of the term "workshop" by the League of Women Voters was
evidence of the use of "revolutionary idiom." Attacks on business enterprise and concern lest its environment be altered led businessmen to
the conclusion that explanations attuned to the needs of the times were

required if the public's faith in business were to be maintained and "a whole nation's economic virtue" protected.[56]

But how was this to be accomplished? James Young, of the National Advertising Council, gave a general answer when he stated, "Advertising techniques effectively employed can more powerfully influence social action than any other means of communication." [57] The reply of the public relations director of the General Foods Corporation, far more specific, revealed the degree to which presentation of Ford by the press conformed to the pattern of presentation preferred by business enterprise itself:

I am convinced that this process of identifying business with the great goals of the human race, the great but simple goals, is all that can maintain today's free corporate system. We have achieved mass production . . . and nowhere have achieved mass serenity of the peoples of this land. Instead we have only contributed to their growing frustration, their decreasing stability, their reduced happiness . . . Let us never for one moment give up our magnificent technologies. But do let us use our every power to identify the owners and managers of those technologies with the simple goals — better education for everybody's children, better health and nutrition, better housing, better opportunities based on ability, more security for the aged and infirm, more respect for the opinion of any man who has opinions.[58]

"The employer organizes the forces of production. He is the natural leader of his workmen," said the National Association of Manufacturers, and "should bring to bear constantly upon them influences for right thinking and action for loyalty to the common enterprise." [59] And how was the employer to do this? By taking "his place alongside of home, and school, and church" as the Ford Motor Company had done when it presented its employees with a list of publications it would be pleased to have them read; by revealing — again as the Ford Motor Company had done in the case of Henry Ford — that "the guiding SPIRIT OF SERVICE," not profit, is the motive of enterprise; by showing that in all essential respects employer was like employee.[60] The General Motors Corporation illustrated these principles admirably in the definition of a businessman which it presented in the magazine it publishes for its employees:

A businessman is one who invests his money in an enterprise which gives employment and provides a regular income to himself and others.

For example, a man paid by GM to drive a truck is an employe. If he saves enough money to start his own trucking business, He's a Businessman.

Although the truck driver is now a businessman, he is pretty much the same fellow as when employed by GM. He looks the same and has the same friends.

True, his responsibilities are very much greater . . . but otherwise he is no different personally than he was before.[61]

In such fashion, too, had Henry Ford been presented by the daily press — different from others only in that he was an employer, which was not such a difference after all.

Nor was this the only parallel in discussion of business enterprise between the daily press and corporation press. No less than the former did the latter identify business enterprise with the nation itself. In the lexicon of corporation house organ editors, "the American system" and "the competitive system" were one and the same, and criticism of the one, which meant criticism of the other, was therefore "alien."

"It belongs to all of us," said Uncle Sam pointing to a map of the United States labeled "B US INESS"; and in defense of what that map symbolized, the General Motors Corporation told its employees: "Of course, there are faults in the American system. Our society is made up of millions of people, none of whom is perfect, so our system cannot be perfect. But our system can be improved, and without changing its form." [62]

In writing their obituaries of Henry Ford, therefore, the daily newspapers were defining the role of the entrepreneur in a manner parallel to that utilized by enterprise itself. In the performance of that task, presentation of factual detail was of less importance than pronouncement of judgment. Years before, Mark Twain, seeing the distinction between the two, offered to pay for the privilege of editing his own obituary:

Of necessity, an Obituary is a thing which cannot be so judiciously edited by any hand as by that of the subject of it. In such a case it is not the Facts that are of chief importance, but the light which the obituarist shall throw upon them, the meanings which he shall dress them in, the conclusions which he shall draw from them, and the judgments which he shall deliver upon them. The Verdicts, you understand . . . not their Facts, but their Verdicts.[63]

With respect to Henry Ford, the verdict of the press was as clear as it was decisive. In his life the American people might see dramatic confirmation of two fundamental precepts: entrepreneur was linked to community by the common attributes of humanity and by principles of motivation which guided his activities in the direction of service to all; enterprise was linked to nation by identification with patriotism and historical tradition. At no time, at least not since the death of Stephen Girard in 1831, were American entrepreneurs given more reason to feel that their activities were thoroughly in accord with national aspirations. In 1947, to be sure, the entrepreneur did not mean to the American people what he had meant in 1831. Emphasis upon personal uniqueness and, with it, the belief that character determines fate had largely disappeared; but they had disappeared because the new conditions of American society imposed new requirements and gave opportunity for new meanings to be seen in the lives of businessmen. Absent was the uniqueness of the entrepreneur, but present was identification with his fellows; absent was the implication that entrepreneurial qualities were everywhere and always applicable, but present was the understanding that entrepreneur and social system were inseparable. The entrepreneur had, indeed, "built himself into the history" of his country.[64]

Conclusion

The poet has described for us the condition of a society in which, within the framework of a common culture, specialization and stratification have shattered uniformity of outlook:

> Malinowski, Rivers,
> Benedict and others
> Show how common culture
>   Shapes the separate lives;
> Matrilineal races
> Kill their mothers' brothers
> In their dreams and turn their
>   Sisters into wives.
>
> Who when looking over
> Faces in the subway
> Each with its uniqueness
>   Would not, did he dare,
> Ask what forms exactly
> Suited to their weakness
> Love and desperation
>   Take to govern there.
>
> Would not like to know what
> Influence occupation
> Has on human vision
>   Of the human fate:
> Do all the clerks for instance
> Pigeon-hole creation,
> Brokers see the Ding-an-
>   sich as Real Estate?
>
> When a politician
> Dreams about his sweetheart,
> Does he multiply her
>   Face into a crowd,
> Are her fond responses

All-or-none reactions,
Does he try to buy her,
Is the kissing loud? [1]

The poet's insight reveals an acute problem. People behave in any situation, we are told, in accordance with the way they see that situation, and their view "is usually the way their particular implicated groups see the situation." [2] If society is "a highly intricate network of partial or complete understandings between the members of organizational units," [3] then what are the consequences of the formation of groups with differing, even conflicting, outlooks for the maintenance of that society? The very existence of stratification presents the possibility that — unless discipline is maintained — the "network of . . . understandings" which is the *sine qua non* of society will be rent.[4] If, then, a society is to maintain itself in accordance with the pattern it has developed, its members must find their membership in that society attractive, act in the way that has come to be expected of them, and accept the system of assorted positions and the behavior associated with those positions characteristic of that society. Fundamental, then, to the continued existence of a particular social order is acceptance of a system of values which establishes the discipline and shared understanding which permit human activity to be carried on with a minimum of friction. Such is the essential meaning of consensus.[5]

Since consensus involves agreement on problems rooted in society itself, semantic solutions alone are inadequate; no society has yet dispensed with policemen, and behind even Goebbels stood Himmler. Still, communication is of vital importance to the creation of consensus, for its primary function is to place whatever is being discussed in such a context as to produce a desired response. If this implies that the communicating persons have at least enough in common to be able to understand each other, it also means that the content of communications — the way persons and problems are presented — may influence the nature of the response toward those persons and problems.[6]

That a man, regardless of the area in which his position of leadership was first attained, may be invested with a symbolic significance far beyond the sphere of his real activity is a fact that has long been recognized. He may be, and often has been, transformed into a social symbol incarnating certain attitudes and forms of behavior and, therefore, serving as a focus about which consensus may be attained and as a stimulus for the voluntary acceptance of the discipline implied in the behavior he symbolizes.[7]

What distinguishes this process in the small group from that in the large, complex community is that in the former each member of the group has the opportunity for viewing the hero himself and judging his actions, while in the latter no such opportunity for a face-to-face relationship exists. Knowledge of what the hero is and what he does is gained through the medium of communications. Under such circumstances, the members of society selected to become its leaders and the aspects of their careers emphasized are functions not only of the individuals so selected, but of those whose judgments control the content of the media of mass communications. Certain characteristics, indeed, when applied to some persons selected by the symbol-makers to become the foci of consensus may be fabricated. "The pseudo-charisma of our time belies its earlier character by the way in which it can be fabricated through the manipulation of the techniques of mass persuasion." [8]

To portray certain persons as heroes, to endow them with particular qualities, to associate them with attitudes considered essential for the preservation of society are among the primary functions of the press. This has been, in effect, the story of the selection by the vast majority of the nation's press of certain representatives of a particular position in society — that of the entrepreneur — to be raised to the level of heroes; of the description of these persons in terms of certain qualities; of the effort to create an area of agreement about that which they have been held to represent.[9] What remains to be explained is why, in terms of the analysis presented here, the mode of presentation adopted by the press has changed.

Briefly, these changes may be summarized as follows:

(1) The entrepreneur of the early nineteenth century is described as a man of certain qualities who performs certain acts directly related to his business position; nonbusiness acts are private and are not, therefore, deemed to be suitable for discussion or even relevant to an understanding of the man.

(2) The source of success of the early nineteenth-century entrepreneur is conceived of as lying in personal qualities; character determines destiny. So long as he has the requisite qualities, success will be his at any time, in any place, under any circumstances.

(3) Favorable or unfavorable attitudes toward the businessman of the early nineteenth century rest not on judgment of his business activities or of the methods by which his fortune was made, but on consideration of the destination of his wealth. Discussion of the sources of wealth, considerably less common, is always a function of critical and antagonistic attitudes toward the businessman.

(4) The entrepreneur of the twentieth century is not discussed by his defenders in terms of his business functions alone; functions associated with his nonbusiness roles — the roles he has in common with the rest of his countrymen — are deemed equally relevant to analysis of his status in society.

(5) Business enterprise itself, not its by-product in the form of philanthropy, becomes the basis for the twentieth-century evaluation of the businessman.

(6) The personal qualities of the entrepreneur are not, in the twentieth century, considered to be sufficient explanations of entrepreneurial success. The economic system itself — sometimes called capitalism, more often called free enterprise — is described as an element without which entrepreneurial success would be an impossibility.

(7) The economic environment in which the businessman operates is presented as synonymous with the nation itself, and nation and economic system are interchangeable parts of the same mechanism.

In short, the problem is to explain why the entrepreneur of the early nineteenth century, presented by his defenders as a man occupying his position by virtue of unique individual capacity and discussed almost exclusively in terms of the business functions associated with that position, becomes at some time near the turn of the century a man discussed not in terms of individual uniqueness but in terms of all that he has in common with the rest of his countrymen, occupying his position as much by virtue of qualities attributed to American society as by his own.

That those at the pinnacle of the economic hierarchy in any society have been wholly immune from criticism may be doubted; that those who occupy such positions in American society have been subjected since the Civil War to increased criticism cannot be doubted. Increasingly, moreover, that criticism has been interpreted by those who have felt themselves to be its targets as being directed not so much against individual businessmen as against the very position of businessman. The former was only a limited threat, for it was directed not against an entire social status but against a particular occupant of that status. More disquieting was the development of opinions which held out alternatives to the existing structure of society, indicated that their believers would no longer accept the discipline essential for the functioning of that society, and portended growing dissent from the values of that society.

One observer, writing in 1843, admitted that the "fact cannot be disguised . . . that a feeling of prejudice and hostility does exist between the wealthy and laboring classes, even in this country . . . Those who prefer to be . . . champions and friends" of the laboring classes "are the assailants, and the rich are compelled to stand upon the defensive; and they cannot fail to look with an evil eye upon those who make them the objects of vindictive and incessant attacks." Who was responsible for "this misplaced clamor about the poor and the rich" which "belongs not to our country"? "That worst pest of human society, the demagogue." [10]

By 1879 it was possible to identify "the demagogue" with more precision. "An end should be put to all plots against society," wrote an anonymous contributor to the *North American Review:*

> The man of capital, and the man whose only capital is his labor, should alike wish it. Let Congress, by investigating the principles and proceedings of the Socialistic Labor party, first assure themselves of its pernicious nature, and then let it proceed to destroy by legislation this network of conspiracies. Let our legislators next assure themselves that the organization is led and inspired by German agitators, and, if they are true to their trust, they will proceed to general revision of our immigration laws.

"Continued ignorance of the true condition of the social substrata which are showing themselves in our land," the writer warned, could "only lead to lawlessness or force" which "might burst upon us as a mighty torrent . . . calculated to threaten the best social and business interests of a country vast in extent of territory and fairly destitute of military protection." [11]

What was later regarded by the spokesmen of the business community itself as the source of this contagion was identified by Elihu Root: "There are two separate processes going on among civilized nations at the present time. One is an assault by Socialism against the individualism which underlies the social system of Western civilization. The other is an assault against existing institutions upon the ground that they do not adequately protect and develop the existing social order." [12]

That the entrepreneur was becoming a focus of dissatisfaction rather than approval and that the particular social structure which supported his activities was being threatened was evidence that old explanations were not relevant to new social conditions.

Hostility could hardly be diverted so long as the entrepreneur continued to be discussed solely in terms of his business functions, precisely the activities which set him apart from others. It might well be allayed, however, if he were presented in such a way that others might see in him something of themselves, if he were shown to be similar to occupants of positions other than his own, if he were described as different from others only in the degree to which he embodied qualities common to all and incarnated universally admired traits. It may be true, as two spokesmen of industry maintain, that "the leader must be everything that he desires his subordinates to become"; [13] but it is also true, when persons depend on the press for information concerning the leader, that he may be presented as embodying everything his subordinates want him to be and want themselves to become. The simple, democratic, human entrepreneur, the entrepreneur as father, husband, grandfather, hobbyist, churchgoer — embodying common qualities to an uncommon degree and performing functions associated with all social levels — becomes, then, a characteristic of twentieth-century discussion. The individualism of the entrepreneur, which once meant his personal uniqueness, now means his conformity with qualities possessed by all.[14]

Consensus needed to be maintained not only in support of the entrepreneur, but also in support of the economic system of which he was a part. So long as the explanation for entrepreneurial success was expressed solely in terms of individual capacities, no opportunity existed to include the economic system within the area for which approval was sought. An explanation which based such success as much, if not more, upon the unique opportunities afforded by that system as upon the unique qualities of the entrepreneur could, however, widen the area of acquiescence. The career of the entrepreneur and his attainment of high status, it could be shown, were objectives within the reach of all. "When he says that one cannot inherit a possibility," said Congressman Rowland Blennerhassett Mahoney, denouncing one of his colleagues, "he strikes down the noblest ideal of this Republic . . . Why, Mr. Speaker, it is possibility, and possibility alone, that glorifies American citizenship . . . The possibility of bettering our conditions, of having all the doors of honor swing wide to merit, is the best heritage conferred upon Americans by the worthies of an elder day." [15] In the struggle for success, failure was a function of individual incapacity, success a function of a system which served the interests of all and which, therefore, deserved the support of all. Characteristically, then, the entrepreneur of the twentieth century is presented not so much as a man of particular qualities who performs particular functions, but as an economic man of distinction who offers a glowing testimonial to the value of the economic system.

But to identify the entrepreneur with those in lesser positions and to attribute his success to qualities inherent in the economic system was only one stage in the new interpretation of the entrepreneur. The next phase was reached when the description of the entrepreneur's position as the higher embodiment of qualities characteristic of every social status was fused with the identification of the economic system and the nation itself. It was against this identification that Mr. Justice Holmes inveighed when he observed tartly: "The fourteenth Amendment does not enact Mr. Herbert Spencer's Social Statics . . . A constitution is not intended to embody a particular economic theory." Significantly, however, Holmes's view was expressed as a dissenting opinion. The majority view found expression in the words of an earlier justice of the Supreme Court, John A. Campbell: "What did the colonists and their posterity seek for and obtain by their settlement of this continent; their long contest with physical evils that attended their colonial condition; their long and wasting struggle for independence . . . ? Freedom. Free action, free enterprise — free competition." [16] It would be difficult, indeed, at least in a secular society, to conceive of any more potent means for the maintenance of consensus than the sanction of patriotism. Not only does it direct loyalty and allegiance toward the objects it sanctifies, but under certain circumstances it transforms criticism directed against the function of a part of society into a threat to the whole of society.

So it was, two thousand years ago, that the emperors of Rome, faced with threats of civil war and foreign invasion and the need to persuade their citizens of many languages, nations, and cultures that they were entitled to their allegiance, identified the position of emperor with the state itself, transformed a part of society into a symbol of the whole, and legitimated it with the sanctions of patriotism and religion. So, too, but more successfully, did the Tudor kings of England, confronted with threats of religious war and Spanish invasion, form a new consensus in support of the position they occupied by transmuting the functional conception of kingship characteristic of medieval political thought into a symbolic conception in which the king, as the embodiment of the whole nation, was deserving of the loyalty of all. And so, too, did the spokesmen of the Prussian nobility, faced with elimination as a social type by forces set loose by the French Revolution, respond to the challenge by exalting the nobility to the status of "Träger des Staats," by identifying the preservation of the nobility with *raison d'état,* by transforming the symbol in terms of which that group was to be understood into one which, though it represented only a fragment of society, was held to be expressive of the whole and therefore to be defended as though it were the state itself. [17]

That the symbolism of the entrepreneur has changed through a century and a quarter of American history is clear. Those changes, deriving from the increased self-consciousness that was the result of growing attacks on entrepreneur and economic system, provide a striking illustration of the manner in which mass communications contribute to the maintenance of the consensus required for the functioning of society. But if those changes are, in one sense, the result of the need to change, the ability to change is, in another sense, evidence of the continued vitality of the functions performed by the entrepreneur in American society. For only as a symbol takes new meanings relevant to new social conditions may it live.

Notes

To economize space, note references to obituaries in contemporary periodicals have had to be eliminated except where they refer to material quoted directly in the text. The accompanying table provides a summary view of the major categories of periodical sources which were used for this study and indicates both the total number of periodicals in each category and the number which contained relevant material. Those who desire more complete documentation and who wish to know the titles of all the periodicals examined may consult the doctoral thesis upon which this book has been based, in Widener Library, Harvard University.

	Girard	Astor	Vanderbilt	Morgan	Rockefeller	Ford
Newspapers						
With material	129	164	100	136	136	138
Total examined	142	194	113	141	143	151
Magazines						
With material	8	12	15	53	30	28
Total examined	24	54	59	233	224	296
Trade Union Publications						
With material				7	7	12
Total examined				66	64	150
Company House Organs						
With material				4	2	1
Total examined				4	24	73

INTRODUCTION

1. Thomas Carlyle, *On Heroes, Hero-Worship and the Heroic in History* (London, 1841), p. 78.

2. London *Daily News,* June 4, 1853, quoted in John Overton Choules, *The Cruise of the Steam Yacht North Star* (Boston, 1854), pp. 58–61.

3. Leonard William Doob, *Public Opinion and Propaganda* (New York,

1948), pp. 431–432; Bernard Berelson, *Content Analysis in Communication Research* (Glencoe, Illinois, 1952), pp. 18–20, 98; Mahlon Brewster Smith, *Functional and Descriptive Analysis of Public Opinion* (Unpublished Ph.D. thesis, Harvard University, 1947), p. 518; Joseph T. Klapper, *The Effects of Mass Media: A Report to the Director of the Public Library Inquiry* (New York, 1949), sect. IV, p. 3, sect. IV, pp. 47–51.

4. William Isaac Thomas, *The Unadjusted Girl* (Boston, 1923), p. 41.

5. Clyde Kluckhohn, *Mirror for Man* (New York and Toronto, 1949), pp. 146–147; Norman Charles Meier and Harold W. Saunders, eds., *The Polls and Public Opinion* (New York, 1949), pp. 145–146.

6. David Ross Locke (Petroleum V. Nasby, pseud.), *Eastern Fruit on Western Dishes. The Morals of Abou Ben Adhem* (Boston, 1875), p. 201; Curtis Daniel MacDougall, *Interpretative Reporting* (New York, 1946), p. 351.

7. Paul Felix Lazarsfeld and Frank Nicholas Stanton, *Communications Research 1948–1949* (New York, 1949), pp. xvi, 117.

CHAPTER ONE: STEPHEN GIRARD

1. New York *Times,* May 21, 1948.

2. Quoted in Cheesman Abiah Herrick, *Stephen Girard Founder* (Philadelphia, 1923), pp. 126–128.

3. Speech of Job R. Tyson, quoted in Herrick, *Stephen Girard Founder,* p. 128.

4. Quoted in Harry Emerson Wildes, *Lonely Midas, the Story of Stephen Girard* (New York and Toronto, 1943), p. 284.

5. Quoted in Wildes, *Lonely Midas,* pp. 276–277.

6. Francis Edward Tourscher, *Diary and Visitation Record of the Rt. Rev. Francis Patrick Kenrick* (Lancaster, Pa., 1916), p. 66. See also John Joseph O'Shea, *The Two Kenricks* (Philadelphia, 1904), p. 88; Hugh Joseph Nolan, *The Most Rev. Francis Patrick Kenrick, Third Bishop of Philadelphia, 1830–1851* (Washington, 1948), p. 138; "Burial and Removal of Stephen Girard," *The American Catholic Historical Researches,* New Series, VII (1911), 17–20.

7. Wildes, *Lonely Midas,* p. 297; Henry Atlee Ingram, *Girard College and Life of Stephen Girard* (Philadelphia, 1898), pp. 5–6; John Bach McMaster, *The Life and Times of Stephen Girard,* 2 vols. (Philadelphia and London, 1918), I, v.

8. Quoted in Wildes, *Lonely Midas,* pp. 299, 301.

9. Joseph Dorfman, *The Economic Mind in American Civilization, 1606–1865,* 2 vols. (New York, 1946), II, 602–603. For a discussion of Raguet's opposition to the Bank of the United States and the laissez-faire philosophy of his group among Jackson's supporters, see Fritz Redlich, *History of American Business Leaders,* 2 vols. in 3 pts. (vol. I, Ann Arbor, 1940; vol. II, pt. I, New York, 1947; vol. II, pt. II, New York, 1951), vol. II, pt. I, 133, 180.

10. Raguet's approval of and confidence in Girard's "caution" as a banker seem to have been somewhat misplaced. At least twice, in 1828 and again in 1832 after Girard's death, the Girard Bank did not have sufficient specie on

hand to meet its immediate specie liabilities. On the first occasion it received a loan of $50,000 and, on the second, one of $100,000 — both from the archenemy of the Jacksonians, Nicholas Biddle. Ralph Charles Henry Catterall, *The Second Bank of the United States* (Chicago, 1903), pp. 432–433. For a contrary view of Jacksonian democracy, in which opposition to privilege and monopoly is construed to mean opposition to the "business community," see Arthur Meier Schlesinger, Jr., *The Age of Jackson* (Boston, 1946), pp. 306–307: "The Jacksonians believed that there was a deep-rooted conflict between the 'producing' and 'non-producing' classes — the farmers and laborers, on the one hand, and the business community on the other . . . The specific problem was to control the power of the capitalistic groups, mainly Eastern, for the benefit of the non-capitalistic groups, farmers and laboring men, East, West, and South."

11. *The Will of the Late Stephen Girard, Esq., with a Short Biography of His Life* (Philadelphia, 1832).

12. Stephen Simpson, *Biography of Stephen Girard,* 2nd ed. (Philadelphia, 1832).

13. Schlesinger, *Age of Jackson,* p. 202.

14. McMaster, *Stephen Girard,* I, v.

15. Simpson, *Stephen Girard,* p. 159.

16. *Ibid.,* p. iv.

17. *Ibid.,* pp. v, iii–iv, 157.

18. *Ibid.,* pp. 46–47, 64–66, 67–68, 113, 142–143, 144, 161, 164, 168–169, 267.

19. *Ibid.,* pp. 62–63, 63–64.

20. *Ibid.,* pp. 12–13, 105, 111–112, 139–140, 151, 154, 169–170, 14.

21. *Ibid.,* pp. 8, 14, 161, 174–175, 156, 270, 212. For a somewhat different interpretation of Simpson's book, which emphasizes solely its "panegyrical" qualities, see L. Hartz, "Laissez-Faire Thought in Pennsylvania, 1776–1860," *Journal of Economic History,* 3:73 (Supplement, 1943), and Schlesinger, *Age of Jackson,* p. 202. McMaster, on the other hand, underscores Simpson's animosity toward Girard. McMaster, *Stephen Girard,* I, v.

22. Alfred McClung Lee, *The Daily Newspaper in America* (New York, 1937), pp. 618–619.

23. On January 23, 1832, in response to a request from the Senate, the Secretary of the Treasury submitted a report disclosing the names of the largest foreign and domestic stockholders of the Bank of the United States. Girard, with 6331 shares, was the largest domestic shareholder and ranked just under Baring Brothers and Co., who, with 7915 shares, were the largest stockholders in both categories. See, for example, Rockville *Maryland Journal and True American,* February 21, 1832, and Philadelphia *Saturday Evening Post,* February 11, 1832.

24. Cotton Mather, *Two Brief Discourses* (Boston, 1695), p. 48.

25. Donald McConnell, *Economic Virtues in the United States* (New York, 1930), pp. 58–61, 64.

26. Quoted in McConnell, *Economic Virtues,* pp. 24–25.

27. Ralph Waldo Emerson, *Complete Works,* 12 vols., Riverside ed. (Boston and New York, 1883–93), VI, 80–81, 56, 99, 100, respectively.

28. Constantine Samuel Rafinesque, *The Pleasures and Duties of Wealth* (Philadelphia, 1840), p. 27.

29. Thomas P. Hunt, *The Book of Wealth; In Which It Is Proved From The Bible, That It Is The Duty Of Every Man To Become Rich* (New York, 1836), pp. 113–116.

30. Nathan Beman, *The Intellectual Position of Our Country: An Introductory Lecture Delivered Before The Young Men's Association For Mutual Improvement, in the City of Troy, December 10th, 1839*, p. 12.

31. B. Hammond, review of Arthur M. Schlesinger, Jr., *The Age of Jackson,* in *Journal of Economic History,* 6:82 (1946); B. Hammond, review of Joseph L. Blau, ed., *Social Theories of Jacksonian Democracy; Representative Writings of the Period 1826–1850,* in *ibid.,* 9:108 (1949); B. Hammond, "Jackson, Biddle and the United States Bank," *ibid.,* 7:1–23 (1947); Redlich, *Business Leaders,* II, pt. I, p. 171; Richard Hofstadter, *The American Political Tradition* (New York, 1948), p. 55; Merle Eugene Curti, *The Social Ideas of American Educators* (New York, 1935), p. 60; Oscar Handlin and Mary Flug Handlin, *Commonwealth: A Study of the Role of Government in the American Economy: Massachusetts, 1774–1861* (New York and London, 1947), pp. 214–215; Alfred Whitney Griswold, *The American Cult of Success* (Unpublished Ph.D. thesis, Yale University, 1933), p. 32.

32. William Charvat, *The Origins of American Critical Thought, 1810–1835* (Philadelphia, 1936), pp. 7–20; Sidney Louis Jackson, *America's Struggle for Free Schools* (New York, 1941), pp. 57, 67, 88; Henry Farnham May, *Protestant Churches and Industrial America* (New York, 1949), chap. I.

33. McMaster, *Stephen Girard,* II, 443.

34. *Hazard's Register,* January 14, 1832.

CHAPTER TWO: JOHN JACOB ASTOR

1. Allan Nevins, ed., *The Diary of Philip Hone,* 2 vols. (New York, 1927), II, 847–848.

2. *Ibid.,* II, 848.

3. New Orleans *Daily Crescent,* April 7, 1848, quoted in Emory Holloway, ed., *The Uncollected Poetry and Prose of Walt Whitman,* 2 vols. (New York and Toronto, 1921), I, 218–219.

4. James Fenimore Cooper, ed., *Correspondence of James-Fenimore Cooper,* 2 vols. (New Haven, 1922), II, 588.

5. Kenneth Wiggins Porter, *John Jacob Astor,* 2 vols. (Cambridge, 1931), I, 46, note 65.

6. Dixon Wecter, *The Saga of American Society* (New York, 1937), pp. 204–205.

7. Moses Yale Beach, *The Wealth and Biography of the Wealthy Citizens of the City of New York,* 10th ed. (New York, 1846), pp. 2–3.

8. *Ibid.,* p. 2.

9. *Ibid.,* p. 3.

10. *Ibid.,* pp. 3, 1, respectively.

11. William Armstrong, *The Aristocracy of New York: Who They Are, and What They Were* (New York, 1848), p. 7.

12. For a contemporary view regarding Astor's loans to the government which differed from Greeley's *New York Tribune*, see W. Andrews, "Gallatin Revisited: John Jacob Astor," *The New-York Historical Society Quarterly*, 36:175–180 (1952).

13. Under the terms of Astor's will, Halleck, who had been an employee of Astor for sixteen years and had been on intimate terms with him, was left an annuity of $200. Nelson Frederick Adkins, *Fitz-Greene Halleck* (New Haven, 1930), pp. 310–312. For the text of Astor's will, see Porter, *Astor*, II, 1260–1296. The size of the legacy to Halleck was the subject of much comment. Even a journal like *Holden's Dollar Magazine* (New York), which defended Astor against charges of penuriousness and felt that every person should be able "to do what he likes with his own," was constrained to add that "it cannot be denied, that it was very mean in Mr. Astor, who had some thirty or forty millions to dispose of, to leave so small a sum to a gentleman whom he called his 'friend' . . . We must ease our conscience, John Jacob, by stating frankly our opinion, that the magnificent gift of four hundred thousand dollars for a public library, weighs but lightly in the balance against the meanness of the annuity to Mr. Halleck. That is our opinion, and we don't care who knows it." *Holden's Dollar Magazine*, 1:318–319 (May 1848). Even during Astor's life, his relations with Halleck had been the subject of much discussion that was uncomplimentary to him. On July 30, 1842, the New York *Mirror* expressed the hope "that there is truth in the buzz that Halleck has roused himself from his long devotion to the affairs of the counting house, and is about to complete his innumerable unfinished poems." Quoted in Adkins, *Halleck*, p. 303. The *Knickerbocker Magazine*, in May, 1844, was saddened

> To think than e'en a millionaire . . .
> Should have withal the hard assurance
> To hold a Son of Song in durrance.

Quoted in Adkins, *Halleck*, p. 304. And some anonymous poet wrote:

> Methought that brow, so full and fair,
> Was formed a poet's wreath to wear;
> And as those eyes of azure hue,
> One moment lifted, met my view,
> Gay worlds of starry thoughts appeared
> In their blue depths serenely sphered,
> Still to his task the bard applied,
> Unrecked, unheeded all beside;
> And as he closed the solemn sheet,
> I heard his murmuring lips repeat —
> Total a semi-million clear
> Income received for one short year;

Aladdin's wealth scarce mounted faster
At its spring-tide than thine, Herr Astor.

Quoted in James Grant Wilson, *The Life and Letters of Fitz Greene Halleck* (New York, 1869), p. 393.

14. Robert Ernst, *Immigrant Life in New York City, 1825–1863* (New York, 1949), p. 20; Porter, *Astor*, II, 950, note 36.

15. The Odd Fellows saw an opportunity to drum up business on their own account: "It behooves the firemen, in view of the hazardous nature of the duties they are called on to discharge, to think of something by which provision more ample than that now possible, may be made by those who may be left behind, as well as for themselves, when prostrated by sickness or disabled by accident . . . the firemen, by adopting a plan similar to that obtaining in the Institution of Odd Fellows, would insure to themselves comfort and ease." In 1846, Astor made two contributions, of $500 and of $200, to the New York Fire Department Fund. Porter, *Astor*, II, 1089.

16. See E. N. Curtis, "American Opinion of the French Nineteenth-Century Revolutions," *American Historical Review*, 29:249–270 (1923).

17. The New York *Journal of Commerce* provides a typical example of this scaling down of the size of Astor's estate. On March 30, it estimated the estate to be worth $40,000,000; on April 3, less than $20,000,000; on April 15, $7,500,000.

18. Handlin and Handlin, *Commonwealth*, pp. 199–204.

19. Francis Joseph Grund, ed., *Aristocracy in America*, 2 vols. (London, 1839), II, 113–115.

20. Edwin Troxall Freedley, *A Practical Treatise on Business*, 3rd ed. (Philadelphia, 1852), pp. 161–162.

21. Philadelphia *Public Ledger*, March 25, 1836, and *Family Magazine*, May 17, 1834, quoted in Frank Luther Mott, *American Journalism*, rev. ed. (New York, 1950), pp. 241–242; Lee, *Daily Newspaper*, pp. 136–138.

22. *Sketches of Mrs. Martha E. Walker and John Jacob Astor* (New York [?], 1849).

23. Horace Mann, *A Few Thoughts for a Young Man* (Boston, 1850), pp. 55–57.

24. *Ibid.*, pp. 57–62.

25. *Ibid.*, pp. 63–64.

26. *Ibid.*, pp. 64–65.

27. Porter, *Astor*, II, 1260–1296.

28. Charles Astor Bristed, *A Letter to the Hon. Horace Mann* (New York, 1850), pp. 8–14.

29. *Ibid.*, pp. 14–18.

30. *Ibid.*, p. 18.

31. *Ibid.*, pp. 24–25. Charles Sumner claimed that the conservative political enemies of Mann circulated Bristed's pamphlet during the campaign against Mann's re-election to Congress. Curti, *American Educators*, p. 117.

32. Helen MacGill Hughes, *News and the Human Interest Story* (Chicago, 1940), p. 6.

33. Freedley, *Practical Treatise*, pp. 61–62, 237, 235–236, respectively.

34. Quoted in Merle Eugene Curti, *The Growth of American Thought* (New York and London, 1943), p. 299.

35. W. B. Sprague, D.D., "Men of Business: Their Responsibility In Respect to Governments, Churches, and Benevolent Institutions," in *The Man of Business, Considered in His Various Relations* (New York, 1851), chap. III.

36. Abner Forbes and J. W. Greene, *The Rich Men of Massachusetts* (Boston, 1851), summary.

37. *"Our First Men:" A Calendar of Wealth, Fashion and Gentility, Containing a List of Those Persons Taxed in the City of Boston, Credibly Reported To Be Worth $100,000*, rev. ed. (Boston, 1846), p. 5.

38. New Orleans *Le Courrier de la Louisiane*, April 7, 1848.

39. J. Todd, D.D., "Men of Business: Their Position, Influence, and Duties To Themselves, To Society, and Especially To Their Employees," in *Man of Business*, pp. 4, 43–44. See also H. J. Wexler, "How to Succeed in Business, 1840–1860," *Explorations in Entrepreneurial History*, 1:26–29 (1949).

40. Francis Bowen, *The Principles of Political Economy* (Boston, 1856), pp. 75, 123, 125.

41. George Robert Russell, *The Merchant. An Oration Before the Rhode Island Alpha of the Phi Beta Kappa Society, at Providence* (Boston, 1849), p. 59.

42. *Thirty-Four Sermons by the Rev. Jonathan Mayhew Wainwright* (New York, 1856), pp. 173–175.

43. *Morning Courier and New York Enquirer*, April 3, 1848.

CHAPTER THREE: CORNELIUS VANDERBILT

1. *Address of the Hon. Chauncey M. Depew, LL.D., at the Unveiling of the Statue of Commodore Vanderbilt at the Vanderbilt University, Nashville, Tennessee, October 11th, 1897* (n.p., n.d.), pp. 1–3.

2. Quoted in New York *Herald*, January 6, 1877.

3. "Open Letter to Commodore Vanderbilt," *Packard's Monthly*, 1:89–91 (1869).

4. "The Vanderbilt Memorial," *The Nation*, 9:431–432 (1869).

5. Quoted in New York *Herald*, January 6, 1877.

6. *Harper's Weekly*, 21:46 (1877); *The Independent*, January 11, 1877, pp. 8, 13; *Scientific American*, 36:36–37 (1877); New York *Times*, January 5, 7, 8, 1877; New York *Daily Bulletin*, January 5, 1877. The newspapers may have been misled as to the nature of Vanderbilt's gift of a ship to the Union; his offer was apparently meant only for the duration of the emergency caused by the construction of the ironclad *Merrimac*. The messenger who brought Vanderbilt the resolution of acknowledgment passed by Congress on January 28, 1864, reported: "After reading it carefully, the Commodore looked at me and said . . . ; 'Congress be *damned!* I never gave that ship to Congress. When the Government was in great straits for a suitable vessel

of war, I offered to give the ship if they did not care to buy it; however, Mr. Lincoln and Mr. Welles think it was a gift, and I suppose I shall have to let her go.' " Wheaton Joshua Lane, *Commodore Vanderbilt: An Epic of the Steam Age* (New York, 1942), pp. 178–179.

7. New York *Daily Graphic,* January 5, 1877; *The Independent,* January 11, 1877, p. 22; New York *Sun,* January 5, 1877; *The Railroad Gazette,* January 12, 1877; New York *Post,* January 4, 1877.

8. Sparta *Wisconsin Greenback,* January 11, 1877.

9. Savannah *Morning News,* January 5, 1877; Chicago *Daily Tribune,* January 5, 1877; Cincinnati *Daily Gazette,* January 5, 1877; San Francisco *Pacific Rural Press,* January 13, 1877.

10. Boston *Watchman,* January 18, 1877; Dubuque *Daily Times,* January 6, 1877.

11. Chicago *Inter Ocean,* January 5, 1877; Portland *Eastern Argus,* January 5, 1877; Cincinnati *Daily Gazette,* January 5, 1877.

12. *In Memoriam — Cornelius Vanderbilt* (Vanderbilt University, Nashville, 1877), p. 8.

13. *Ibid.,* p. 9.

14. *Ibid.,* p. 17.

15. *Ibid.,* p. 16.

16. *Ibid.,* p. 44.

17. Springfield *Illinois State Journal,* January 6, 1877; Washington *National Republican,* January 5, 1877; Chicago *Daily Tribune,* January 8, 1877; Philadelphia *Inquirer,* January 5, 1877.

18. San Francisco *Weekly Alta California,* January 13, 1877; Washington *Evening Star,* January 7, 1877; New Orleans *Times,* January 5, 1877; Philadelphia *North American,* January 5, 1877; Indianapolis *Daily Sentinel,* January 5, 1877; Toledo *Blade,* January 4, 1877.

19. Locke, *Abou Ben Adhem,* pp. 20, 121–122.

20. "The Symphony," in Charles Roberts Anderson, *The Centennial Edition of the Works of Sidney Lanier,* 10 vols. (Baltimore, 1945), I, 46–56.

21. For a discussion of novelists' views toward businessmen, see Gordon Wilson Clarke, *The Changing Conception of the Businessman in the American Novel* (Unpublished Ph.D. thesis, University of Illinois, 1949), pp. 60–63.

22. E. L. Godkin, "Commercial Morality and Political Corruption," *The North American Review,* 107:250 (1868).

23. Charles Loring Brace, *The Dangerous Classes of New York, and Twenty Years' Work Among Them,* 3rd ed. (New York, 1880), pp. 110–111.

24. *Ibid.,* pp. 111–113.

25. Robert King Merton, *Social Theory and Social Structure* (Glencoe, Illinois, 1949), p. 154.

26. Chester McArthur Destler, *American Radicalism 1865–1901* (New London, 1946), pp. 25–58, 76; May, *Protestant Churches,* pp. 91, 112.

27. N. P. Gilman, "Profit-Sharing," *The Forum,* 4:96 (1887).

28. J. Bascom, "The Gist of the Social Question," *The Forum,* 4:87–89 (1887).

29. Sacramento *Daily Union,* January 5, 1877.

30. Quoted in Destler, *American Radicalism,* p. 11.

31. *Methodist Review,* 73:285 (1891).

32. Brace, *Dangerous Classes,* pp. 29–30.

33. *Cummings v. Missouri* (1867), 4 Wallace 277, 321, quoted in Robert Green McCloskey, *American Conservatism in the Age of Enterprise* (Cambridge, 1951), p. 108; see also chapter V, "Judicial Conservatism and the Rights of Man."

34. Christopher Tiedeman, *Treatise on the Limitations of the Police Powers,* quoted in Benjamin Twiss, *Lawyers and the Constitution* (Princeton, 1942), pp. 124–125.

35. Curti, *American Educators,* p. 220.

36. Richard David Mosier, *Making the American Mind: Social and Moral Ideas in the McGuffey Readers* (New York, 1947), pp. 88–122.

37. Arthur Latham Perry, *Elements of Political Economy,* quoted in Henry Steele Commager, *The American Mind* (New Haven, 1950), p. 231.

38. Curti, *American Educators,* p. 222.

39. Joseph Tuckerman, *On the Elevation of the Poor* (Boston, 1874), pp. 27–29.

40. June 21, 1876, p. 196.

41. Rudyard Kipling, *American Notes* (New York, n.d.), p. 82. See also May, *Protestant Churches,* pp. 55–56, 163.

42. Curti, *American Thought,* pp. 605, 634–635, 645–646.

43. Carl Sandburg, reminiscing about his youth in Galesburg, Illinois, reveals how impressed he was by the biography of Commodore Vanderbilt, one of fifty dealing with the lives of "poor boys who have become rich," which could be obtained by the purchase of a ten-cent package of Duke's Cameo or Cross-Cut cigarettes. Sandburg, afraid of nicotine, was not interested in the cigarettes; but he carefully collected the biographies which demonstrated that "America [is] the land of self-made men — the one country in the world where it is possible for a man to rise by his own effort from obscurity and poverty not only to the highest place in society, but to the more courted rank of millionaire as well." Carl Sandburg, *Always The Young Strangers* (New York, 1953), pp. 259, 261–262.

44. Merton, *Social Theory,* pp. 132–133; Robert Staughton Lynd, *Knowledge for What?* (Princeton, 1940), pp. 76–79; R. E. Park, "Reflections on Communications and Culture," in Bernard Berelson and Morris Janowitz, eds., *Reader in Public Opinion and Communications* (Glencoe, Illinois, 1950), p. 165.

45. Jay Gould, *History of Delaware County* (Roxbury, 1856), pp. 1–2.

46. Wheeling *Intelligencer,* January 6, 1877.

CHAPTER FOUR: J. P. MORGAN

1. G. S. Viereck, "The Conqueror," in *The International,* 7:119 (1913).

2. *The Century,* 86:466 (1913).

3. For a denial of the charge that Morgan supplied defective rifles to

the Union Army, see Robert Gordon Wasson, *The Hall Carbine Affair; A Study in Contemporary Folklore*, rev. ed. (New York, 1948).

4. Denver *Rocky Mountain News,* April 1, 1913.

5. Sioux Falls *Daily Argus-Leader,* March 31, 1913.

6. *The Conservator,* 24:17–20 (1913).

7. New Orleans *Daily Picayune,* April 1, 1913; Columbia *State,* April 1, 1913.

8. Baltimore *American and Commercial Advertiser,* March 31, 1913; Atlanta *Georgian,* March 31, 1913.

9. Houston *Post,* April 1, 1913; Denver *Republican,* April 1, 1913; Memphis *Commercial Appeal,* April 1, 1913.

10. Washington *Herald,* April 1, 1913; Brooklyn *Daily Eagle,* March 31, 1913; Boston *Press,* April 1, 1913; Boston *Evening Transcript*, March 31, 1913; New York *Herald,* April 2, 1913; Cincinnati *Enquirer,* April 1, 1913; Des Moines *Register and Leader,* April 1, 1913.

11. Boston *Christian Science Monitor,* March 31, 1913; Savannah *Morning News,* April 1, 1913; New York *Herald,* April 1, 1913; Anaconda *Standard,* April 1, 1913; Chicago *Broad-Ax,* April 5, 1913.

12. Laramie *Boomerang,* April 1, 1913; Reno *Evening Gazette,* April 1, 1913.

13. New York *American,* April 1, 1913; Washington *Post,* April 1, 1913; Kansas City *Star,* March 31, 1913.

14. Newark *Evening News,* March 31, 1913; Dallas *Morning News,* April 1, 1913; Baltimore *Evening Sun,* March 31, 1913.

15. Quoted in *Harper's Weekly,* 57:7 (April 26, 1913).

16. Bryan's wife had a somewhat different view of the situation. "If Mr. Morgan knew that Mr. Bryan was dallying with his funeral arrangements . . ." [the dots are Mrs. Bryan's] she noted. "The papers took notice of the circumstance." Morris Robert Werner, *Bryan* (New York, 1929), pp. 225–226.

17. *The Market World and Chronicle,* April 5, 1913; *The Bond Buyer,* April 5, 1913, p. 1053; *American Exporter,* May, 1913, p. 73; *The Commercial and Financial Chronicle,* April 5, 1913. On May 12, 1913, Frederick H. Prince, Boston banker and railroad executive, told business publicist C. W. Barron that "the Pujo Committee Investigation killed Morgan. Morgan was a very sensitive, shrinking man and all his exterior bluff was simply a protective coating." Prince had apparently forgotten that nineteen years earlier he had predicted the imminent death of the financier. On June 1, 1894, he had told Barron: "J. P. Morgan will live but two years. He has had fits and will die suddenly." Arthur Pound and Samuel Taylor Moore, *More They Told Barron* (New York and London, 1931), pp. 157, 144.

18. *The Economist,* April 5, 1913; *American Exporter,* May, 1913, pp. 75–78; *Monthly Bulletin of the American Iron and Steel Institute,* May, 1913.

19. Frederick Townsend Martin, *The Passing of the Idle Rich* (New York, 1911), p. 93.

20. *Ibid.,* pp. 109–127.

21. James Ford, *Slums and Housing,* 2 vols. (Cambridge, Mass., 1936), I, 187.

22. Robert Hunter, *Poverty* (New York and London, 1907), p. 337.

23. Charles Edward Russell, *Business The Heart of the Nation* (New York, 1911), pp. 250–251.

24. Richard Theodore Ely, *Social Aspects of Christianity* (New York, 1889), pp. 97–98.

25. William James Ghent, *Our Benevolent Feudalism* (New York and London, 1902), pp. 124–125, 158. See also Charles Howard Hopkins, *The Rise of the Social Gospel in American Protestantism* (New Haven, 1940), pp. 318–319; Martin, *Idle Rich,* p. 91.

26. "Great Fortunes," *The Atlantic Monthly,* 96:40 (1905).

27. Clarence Elmore Bonnett, *Employers' Associations in the United States* (New York, 1922), pp. 23–25.

28. Quoted in John Alfred Ralph Pimlott, *Public Relations and American Democracy* (Princeton, 1951), p. 236.

29. Kenneth Burke, *A Rhetoric of Motives* (New York, 1950), p. 22; Kenneth Burke, *A Grammar of Motives* (New York, 1945), pp. 91–94.

30. "The Freedom of Wealth," *The Outlook,* 76:775 (1904).

31. Quoted in Charles Austin Beard and Mary Ritter Beard, *The American Spirit* (New York, 1942), p. 446.

32. William Jewett Tucker, *Public Mindedness* (Concord, N.H., 1910), pp. 168–169, 176.

33. Martin, *Idle Rich,* p. 171.

34. William Stephen Rainsford, *The Story of a Varied Life* (London, 1923), p. 291.

35. The Reverend W. Lawrence, "The Relation of Wealth to Morals," *World's Work,* 1:287 (1900–01); Edgar Watson Howe, *The Blessing of Business* (Topeka, 1918), pp. 46, 19; Edward Bok, *The Young Man in Business* (Boston, 1900), p. 6. See also McConnell, *Economic Virtues,* pp. 114–115, 118–119, 122, 142–149.

36. Curti, *American Thought,* pp. 634–635; Clarke, *Changing Conception,* p. 220; Curti, *American Educators,* p. 583; Anna Youngman, *The Economic Causes of Great Fortunes* (New York, 1909), p. 148; McCloskey, *American Conservatism,* pp. 15–16, 69–71.

37. For a discussion, in another context, of how newspapers utilize the slogans of patriotism to achieve particular ends, see Earle Leslie Hunter, *A Sociological Analysis of Certain Types of Patriotism* (New York, 1932), pp. 23, 249–250.

38. Ambrose Bierce, *The Devil's Dictionary* (New York and Washington, 1911), pp. 87–89.

39. Orison Swett Marden, *Success* (Boston and Chicago, 1897), p. 153.

40. *Autobiography of Andrew Carnegie* (Boston and New York, 1920), p. 17.

41. A. A. Levey, "The Newspaper Habit and Its Effects," *The North American Review,* 143:309 (1886).

42. Thomas Childs Cochran and William Miller, *The Age of Enterprise* (New York, 1949), p. 269.

43. Curti, *American Thought,* p. 653; Ferdinand Lundberg, *America's 60 Families* (New York, 1937), pp. 116–118, 252–258.

44. Hughes, *Human Interest,* pp. 71–72; H. A. Innis, "The Newspaper in Economic Development," *Journal of Economic History,* 2:22 (supplement, 1942).

45. Bierce, *Devil's Dictionary,* pp. 334–335. See also Ghent, *Feudalism,* p. 160; Martin, *Idle Rich,* pp. 139–141.

46. Hughes, *Human Interest,* p. 275; Curti, *American Thought,* p. 653.

47. Speeches of John Claflin, Elihu Root, Joseph Choate, and Seth Low at the memorial meeting for J. P. Morgan, April 3, 1913, in *Chamber of Commerce of the State of New York: Memorial of J. Pierpont Morgan* (New York, 1913), pp. 4, 8, 11, 23.

48. *John Pierpont Morgan: A Memorial Address Delivered in the Chapel of the Intercession, Trinity Parish, New York City, at a Special Service Held on Sunday Evening, June 1st, 1913, by George F. Parker (A Member of the Congregation),* p. 3.

49. *John Pierpont Morgan: An Appreciation — A Sermon Preached at the Daily Noon Service at Wall and Broad Sts., New York City, April 2, 1913, by William Wilkinson, Trinity Parish,* p. 14.

CHAPTER FIVE: JOHN D. ROCKEFELLER

1. Quoted in Chicago *Herald and Examiner,* May 28, 1937.

2. S. K. Bigman, "Rivals in Conformity: A Study of Two Competing Dailies," *Journalism Quarterly,* 25:127–131 (1948).

3. Denver *Colorado Labor Advocate,* June 3, 1937; *The Brewery Worker,* June 5, 1937.

4. The writer is referring to the attack on CIO organizers who were distributing leaflets at the River Rouge plant of the Ford Motor Company in Dearborn, Michigan.

5. *International Molders' Journal,* July, 1937, pp. 400–401.

6. Merton, *Social Theory,* pp. 144–146.

7. Quoted in *Time,* 22:30 (September 11, 1933).

8. January 14, 1932.

9. *Editor and Publisher,* 70:44 (May 29, 1937). No newspaper in the United States devoted more space to Rockefeller's death than the *Herald-Tribune,* but two — the Cleveland *Plain Dealer* and the Philadelphia *Inquirer* — devoted a slightly higher percentage of their total editorial space to the event.

10. New York *Evening Journal,* May 24, 1937; Chicago *Daily News,* May 25, 1937; Birmingham *News,* May 25, 1937; Detroit *Free Press,* May 25, 1937; Asheville *Citizen,* May 24, 1937.

11. San Francisco *Chronicle,* May 25, 1937; Augusta *Daily Kennebec Journal,* May 25, 1937; Jackson *Daily Clarion-Ledger,* May 25, 1937; Washington *Evening Star,* May 24, 1937.

12. Montgomery *Advertiser,* May 30, 1937; New York *Daily News,* May 25, 1937; Rochester *Democrat and Chronicle,* May 24, 1937.

13. Denver *Rocky Mountain News,* May 25, 1937; Boise *Capital News,* May 24, 1937; New York *World-Telegram,* May 24, 1937; Des Moines *Register,* May 24, 1937; Newark *Evening News,* May 24, 1937; Little Rock *Arkansas Democrat,* May 26, 1937.

14. Quoted in New York *Daily Mirror,* May 24, 1937; Omaha *Evening World-Herald,* May 24, 1937; San Francisco *Examiner,* May 24, 1937.

15. Youngstown *Vindicator,* May 24, 1937; Topeka *Daily Capital,* May 25, 1937.

16. New York *Wall Street Journal,* May 24, 1937; Mobile *Register,* May 25, 1937; Butte *Montana Standard,* May 25, 1937; Sacramento *Union,* May 25, 1937.

17. Boston *Herald,* May 24, 1937; Bismarck *Tribune,* May 26, 1937; Indianapolis *News,* May 24, 1937; New York *Daily Tribune,* May 24, 1937.

18. Rochester *Democrat and Chronicle,* May 24, 1937; New York *Times,* May 24, 1937; Pittsburgh *Sun-Telegraph,* May 24, 1937; Chicago *Herald and Examiner,* May 24, 1937; Los Angeles *Times,* May 24, 1937.

19. It was as if in recognition of this, two historians of show business report, that shortly after the first World War "Fox Films led a movie industry campaign against Red Bolshevism by preparing a film in which they asked members of America's '400' to appear, showing their happy, quiet family lives. The idea was apparently to sell . . . the notion that J. P. Morgan and his coterie were 'just folks.' " Abel Green and Joe Laurie, Jr., *Show Biz from Vaude to Video* (New York, 1951), p. 205.

20. Washington *Evening Star,* May 24, 1937; Washington *Times,* May 24, 1937; New York *Times,* May 24, 1937; Los Angeles *Times,* May 24, 1937.

21. Kenneth Burke, *The Philosophy of Literary Form* (Baton Rouge, 1941), pp. 293–294, 296–298, 300.

22. Quoted in Chicago *Herald and Examiner,* May 26, 1937; New York *Times,* May 24, 1937.

23. New York *Evening Journal,* May 24, 1937; New York *Daily Mirror,* May 24, 1937; Seattle *Daily Times,* May 24, 1937; Philadelphia *Evening Bulletin,* May 24, 1937; Little Rock *Arkansas Democrat,* May 24, 1937; Springfield *Daily Republican,* May 24, 1937; Augusta *Daily Kennebec Journal,* May 25, 1937; Jacksonville *Florida Times-Union,* May 25, 1937; Grand Rapids *Herald,* May 25, 1937; Oklahoma City *Daily Oklahoman,* May 25, 1937. For evidence that the press was mistaken in considering Rockefeller's career as a replica of the Alger pattern of rags to riches, see K. Lynn, "Allan Nevins: An Algerine Captive," *Explorations in Enterpreneurial History,* 2:245–261 (July 15, 1950).

24. New York *World-Telegram,* May 24, 1937; Cleveland *Plain Dealer,* May 24, 1937; New York *American,* May 24, 1937; San Francisco *Examiner,* May 24, 1937; Springfield *Illinois State Register,* May 24, 1937.

25. Lincoln *Nebraska State Journal,* May 25, 1937; New York *Times,* May 24, 1937.

26. Phoenix *Arizona Republic,* May 25, 26, 1937; Detroit *Free Press,* May 24, 1937; Toledo *Blade,* May 25, 1937.

27. *News-Week,* 9:33–34 (May 29, 1937); *Time,* 29:72–75 (May 31, 1937).

28. *News-Week,* 9:33–34 (May 29, 1937); "Finis," *Pathfinder,* June 5, 1937; L. J. Roney, "John Davison Rockefeller," *The New York Genealogical and Biographical Record,* 68 (October 1937).

29. *Time,* 29:72–75 (May 31, 1937); *Pathfinder,* June 5, 1937; *The Christian Leader,* 119 (June 12, 1937).

30. Quoted in *Oil, Paint and Drug Reporter,* 131 (May 31, 1937).

31. *The Oil and Gas Journal,* May 27, 1937, pp. 8–11; *Oil, Paint and Drug Reporter,* 131 (May 31, 1937); *Business Week,* May 29, 1937; *The Oil Weekly,* May 31, 1937.

32. Quoted in *The Autobiography of William Allen White* (New York, 1946), p. 629.

33. *Problems of Journalism: Proceedings of the Sixteenth Annual Convention of the American Society of Newspaper Editors* (Washington, 1938), pp. 133–134.

34. Quoted in Chicago *Times,* July 2, 1939.

35. See, for example, A. Barth, "Position of the Press in a Free Society," in Willard Hayes Yeager and William Emil Utterback, eds., "Communication and Social Action," *Annals of the American Academy of Political and Social Science,* 250:82–88 (1947); William Albig, *Public Opinion* (New York and London, 1939), p. 407; Helen Ogden Mahin, *The Development and Significance of the Newspaper Headline* (Ann Arbor, 1924), pp. 45–47.

36. P. F. Lazarsfeld and R. K. Merton, "Mass Communication, Popular Taste and Organized Social Action," in Wilbur Lang Schramm, ed., *Mass Communications* (Urbana, 1949), p. 470.

37. Lazarsfeld and Merton, "Mass Communication," pp. 475–477, 480. For evidence relating to monopolization of the press, see R. B. Nixon, "Concentration and Absenteeism in Daily Newspaper Ownership," in Berelson and Janowitz, eds., *Public Opinion,* p. 196, and *A Free and Responsible Press. Report of the Commission on Freedom of the Press* (Chicago, 1947), pp. 37–38, 46–48. For an indication of the potential power which monopolization of the press gives to newspaper publishers, see the statement of Alfred H. Kirchhofer of the Buffalo *Evening News* in his presidential address to the American Society of Newspaper Editors: "A late, revered president of this society, Fred Fuller Shedd, once remarked that he never let pass an opportunity to knock down attacks upon the press. We might well adopt it as a collective policy not to print them in the first place, and to refute them if they have to be printed because they are news." *Problems of Journalism,* p. 18.

38. Lazarsfeld and Merton, "Mass Communication," pp. 464–468.

39. Lundberg, *60 Families,* pp. 247–251, 259–284.

40. *Labor Policies of Employers' Associations; Part III: The National Association of Manufacturers,* report no. 6, pt. 6, United States Senate Committee on Education and Labor (Washington, 1939), p. 281. See also Carl Dean Thompson, *Confessions of the Power Trust* (New York, 1932), p. 652.

41. The play, Charles Klein's *The Lion and the Mouse,* ran for two years in New York while four road shows toured the country. Green and Laurie, *Show Biz,* p. 59.

42. John Davison Rockefeller, *Random Reminiscences of Men and Events* (New York, 1933), p. 62.

43. *Autobiography of Mother* [*Mary*] *Jones* (Chicago, 1925), pp. 189, 191. See also pp. 182, 201–202.

44. Theodore Dreiser, *Hey Rub-A-Dub-Dub* (New York, 1920), p. 75.

45. Omaha *Evening World-Herald,* May 24, 1937.

46. *Autobiography of Mother Jones,* pp. 81, 216.

47. Cochran and Miller, *Age of Enterprise,* pp. 331–332.

48. L. Lowenthal, "Biographies in Popular Magazines," in Paul Felix Lazarsfeld and Frank Nicholas Stanton, *Radio Research 1942–1943* (New York, 1944), p. 510; P. Johns-Heine and H. H. Gerth, "Values in Mass Periodical Fiction, 1921–40," *Public Opinion Quarterly,* 13:105–118 (1949); Clarke, *Changing Conception,* pp. 271, 273, 316–319.

49. Baltimore *Sun,* May 24, 1937; Newark *Evening News,* May 25, 1937.

50. Talcott Parsons, *Essays in Sociological Theory Pure and Applied* (Glencoe, Illinois, 1949), pp. 267–268.

51. Albig, *Public Opinion,* pp. 8, 31, 283, 290; Elton Mayo, *The Social Problems of an Industrial Civilization* (Boston, 1945), p. 54.

52. Bronson Batchelor, *Profitable Public Relations* (New York and London, 1938), pp. 83–84.

53. C. A. Eaton (Republican, New Jersey), "The Declaration of Independence," in *Congress of American Industry — Discussions by Leading Authorities — 1776–1926* (Philadelphia, 1926), p. 21.

54. J. H. Pew, "The Oil Industry: A Living Monument to the American System of Free Enterprise," in *Proceedings: Nineteenth Annual Meeting, American Petroleum Institute* (Chicago, 1938), section I, pp. 18–20.

55. Don C. Prentiss, *Ford Products and Their Sale: A Manual for Ford Salesmen and Dealers in Six Books* (Detroit, 1923), book 5, p. 581.

56. Robert Leonard Davis, *Invoking the Public Interest* (Unpublished Master's Thesis, Columbia University, 1939), pp. 37–41, 48–59, 60; Robert Alexander Brady, *Business as a System of Power* (New York, 1943), pp. 274, 286–287, 287–289; Carl Dreyfuss, *Occupation and Ideology of the Salaried Employee,* 2 vols. (New York, 1938), II, 69. See also Merle Eugene Curti, *The Roots of American Loyalty* (New York, 1946), p. 235; Curti, *American Thought,* pp. 656, 697–700; Max Radin, review of Harold Laski, *The State in Theory and Practice,* in *New York University Law Quarterly Review,* 13:505 (1935–36).

57. *A Study of American Railway Employe Magazines.* American Railway Magazine Editors' Association (1940), pp. 1–2.

58. Charles Horton Cooley, *Human Nature and the Social Order,* rev. ed. (New York, 1922), p. 309.

59. New York *American,* April 21, 1935, quoted in *Selections from the Writings and Speeches of William Randolph Hearst* (San Francisco, 1948),

p. 15. For a discussion of similar developments in another communications medium — the moving picture industry — see Peter Odegard, *The American Public Mind* (New York, 1930), p. 205.

60. Quoted in Curti, *American Educators,* p. 157.

61. Charlotte *Observer,* May 24, 1937.

62. For a discussion of the effect of social mobility on the conception of the entrepreneur, see Svend Riemer, *Upward Mobility and Social Stratification,* translated from *Archiv für Sozialwissenschaft und Sozialpolitik,* vol. 67 (1932), Arnold Lissance, tr. (New York, 1937), pp. 4–5.

63. Hughes, *Human Interest,* pp. 213–214; Lynd, *Knowledge,* p. 86; Brady, *Business,* pp. 286–287, 259–261. See also Kurt Lewin, *Resolving Social Conflicts* (New York, 1948), p. 68; E. A. Shils, "Primary Groups in the American Army," in Robert King Merton and Paul Felix Lazarsfeld, eds., *Continuities in Social Research* (Glencoe, Illinois, 1950), p. 32; R. K. Merton and A. S. Kitt, "Contribution to the Theory of Reference Group Behavior," in *ibid.,* p. 74; Kluckhohn, *Mirror for Man,* p. 236. For a discussion of the portrayal by novelists of businessmen as "distinct individuals" rather than as types during this period, see Clarke, *Changing Conception,* pp. 273–274.

64. Bertie Charles Forbes, *Men Who Are Making America,* 5th ed. (New York, 1921), p. 299.

65. Cooley, *Human Nature,* pp. 326, 340–341, 346.

66. New York *Socialist Call,* May 29, 1937; New York *Times,* May 27, 1937.

CHAPTER SIX: HENRY FORD

1. Quoted in Keith Theodore Sward, *The Legend of Henry Ford* (New York and Toronto, 1948), p. 127.

2. *Congressional Record,* 93:3277 (April 10, 1947).

3. Quoted in Sward, *Henry Ford,* p. 106.

4. Sward, *Henry Ford,* pp. 389–396.

5. *Congressional Record,* 93:3243 (April 9, 1947).

6. *Ibid.,* p. 3248.

7. *Ibid.,* p. 3246.

8. *Ibid.,* p. 3250.

9. *Appendix to the Congressional Record,* 93:A 3830–3831 (July 25, 1947).

10. Detroit *News,* November 10, 1941; Anonymous pamphlet, *Henry Ford Swims the Red Sea* (Indianapolis 1941), *passim.*

11. Butte *Standard,* April 8, 1947; Mobile *Register,* April 9, 1947; New York *Daily Mirror,* April 9, 1947; Baltimore *News-Post,* April 10, 1947; Indianapolis *News,* April 8, 1947.

12. Sioux City *Journal,* April 9, 1947; Mobile *Register,* April 9, 1947.

13. Reno *Nevada State Journal,* April 10, 1947; Portsmouth *Press Herald,* April 9, 1947; Manchester *New Hampshire Morning Union,* April 9, 1947.

14. Indianapolis *News,* April 8, 1947; Indianapolis *Star,* April 9, 1947;

Rochester *Democrat and Chronicle,* April 8, 9, 1947; Boston *Herald,* April 9, 1947; Harrisburg *Patriot,* April 9, 1947; Houston *Post,* April 9, 1947; Memphis *Commercial Appeal,* April 9, 1947.

15. Mobile *Register,* April 9, 1947; Cincinnati *Enquirer,* April 9, 1947; New York *Herald Tribune,* April 8, 1947.

16. Harrisburg *Patriot,* April 9, 1947; Grand Forks *Herald,* April 8, 1947; Santa Fe *New Mexican,* April 10, 1947; Augusta *Kennebec Journal,* April 9, 1947; San Francisco *Examiner,* April 9, 1947; Augusta *Chronicle,* April 9, 1947; Topeka *Daily Capital,* April 9, 1947.

17. Sioux City *Journal,* April 9, 1947; Boston *Post,* April 9, 1947; Denver *Rocky Mountain News,* April 9, 1947; Washington *Star,* April 8, 1947; Denver *Post,* April 9, 1947.

18. New Orleans *Times-Picayune,* April 9, 1947; Milwaukee *Journal,* April 9, 1947; San Francisco *Examiner,* April 9, 1947; Tucson *Daily Citizen,* April 10, 1947.

19. Manchester *New Hampshire Morning Union,* April 9, 1947; Buffalo *Evening News,* April 8, 1947; *The Ford Idea in Education* (Detroit, 1917), p. 3.

20. Washington *Daily News,* April 9, 1947; Grand Forks *Herald,* April 9, 1947; Grand Rapids *Herald,* April 9, 1947; Boise *Idaho Statesman,* April 9, 1947; Concord *Daily Monitor,* April 9, 1947.

21. Tucson *Daily Citizen,* April 8, 1947; Washington *Daily News,* April 8, 1947; Wilmington *Journal-Every Evening,* April 8, 1947; New Orleans *Item,* April 9, 1947; Augusta *Kennebec Journal,* April 9, 1947; Brooklyn *Eagle,* April 8, 1947.

22. Columbia *State,* April 9, 1947; Norfolk *Virginian-Pilot,* April 9, 1947; Atlanta *Constitution,* April 9, 1947; Indianapolis *Star,* April 9, 1947; Bismarck *Tribune,* April 9, 1947; Sioux City *Journal,* April 9, 1947; Butte *Montana Standard,* April 8, 1947.

23. Chicago *Herald-American,* April 9, 10, 1947; San Francisco *Examiner,* April 9, 1947.

24. Chicago *Herald-American,* April 11, 1947; Jacksonville *Florida Times-Union,* April 9, 1947; Little Rock *Arkansas Democrat,* April 9, 1947; Reno *Evening Gazette,* April 8, 1947; Newark *Evening News,* April 8, 1947; Birmingham *News,* April 8, 1947; Portland *Press Herald,* April 9, 1947; New York *Times,* April 8, 1947; Baltimore *Sun,* April 9, 1947; Wilmington *Journal-Every Evening,* April 8, 1947.

25. Henry Ford, *365 of Henry Ford's Sayings* (New York, 1923).

26. *Ibid.,* pp. 2, 7, 20–21, 28.

27. Detroit *Free Press,* September 7, 1930.

28. Ford, *Ford's Sayings,* pp. 40, 41.

29. Detroit *Times,* July 27, 1930.

30. Dearborn *Independent,* 1919, quoted in Sward, *Henry Ford,* p. 145.

31. New York *World-Telegram,* April 8, 1947; Grand Rapids *Herald,* April 9, 1947; Atlanta *Journal,* April 8, 1947; Chicago *Sun,* April 9, 1947; Los Angeles *Times,* April 8, 1947; Portland *Oregonian,* April 9, 1947.

32. Los Angeles *Times,* April 9, 1947; Phoenix *Arizona Republic,* April

9, 1947; Chicago *Herald-American,* April 8, 1947; New York *Times,* April 9, 1947; Baltimore *Sun,* April 9, 1947.

33. Lansing *State Journal,* April 9, 1947; Washington *Post,* April 9, 1947; Montgomery *Advertiser,* April 10, 1947; New York *Times,* April 9, 1947.

34. Detroit *Free Press,* April 9, 1947; Mobile *Register,* April 11, 1947.

35. Workers Defense League News Service Press Release, New York, April 30, 1947. Local 600, UAW-CIO, filed a grievance against the Ford Motor Company charging that because of the layoff on the day of Ford's funeral employees who worked on Saturday of that week were deprived of the time-and-one-half pay they would have received if they had worked a normal forty-hour week. The umpire decided against the union and pointed out that the company was arranging "to provide a premium day's work for all employees to make up for their lost earnings that week." *The Umpire, Ford Motor Co. and UAW-CIO,* Case No. 4690, Opinion A–242, May 15, 1947.

36. Long Beach *Labor News,* April 18, 1947; North Hollywood *American Aeronaut,* April 18, 1947; Washington *Machinist,* April 17, 1947; Washington *Labor,* April 12, 1947.

37. The statement that Ford was "one of the first industrialists to recognize the CIO" is contrary to the facts. The General Motors Corporation recognized the UAW-CIO in February, 1937; Chrysler, shortly thereafter; and Ford — the last automobile company to recognize the union — not until June 21, 1941.

38. *Automotive and Aviation Industries,* April 15, 1947, p. 17; *Steel,* April 14, 1947, pp. 73–74; *American Machinist,* April 24, 1947, p. 75; *Iron Age,* April 17, 1947, pp. 74–76.

39. In relation to the statement that Ford "saw the dangers of communism" as early as 1917, it should be pointed out that he also saw no contradiction between anticommunism and economic aid to Russia. He accepted his first contract from Russia — for $75.000,000 — in the early 1920's, and throughout the next two decades exported automobiles, tractors, heavy machinery — even an entire rubber-tire plant — and trained Russian technicians in his factories. While the Ford Motor Company was denouncing the so-called "Ford Hunger March" of March 7, 1932, at its River Rouge plant, as a "Red rising," a large group of Russian engineers — who were being trained in Ford production methods in return for $30,000,000 — were within the plant. William C. Richards, *The Last Billionaire Henry Ford* (New York and London, 1948), pp. 224, 345–347; Sward, *Henry Ford,* p. 242.

40. *United Auto Worker* (Detroit, Michigan, UAW-CIO), May 13, 1939.

41. John Dos Passos, *The Big Money* (New York, 1933), p. 56.

42. Cooley, *Human Nature,* pp. 310–311; Thomas Humphrey Marshall, *Citizenship and Social Class* (Cambridge, England, 1950), pp. 125–127.

43. R. Centers, "Attitude and Belief in Relation to Occupational Stratification," *Journal of Social Psychology,* 27:168–173 (1928).

44. Lynd, *Knowledge,* p. 81.

45. For a discussion, though relating to a different medium of com-

munication, of the social consequences of presenting a public figure in terms of multiple roles, see Robert King Merton, *Mass Persuasion: The Social Psychology of a War Bond Drive* (New York and London, 1946), pp. 143–171. See also Merton, *Social Theory*, pp. 131–132; Lowenthal, "Biographies," in Lazarsfeld and Stanton, *Radio Research 1942–1943*, pp. 513–548; Kluckhohn, *Mirror for Man*, p. 233.

46. Rockefeller, *Random Reminiscences*, pp. 153–154.

47. Merton, *Mass Persuasion*, p. 153; Merton, *Social Theory*, pp. 130–131.

48. For a discussion of the identification of nation and economic system, see Curti, *American Loyalty*, pp. 235, 240; McCloskey, *American Conservatism*, pp. 131–132.

49. George Sawyer Pettee, *The Process of Revolution* (New York, 1937), pp. 42–43; Pimlott, *Public Relations*, pp. 238, 243; Robert Staughton Lynd, preface, in Brady, *Business*, pp. xii–xiv.

50. J. B. Sheridan, director, Missouri Committee on Public Utility Information, quoted in A. M. Lee, "Power-Seekers," in Alvin Ward Gouldner, ed., *Studies in Leadership* (New York, 1950), p. 672.

51. For a discussion of the importance of "monopoly" presentation by the press, see J. T. Klapper, "Mass Media and the Engineering of Consent," *The American Scholar*, 17:427 (1948); Merton, *Mass Persuasion*, p. 171.

52. Walter Lippmann, *Public Opinion* (New York, 1922), p. 166.

53. *Union Reporter*, May, 1947.

54. Herbert Brucker, *Freedom of Information* (New York, 1949), p. 69.

55. B. C. Forbes, "Industry Missing Fire on Public Relations," *Forbes Magazine*, May 1, 1947, pp. 19–20, 37.

56. S. Mangan, "State of the Nation," *Fortune*, 28:262 (1943); M. Dodge, "Labor," *Public Relations Journal*, 2:4, 6 (1946); Lucille Cardin Crain and Ann Burrows Hamilton, *Packaged Thinking for Women* (National Industrial Conference Board, New York, 1948), p. 16. For a discussion of the history of corporate public relations and its objectives, see L. A. Sussman, "The Personnel and Ideology of Public Relations," *Public Opinion Quarterly*, 12:697–708 (1948–49).

57. Quoted in "Advertising and Public Relations," *The Oil Forum*, June, 1947, p. 147.

58. W. H. Chase, "Human Relations — Key To A New Era," *Journal of Communication*, 1:14–15 (1951).

59. *Proceedings of the 28th Annual Meeting of the National Association of Manufacturers*, Open Shop Report (n.p., 1923), pp. 156–159.

60. Carl F. Braun, *Management and Leadership* (Alhambra, California, 1948), pp. 21–22, 24. The list prepared by the Ford Motor Company was as follows: "All Ford publications, including Dearborn *Independent;* all Ford biographies; auto trade publications; farm publications; *Administration, Advertising and Selling, American Magazine, Business Philosopher, Forbes Magazine, Printers' Ink, Sales Management, System, Success* (Marden's); *Scientific American, Science and Invention, Popular Science, Popular Mechanics; Correct English: How to Use It; Saturday Evening Post, Collier's, Cosmopolitan, Current Opinion, Hearst's International, Literary Digest, McClure's, National*

Geographic; Alexander Hamilton Institute course, LaSalle Extension University course, Sheldon School course; Newspapers; Spencer's *First Principles,* Emerson's *Essays."* Prentiss, *Ford Products,* book 5, pp. 563–565. See also book 6, p. 641.

61. *GM Folks,* September, 1947.

62. *GM Folks,* December, 1948. See also *ibid.,* October, 1948, November, 1948; *Corning Glass Works Gaffer,* March, 1947. For a discussion of the way in which corporation-sponsored radio programs and motion pictures similarly identify the businessman with all men and enterprise with the nation, see R. Arnheim, "The World of the Daytime Serial," in Lazarsfeld and Stanton, *Radio Yearbook,* pp. 34–85, and A. Sturmthal and A. Curtis, "Program Analyzer Tests of Two Educational Films," in *ibid.,* pp. 485–506.

63. "Amended Obituaries," in *The Writings of Mark Twain,* De Luxe ed. (Hartford, 1899–1907), pp. 231–232.

64. Memphis *Commercial Appeal,* April 9, 1947.

CONCLUSION

1. "Heavy Date," *The Collected Poetry of W. H. Auden* (New York, 1945), pp. 106–107.

2. Walter Coutu, *Emergent Human Nature* (New York, 1949), p. 251.

3. Edward Sapir, "Communication," quoted in Louis Wirth, "Consensus and Mass Communication," in Schramm, *Communications,* p. 527.

4. Coutu, *Human Nature,* p. 351; Merton, *Social Theory,* pp. 319–320; Pettee, *Revolution,* p. 44.

5. Theodore Mead Newcomb, *Social Psychology* (New York, 1950), pp. 280, 284, 567–571, 634–637; Logan Wilson and William Lester Kolb, *Sociological Analysis* (New York, 1949), pp. 513–514.

6. Ernest Kris and Hans Speier, *German Radio Propaganda* (New York, London, and Toronto, 1944), pp. 48–49; Howard Russell Huse, *The Illiteracy of the Literate* (New York and London, 1933), p. 43; Newcomb, *Psychology,* pp. 268, 292–295.

7. Wirth, "Consensus," pp. 529–530; Hans Heinrich Gerth and Charles Wright Mills, *From Max Weber: Essays in Sociology* (New York, 1946), pp. 79–81, 262; Edward Alsworth Ross, *Social Control* (New York, 1924), pp. 220, 245; O. E. Klapp, "The Creation of Popular Heroes," *American Journal of Sociology,* 54:135–141 (1948–49); Pettee, *Revolution,* pp. 42–43, 70; Newcomb, *Psychology,* pp. 661–662; Albig, *Public Opinion,* pp. 98, 106, 121–124; Max Weber, *The Theory of Social and Economic Organization,* A. M. Henderson and Talcott Parsons, trs. (New York, 1947), pp. 382–383; Gouldner, *Leadership,* p. 20. It should perhaps be repeated here that it is precisely this tendency of the press to transform men into symbols and to utilize these symbols to elicit desired forms of behavior that affects its understanding and description of the real activities of the entrepreneur and, accordingly, limits its reliability as an historical source. But these very limitations are, from the point of view of the historian of ideas, of considerable interest and importance for the study of value systems.

8. J. F. Wolpert, "Toward a Sociology of Authority," in Gouldner, *Leadership*, p. 681. See also A. M. Lee, "Power-Seekers," in *ibid.*, pp. 673–674; Albig, *Public Opinion*, pp. 106, 123–124, 127, 131–135; Hugh Dalziel Duncan, *Language and Literature in Society* (Chicago, 1953), pp. 8–9, 140.

9. For a discussion of the use of the press to achieve consensus, see: William Isaac Thomas and Florian Znaniecki, *The Polish Peasant in Europe and America*, 5 vols. (Chicago, 1918–20), IV, 243; Klapper, *Mass Media*, sect. IV, pp. 1–3, 20–51; C. L. Allen, "The Press and Advertising," in Malcolm Macdonald Willey and Ralph Droz Casey, "The Press in the Contemporary Scene," *Annals of the American Academy of Political and Social Science*, 219:90 (1942); M. Sherif and S. S. Sargent, "Ego-Involvement and the Mass Media," *The Journal of Social Issues*, 3:8–16 (1947).

10. Hon. H. G. O. Colby, *Anniversary Address before the American Institute of the City of New York* (New York, 1843), pp. 14, 16.

11. "German Socialists in America," *North American Review*, 128:384, 490, 492 (1879).

12. E. Root, "Experiments in Government," *North American Review*, 198:2 (1913).

13. General Charles P. Summerall, quoted in James David Mooney and Alan Campbell Riley, *Onward Industry!* (New York and London, 1931), pp. 33–34.

14. For a discussion of the importance of identification in reducing hostility, see R. K. Merton, "Patterns of Influence: A Study of Interpersonal Influence and of Communications Behavior in a Local Community," in Lazarsfeld and Stanton, *Communications Research 1948–1949*, pp. 180–222; R. M. Williams, Jr., "Propositions on Intergroup Hostility and Conflict," in Wilson and Kolb, *Sociological Analysis*, p. 752; Duncan, *Language and Literature*, pp. 105–107, 113.

15. "American Possibility," *Speech of the Hon. Rowland Blennerhassett Mahoney of New York in the House of Representatives, Saturday, April 25, 1895* (Washington, 1896), pp. 3–4.

16. Quoted in Twiss, *Lawyers*, pp. 54, 137.

17. The following works are among the more important of those consulted which contain material supporting this hypothesis: W. S. Ferguson, "Legalized Absolutism En Route from Greece to Rome," *American Historical Review*, 18:29–47 (1912–13) Lily Ross Taylor, *The Divinity of the Roman Emperor* (Middletown, Conn., 1931), *passim;* Floyd Seyward Lear, "The Idea of Majesty in Roman Political Thought," in *Essays in History and Political Theory in Honor of Charles Howard McIlwain* (Cambridge, 1936), pp. 188, 190–195; Samuel Rezneck, "The Trials of Treason in Tudor England," in *ibid.*, p. 275; Ludwig Hahn, *Das Kaisertum* (Leipzig, 1913), pp. 11, 21, 57; *The Cambridge Ancient History*, 12 vols. (New York and Cambridge, 1924–39), X, 177, 352–383, 488–501, 626–631, 654, 731–732; Charles Howard McIlwain, *The Growth of Political Thought in the West* (New York, 1932), pp. 141–142; M. P. Charlesworth, "The Virtues of a Roman Emperor: Propaganda and the Creation of Belief," *Proceedings of the British Academy*, 23:105–133 (1937); Franklin Le Van Baumer, *The Early Tudor Theory of Kingship* (New

Haven, 1940), pp. 5, 85, 88, 92, 119, 224; Herbert Albert Laurens Fisher, ed., *The Collected Papers of Frederick William Maitland*, 3 vols. (Cambridge, England, 1911), III, 246–250; Richard Henry Gretton, *The King's Majesty* (London, 1930), pp. 54–57, 65–70; John Neville Figgis, *The Divine Right of Kings*, 2nd ed. (Cambridge, England, 1922), *passim;* Joseph Robson Tanner, *Tudor Constitutional Documents* (Cambridge, England, 1930), pp. 1–8, 12, 314–315, 332, 335, 375–379, 383, 413; Percy Ernest Schramm, *A History of the English Coronation* (Oxford, 1937), pp. 213–216; Fritz Kern, *Kingship and Law in the Middle Ages* (Oxford, 1939), pp. 135–139; Sir William Searle Holdsworth, *A History of English Law*, 13 vols. (London, 1903–52), II, 198–200; III, 459–468; Reinhold Aris, *History of Political Thought in Germany from 1789 to 1815* (London, 1936), pp. 252, 304–314, 391–400; Lysbeth Walker Munch, *The Junker in the Prussian Administration Under Wilhelm II, 1888–1914* (Providence, 1944), 8–13, 19–23, 27–32; Johanna Schultze, *Die Auseinandersetzung zwischen Adel und Bürgertum in der deutschen Zeitschriften der letzten Jahrzehnte des 18. Jahrhunderts* (Berlin, 1923), pp. 75, 95; Karl Mannheim, "Das Konservative Denken," *Archiv für Sozialwissenschaft und Sozialpolitik*, 57:112–142 (1927); Friedrich Meinecke, *Weltbürgertum und Nationalstaat* (Munich and Berlin, 1914), *passim;* Frieda Braune, *Edmund Burke in Deutschland* (Heidelberg, 1917), pp. 213–215; Otto Tschirch, *Geschichte der öffentliche Meinung in Preussen von Baseler Frieden bis zum Zusammenbruch des Staates (1795–1806)*, 2 vols. (Weimar, 1934), *passim.*

Index

HARPER COLOPHON BOOKS